Schizophrenia from a Neurocognitive Perspective

▶

Schizophrenia from a Neurocognitive Perspective

Probing the Impenetrable Darkness

Michael Foster Green

*University of California, Los Angeles, Department of
Psychiatry and Biobehavioral Sciences*
West Los Angeles Veterans Affairs Medical Center

Allyn and Bacon

Boston • London • Toronto • Sydney • Tokyo • Singapore

Series Editor: Carla F. Daves
Series Editorial Assistant: Susan Hutchinson
Manufacturing Buyer: Suzanne Lareau

Copyright © 1998 by Allyn & Bacon
A Viacom Company
Needham Heights, MA 02194

Internet: www.abacon.com

Library of Congress Cataloging-in-Publication Data

Green, Michael Foster.
    Schizophrenia from a neurocognitive perspective : probing the
impenetrable darkness/ Michael Foster Green.
        p.   cm.
    Includes bibliographical references and index.
    ISBN 0-205-18477-4
    1. Schizophrenia. 2. Cognitive disorders. I. Title
    [DNLM: 1. Schizophrenia. 2. Psychiatric Disorders.
    3. Cognitive Disorders. 4. Behavior. 5. Neuropsychological Tests.
    WM 203 G797s   1998]
    RC514.G693   1998
    616.89'82—dc21
    DNLM/DLC   97-26855
    for Library of Congress   CIP

Printed in the United States of America

10 9 8 7 6 5 4 3   01 00 99 98

To the memory of Victoria Lia Green

Contents

Preface

The causes of dementia preacox are at the present time still wrapped in impenetrable darkness.

—Emil Kraepelin

To a large extent, the origins of schizophrenia continue to be "wrapped in impenetrable darkness." Schizophrenia remains a mystery, but nearly a century's worth of investigations have turned up some clues. The clues can be followed in two directions. We may opt to "look inward" to examine the neurochemistry or neuroanatomy of the disorder, or even further inward to consider intracellular and genetic contributions. Alternatively, we may decide to "look outward" to determine how the disorder affects the patient's functioning in the world.

The premise of this book is simple: that a neurocognitive perspective of schizophrenia provides a vantage point for views of both directions. Any perspective in isolation will be insufficient for describing, let alone explaining, such a complex disorder. One advantage of viewing schizophrenia from a neurocognitive perspective is that neurocognitive processes lie at the intersection of biological and behavioral processes. Hence, a systematic exploration of neurocognition can provide a scientific base for forays into virtually any other area of schizophrenia research.

This book was written in an effort to appeal to a broad spectrum of readers. My goal was to present concepts and challenges that my colleagues and I struggle with daily, but to make the material accessible to anyone who has a firm grounding in the basics of physiological psychology and psychopathology.

In writing this book, I have attempted to represent the excellent contributions of a large number of clinical research laboratories. At the same time, I have drawn liberally and unabashedly from the work of my colleagues at the UCLA Clinical Research Center for the Study of Schizophrenia. In particular, many sections of this book are mercifully shortened versions of marathon discussions with Keith Nuechterlein and Jim Mintz. If the book appears somewhat "UCLA-centric" as a result of this emphasis, then it can be considered a tribute to inspiring mentors and outstanding associates.

My appreciation goes to the following reviewers for their comments on the manuscript: Patrick W. Corrigan, University of Chicago Center for Psychiatric Rehabilitation; William D. Spaulding, University of Nebraska-Lincoln; Elaine F. Walker, Emory University; Barbara Cornblatt, Hillside Hospital; and Sohee Park, Northwestern University.

To the extent that the writing has any clarity and flow, it is largely due to the unwavering efforts of Mary Jane Robertson and Kimmy Kee. As the book evolved through its incarnations, these two individuals read every single word, and gently asked me to change most of them.

Schizophrenia from a Neurocognitive Perspective

▶ 1

The Neurodevelopmental
Model of Schizophrenia

A BIG SHIFT

It seemed as if schizophrenia changed during the 1980s. Of course the disease itself did not change; what changed was our view of the disorder. Until that time, schizophrenia was seen as a disorder of early adult onset and progressive deterioration. That view, however, was substantially and irreversibly altered. Simple, clear terms such as "age of onset" became complicated and murky. Just because a man first hears voices at the age of 18, or a woman first describes paranoid delusions at the age of 22, does that mean that the disorder began at those ages? The notion of a discrete age of onset became hard to reconcile with evidence that the development of schizophrenia could be influenced by events that occurred early in life—very early.

Another notion about schizophrenia, "progressive deterioration," seemed out of place in a world that was increasingly preoccupied with true progressive disorders such as Alzheimer's disease and AIDS. It is unfortunately true that a minority of schizophrenic patients experiences a poor course and outcome. However, instead of worsening with time (which would be expected from a deteriorating condition), symptoms generally mellow with age.

It was during the 1980s that schizophrenia began to be viewed within a *neurodevelopmental* model. According to this model, schizophrenia is a long-term consequence of an early (most likely prenatal) abnormality in neural development. Although the abnormality occurs quite early in life, it lies silent (or at least fairly quiet) until an affected region of the brain matures and is called upon to function (Weinberger, 1987). At this time, the clinical symptoms of schizophrenia appear. The neurodevelopmental model provides a

1

foundation for the neurocognitive perspective of schizophrenia, and will serve as our starting point.

Previous studies had suggested the importance of neurodevelopmental processes in schizophrenia, but to bring about a major shift something more was required. What was needed was a critical mass of data from a variety of sources. It is inherently difficult to gather empirical support for the neurodevelopmental model because of a thorny methodological obstacle: The onset of symptoms in schizophrenia typically occurs in early adulthood, but the periods of interest (usually pre- or perinatal) are some decades earlier. How does one overcome such an obstacle? Table 1.1 lists several creative approaches that have been used.

EPIDEMIOLOGICAL STUDIES

During the autumn of 1957 the city of Helsinki experienced an A2 influenza epidemic. Although influenza was no stranger to this Scandinavian city, the epidemic of 1957 was unusual in two respects. First, it was short-lived. The flu started on October 8th and then ended five weeks later on November 14th. Second, it was fairly widespread. An estimated two thirds of the population are thought to have experienced some signs of infection. The qualities of this particular influenza epidemic make it highly suitable for evaluating long-term effects.

Is it possible that exposure to the influenza virus during pregnancy could increase the risk for schizophrenia in the offspring? To test this possibility, Mednick and his colleagues (Mednick, Machon, Huttunen, & Bonett, 1988) determined the rates of schizophrenia in offspring who were in utero during the influenza epidemic and compared the rates to those of controls. The study focused on whether certain periods of fetal development were more risky than others, so the sample was divided according to trimesters. Offspring who were born in the three months after the epidemic would have been in

TABLE 1.1   Methods for Testing the Neurodevelopmental Model of Schizophrenia

Epidemiological Studies	• Influenza • Famine
Neurohistological Studies	• Cell Orientation • Cell Placement
Archival-Observational Studies	• Home Movies
Markers of Abnormal Neurodevelopment	• Minor Physical Anomalies • Dermatoglyphics • Atypical Handedness

their third trimester at the time of the epidemic. Those born 4–6 months after the epidemic would have been in their second trimester, and those born 7–9 months afterwards would have been in their first trimester. Control subjects were born in the same hospitals during the same months of previous years. Controlling for the calendar months of birth is important for a study like this because the rates of schizophrenia may vary with the season of birth.

As shown in Figure 1.1, the offspring of mothers who were exposed to the influenza virus during the second trimester of pregnancy were at increased risk for schizophrenia. However, the rates for the first and third trimesters were nearly the same as those of the control subjects. The results suggest a critical period of vulnerability for the fetus. Although the magnitude of the effect appears substantial from this study, influenza viruses probably account for a small proportion of the total number of patients with schizophrenia. Influenza epidemics are relatively rare occurrences so the influenza virus could not account for the vast majority of cases of schizophrenia. Also, schizophrenia is a relatively rare disorder with roughly 1% of the general population affected. Even with a substantial increase in risk, only a small minority of mothers who were exposed to the virus in the second trimester gave birth to a pre-schizophrenic child. Despite the relatively small number of total cases, this finding is still important because it shows that a specific environmental factor occurring at a specific time in fetal development can increase risk for schizophrenia.

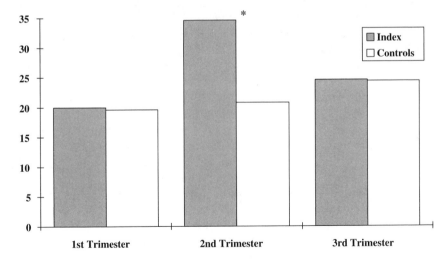

* = p < .01

FIGURE 1.1   **Percent of Schizophrenic Patients Among Hospital Admissions**

Source: From Mednick et al. (1988)

Several studies from other geographic regions have shown increased risk of schizophrenia with exposure to influenza during the second trimester (Barr, Mednick, & Munck-Jorgenson, 1990; O'Callaghan, Sham, Takei, Glover, & Murray, 1991b). There have been failures to replicate and the issue is not without controversy (Crow, 1994). However, the bulk of the evidence across studies suggests that a virus may lead to disruption of neural development in the second trimester and that this disruption is linked to the eventual development of schizophrenia.

One possible mechanism through which a virus could increase risk for schizophrenia would be by eliciting autoantibody production in the mother. An alternative way to examine the role of maternal antibodies is to consider the effects of Rhesus (Rh) incompatibility. Incompatibility of the RhD antigen (RhD-negative mother/RhD-positive infant) can cause hemolytic disease and brain damage in the fetus during the second trimester of neurodevelopment when the transfer of maternal antibodies to the fetus is occurring. A RhD-negative mother generally develops RhD antibodies following her first pregnancy with a RhD-positive infant, so the damaging effects of incompatibility rarely develop for the firstborn RhD-positive infant. Data from a large perinatal project in Denmark in 1959–1961 were combined with data from the National Psychiatric Registry (Hollister, Laing, & Mednick, 1996). In this way, the rates of schizophrenia could be compared for Rh compatible and incompatible groups. When the offspring of RhD-negative mothers were RhD-positive, their rates of schizophrenia were nearly three times greater than when the mother and offspring were RhD compatible. This epidemiological study, like the influenza studies, pinpoints a specific etiological route for schizophrenia. Moreover, because the effects of Rh incompatibility can be effectively treated, it indicates that some forms of schizophrenia may be preventable (Wyatt, 1996).

The tragedies of World War II gave rise to two epidemiological studies, which also inform us about the neurodevelopmental origins of schizophrenia. On the last day of November 1939 the Soviet Union launched an invasion of Finland in what became known as the Winter War of 1939. The invasion force was estimated at over 1 million men, more than three times the entire Finnish Armed Forces at that time. With such a wide disparity in number of troops, many of the Soviet soldiers wore summer uniforms in anticipation of a fast victory. The Finnish troops, which moved on skis, were highly resourceful and found ways to stall the invasion. The Molotov Cocktail was born of this conflict as the Finns learned how to stop Soviet tanks by throwing lighted bottles of fuel into their turrets. Following three and a half months, the Winter War ended with high casualties on both sides. Roughly 25,000 Finnish soldiers were killed. Some of these soldiers left behind pregnant wives and some left behind wives with newborn children. The offspring of these soldiers became experimental and control groups, respectively, in an informative study (Huttunen & Niskanen, 1978). Obviously the family trauma was extreme in both groups, but the effects on neurodevelopment were quite different. A newborn child would be much less susceptible to neurodevelopmental disruption than would a developing fetus. The sample for this study included fathers who died of other causes, but the vast majority of the fathers in both groups died during World War II conflict with the Soviet Union. The experimental group that experienced prenatal loss had significantly more cases of schizophrenia than the controls whose fathers died within the first year of life. All of the cases of schizophrenia in the experimental group ($n = 6$) were from mothers who received the news during the second trimester or the last month of pregnancy. Here again, we have evidence of a nongenetic second trimester event that contributes to risk for schizophrenia.

Near the end of World War II the Allies invaded France. By September of 1944 they had crossed two branches of the Rhine River, but were unable to capture key bridges that connected the Netherlands to Germany. This unsuccessful effort was depicted in the book by Cornelius Ryan and the 1977 film, *A Bridge Too Far*. When the Dutch railroad workers went on strike to support the Allies, the Germans retaliated by imposing a highly effective blockade of western Holland. The result was the Dutch Hunger Winter, a severe famine in this region from October 1944 until the end of the war in May 1945. The famine reached its peak from February to April 1945, during which time bread and potatoes formed nearly the entire ration. Susser and Lin (1992) followed the offspring of women who were pregnant during the Hunger Winter to examine the risk for development of subsequent psychiatric disorders. There were no special food supplements for pregnant women during the famine period. The offspring of women who were exposed to severe famine during their first trimester of pregnancy had increased rates of hospitalization for schizophrenia. In the initial report, the increased risk for schizophrenia was true for female, but not male, offspring. However, a subsequent report with a larger sample observed a two-fold increase in the risk for schizophrenia for both men and women who were conceived at the height of the famine (Susser et al., 1996). Unlike the studies of influenza, which implicated the second trimester, these studies suggest that starvation exerts its effects on risk for schizophrenia slightly earlier in development. Perhaps the period of risk varies according to the type of neurodevelopmental stressor.

The notion that fetal development influences psychiatric disorder is not new. Consider the following statement:

> People are born to have the illness of craziness, how does it come about?… it is an illness started in the womb, resulting from a bad scare of the mother when she was pregnant…(translated in Lam & Berrios, 1992, p. 122)

This quote comes from the *Yellow Emperor's Classic of Internal Medicine*. It is a Chinese medical text that is roughly 2,000 years old.

Assuming that exposure to a virus or other environmental stressors during the second trimester increases risk for schizophrenia, what is a plausible mechanism for the effect? What is the nervous system doing during the second trimester of development? The second trimester is the time of *cell migration* in which neurons move out of the proliferation zones and into more distal locations in which they establish connections with other neurons. Do we have any evidence that schizophrenic patients had abnormalities in cell migration?

NEUROHISTOLOGICAL STUDIES

Even with the advent of sophisticated neuroimaging techniques that allow us to see the brain *in vivo*, the answers to some questions still require a microscopic view of the brain that can only be obtained upon autopsy. Several neurohistological studies have been conducted using the brains of schizophrenic patients. In one study, the authors examined the orientation of the pyramidal cells of the left hippocampus (Kovelman & Scheibel, 1984). In normal controls, the pyramidal cells were neatly aligned in rows. However, in schizophrenic patients, the cells showed considerable disarray. This finding of cell disorientation was later replicated in a larger sample of patients and was reported in both hemispheres (Conrad, Abebe, Austin, Forsythe, & Scheibel, 1991; Conrad & Scheibel, 1987).

Recent studies have examined the cytoarchitecture of the cortex with specialized staining techniques. The strict laminar organization of the cortex can provide clues about the development of the brain. For instance, studies using staining techniques have shown a type of neural displacement in schizophrenia. There appear to be too few cells in the superficial layers of the cortex and too many cells in the deeper layers (Arnold, Hyman, Van Hoesen, & Damasio, 1991; Jakob & Beckman, 1986). This finding was replicated using a different method; neurons that were stained for the enzyme nicotinamide-adenine dinucleotide phosphate (NADPH)-diaphorase were located in deeper layers in the prefrontal and temporal regions of patients compared with controls (Akbarian et al., 1993; Akbarian et al., 1996). In each of these studies, the distribution of neurons appears to be displaced inwards into deeper layers of the cortex (see Figure 1.2). Because the cortex develops in an "inside-out" fashion, the inward displacement of cells strongly suggests that the neurons failed to migrate as far as they should have.

If some neurons arrived at the wrong locations, some of the connections among these neurons are likely to be anomalous. The displacement of cells could lead to a situation in which the neurons show aberrations in the degree

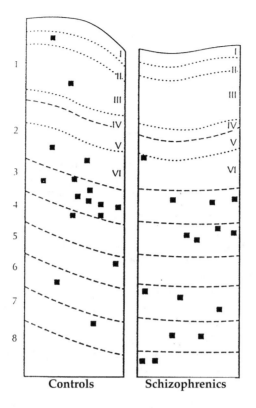

Controls   Schizophrenics

FIGURE 1.2

Source: From "Altered Distribution of Nicotinamide-Adenine Dinucleotide Phosphate-Diaphorase Cells" in Frontal Lobe of Schizophrenics Implies Disturbances of Cortical Development by S. Akbarian et al., 1993, *Archives of General Psychiatry, 50:* p. 172. Copyright 1993, American Medical Association. Reprinted with permission.

of synaptic "pruning." Synaptic pruning is a fine tuning process in which the neuron selectively loses unnecessary synaptic connections by reducing its dendritic branching. Abnormalities in synaptic pruning could leave the patients with too few (Hoffman & McGlashan, 1993) or too many synapses (David, 1994); both conditions resulting in non-optimal processing. The notion of excessive pruning is consistent with the observation that the cortical neurons of schizophrenic patients tend to be packed more tightly than those of controls in the prefrontal and the occipital regions (Selemon, Rajkowska, & Goldman-Rakic, 1995). Putting these findings together, we can speculate that the neurons of patients fail to migrate normally to the outer layers of cortex, but instead stop short in their migration at deeper cortical layers. This displacement prevents the optimal establishment of neural connections, which in turn causes a more severe pruning process and a denser packing of neurons. As we will see later in this chapter, these abnormalities in neural placement and neural connections have substantial implications for neurocognition.

Could these findings of cell disorientation and misplacement have occurred as the result of medications, institutionalization, or some other aspect of being treated for schizophrenia? Not likely. Once the neurons are in position after migration, they become "packed in" with other neurons and glial cells. There is essentially no room to move. The cell disorientation and misplacement appear to result from abnormalities of cell migration during neurodevelopment, most likely in the second trimester.

The bulk of the findings from both the epidemiological and neurohistological studies converge, suggesting that the second trimester is a critical period of risk. Perhaps the influenza virus increases risk for schizophrenia by disrupting the process of cell migration. But what about the vast majority of schizophrenic patients who were never exposed to the influenza virus or other stressful prenatal events during the second trimester? Let us suppose that problems in cell migration are necessary for the development of schizophrenia, but that there are several ways for these problems to occur. Migration might be disrupted by processes that are under genetic control, or alternatively, by the presence of a nongenetic event such as a virus. In this way, the relatively small number of cases that result from the virus may be "mimicking" the genetic predisposition for schizophrenia.

In any event, the evidence is consistent in suggesting the importance of neurodevelopmental processes in schizophrenia. The next sections will consider how these problems in neurodevelopment begin to reveal themselves behaviorally.

ARCHIVAL-OBSERVATION STUDIES

Despite the differences in the way we perceived and coped with the world, Andy and I were unusually close as children. His presence in my life and mine in his was more constant than that of either of our parents. I adored and emulated my older brother, tagged after him, and vied for his attention; he was my daily companion, my playmate, and so I believed, my protector.

However, a recent look at old family photos has given my memories a jolt, and made me question who was really protecting whom. Paradoxically, these snapshots belie my memories of Andy as my caretaker. In each and every one, I stand in the foreground with Andy several paces behind me, even though he is older by a year-and-a-half and there are only two of us in the picture. I am sturdy and smiling; Andy is frail, his handsome features scrunched up into a scowl. He holds his body in an odd, concave position, sucking in the center of his body, with his head pitched awkwardly forward. Thin arms, bent at the elbows, hang lank behind his torso as if he holds onto a set of invisible supporting bars. Occasionally, he smiles, but these pictures are the most disturbing of all: My brother's taut, clenched smile, baring most of his upper and lower front teeth, conveys only great tension and pain: it is a frozen, soundless scream. (Brodoff, 1988, pp. 114–115)

In this excerpt, photos served as a check on memories of a pre-schizophrenic sibling. In addition, photos can serve as a unique type of data base. Imagine a family with two adult siblings: one sibling has developed schizophrenia, and one has not. Think how valuable it would be if we could observe the two siblings as children, long before the symptoms of schizophrenia, to identify precursors to the disorder. Of course we could ask the parents what they remember of the two children, but that would be a long time ago, and the parents' recollection could be influenced by their current knowledge that one child developed schizophrenia.

Walker and colleagues have used home movies as a way to study the childhood precursors of schizophrenia. They have obtained home movies from families in which a child developed schizophrenia, and at least one sibling did not. As it turns out, the families tend to take movies of their children at certain times (e.g., the first birthday, the first steps) so that the siblings can be compared in roughly similar situations. These home movies were shown to raters who were asked to choose the pre-schizophrenic child. The raters were generally successful. How do they make such judgments? The pre-schizophrenic child often shows more negative emotions compared with the control sibling (Walker, Grimes, Davis, & Smith, 1993). Importantly, they also have unusual motoric features and a higher rate of neuromotor dysfunction (Walker, Savoie, & Davis, 1994). For example, Figure 1.3 is a frame from a home movie in which a pre-schizophrenic child displays an atypical hand posture. The abnormal motoric features are especially noticeable in the first two years and then become less common as the child develops. Walker (1994) has speculated that these motoric abnormalities are a reflection of underlying dysregulation in dopamine that is most apparent in the first two years before compensatory mechanisms are established. Later in life, the dopamine dysregulation may lead to the development of psychotic symptoms.

The archival-observational method provides compelling evidence that abnormalities in neurodevelopment are revealed early in life, although not as psychotic symptoms. Instead they are shown as behavioral abnormalities

FIGURE 1.3

Source: From "Developmentally Moderated Expressions of the Neuropathology Underlying Schizophrenia" by E. F. Walker, 1994, *Schizophrenia Bulletin, 20,* p. 455. Reprinted with permission.

in motor and emotional development. One intriguing aspect of these findings is that the motor abnormalities are less noticeable as the child develops. Next, we will consider whether signs of abnormal neurodevelopment are also observable in adult patients.

MARKERS OF ABNORMAL NEURODEVELOPMENT

At the end of the last century Thomas Clouston, a professor from the University of Edinburgh in Scotland, identified a psychotic condition that he believed to be the result of a neurodevelopmental failure (cited in Murray & Jones, 1995). As evidence for the involvement of developmental problems, Clouston noted that 55% of these patients with "developmental or adolescent insanity" had a deformed palate compared with 19% of the general population. In all likelihood, this was the first study of markers of abnormal neurodevelopment in schizophrenia.

Markers of abnormal neurodevelopment in schizophrenic patients are usually measurable physical characteristics that reflect abnormal neurodevelopmental processes that occurred before or shortly after birth. Some of the most commonly employed markers include minor physical anomalies (Green, Satz, & Christenson, 1994b; Green, Satz, Gaier, Ganzell, & Kharabi, 1989a; Gualtieri, Adams, Shen, & Loiselle, 1982; Guy, Majorski, Wallace, & Guy, 1983; O'Callaghan, Larkin, Kinsella, & Waddington, 1991a), dermatoglyphic signs (Bracha, Torrey, Bigelow, Lohr, & Linington, 1991; Bracha, Torrey, Gottesman, Bigelow, & Cunniff, 1992; Mellor, 1992), and atypical handedness (Clementz, Iacono, & Beiser, 1994; Green, Satz, Smith, & Nelson, 1989b).

Minor Physical Anomalies

Minor physical anomalies (MPAs) are minor abnormalities of the head, feet, hands, and face (e.g., high steepled palate, large or small distance between tear ducts, malformed ears, or webbing between the toes). Normal controls often have one, but they rarely have several MPAs. There are a couple of reasons to expect that MPAs reflect, although indirectly, the development of the central nervous system. First, MPAs and the nervous system both derive from the ectodermal layer. Second, high rates of MPAs are associated with disorders that have known prenatal neural involvement such as Down's Syndrome. Although the specific timing of the MPAs is not well known, they likely reflect processes in the second trimester of neurodevelopment (Green, Bracha, Satz, & Christenson, 1994a), a time frame that fits well with the epidemiological and histological studies.

Compared with other methods of studying abnormal neurodevelopment, MPAs have certain advantages: they can be assessed with a brief examination, the assessments can be conducted reliably, and the exam requires minimal supplies (only a tape measure and a ruler). When used in research, MPAs have a major limitation: The assessment of MPAs generally requires an in-person examination that makes it difficult for the raters to be completely blind to group assignment when assessing symptomatic patients.

If schizophrenia has neurodevelopmental origins, then the patients should have an excess of MPAs. Indeed, this is the case. All of the studies that have compared MPAs in schizophrenic patients to normal controls have found an excess of MPAs in schizophrenia and this excess does not seem to be an artifact of socio-economic status (Green et al., 1989a). MPAs in schizophrenia are not limited to one body region, but often include abnormalities of the mouth (e.g., steepled palate), as well as unusually large and small head circumferences. MPAs do not occur with such high frequency in other psychotic disorders, suggesting some degree of specificity to schizophrenia among the psychotic disorders (it is not wholly specific because other developmental disorders have MPAs). In addition, the siblings of the schizophrenic patients do not appear to have an increase in MPAs, suggesting that

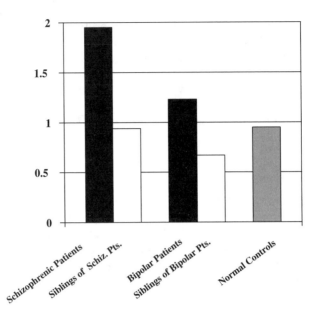

FIGURE 1.4   Minor Physical Anomaly Score

the neural events reflected by MPAs may be nongenetic in origin (see Figure 1.4). More on this point later.

Dermatoglyphics

Dermatoglyphics (literally skin carvings) are finger-, hand-, and footprints. People are well aware that the uniqueness of fingerprints makes them valuable for identifying an individual. However, dermatoglyphics can also be used as a record of neurodevelopment. Ridges on the fingers are set down between weeks 14–22 of gestation, so disruptive events that occur during these weeks are likely to be reflected in a subtle alteration of the dermatoglyphics. It is rather like a developmental fossil record; we have a recording of the events, but not many details about the reasons for the events.

One measure that is derived from dermatoglyphics is total number of ridges on each finger. A comparison of total ridge counts in monozygotic twin pairs discordant for schizophrenia (i.e., one twin has schizophrenia and one does not) suggested two subgroups of patients. One subgroup of schizophrenic patients showed decreased ridge counts, indicating that they were smaller than their unaffected co-twin during the second trimester, perhaps due to reduced blood supply. However, a second subgroup had higher ridge counts than their co-twin, suggesting that they were larger at this point of neurodevelopment, perhaps due to swelling (Bracha et al., 1992).

Aside from total ridge counts, dermatoglyphic asymmetry (also called fluctuating asymmetry) has been of interest in schizophrenia. Dermatoglyphic asymmetry is a measure of the variability in the ridge counts between the left and right hands. A large asymmetry between the left and right hands is considered a sign of disturbance in fetal neurodevelopment and/or reduced developmental stability. It is interpreted as evidence that the fetus had a reduced ability to buffer against adverse environmental effects. Several studies have found that schizophrenic patients have an increase in dermatoglyphic asymmetry (Markow & Gottesman, 1989; Markow & Wandler, 1986; Mellor, 1992). Dermatoglyphic asymmetry is especially ap-propriate for studies of non-twins because it reduces between-subject variability by comparing the right and left side of the same individual.

Atypical Handedness

Handedness is such a simple behavioral index that one might be surprised at its utility for exploring complex theories of neurodevelopment. Studies of handedness have been quite informative with a variety of neurodevelopmental disorders such as autism, mental retardation, and disorders of focal brain insult such as epilepsy and stroke. As a group, schizophrenic patients show a shift away from right-handedness. Initially, reports attributed this shift to an increase in left-handedness. More thorough assessments have determined that the shift is largely due to an increase in mixed-handedness. Not only do schizophrenic patients tend to switch hands between different items (e.g., write with their right hand and throw with their left), but they also tend to switch hands for the same item over time (Green et al., 1989b).

How can we explain this shift in handedness? It makes some sense to view atypical handedness as another marker (like MPAs and dermatoglyphics) of problems in neurodevelopment. The abnormalities in neurodevelopment are bilateral and probably diffuse. The neural substrate for manual dominance is located in the left hemisphere for right-handers. A bilateral problem in neurodevelopment could partially erode the substrate for manual dominance, resulting in less complete dominance and a mixed-handedness presentation.

Genetic versus Nongenetic Factors

The problems in neurodevelopment reflected by markers such as MPAs, dermatoglyphics, and handedness might be associated with genetic predisposition for schizophrenia, or they might reflect largely nongenetic events. Data from several laboratories are starting to favor the latter interpretation. In a study of monozygotic twins discordant for schizophrenia, the affected twin had more signs of subtle upper limb dysmorphology, including abnormal dermatoglyphic patterns (Bracha et al., 1991). Genetic factors are obviously unable to account for differences in genetically identical twin pairs. Additional support for nongenetic factors comes from the observation that twins discordant for schizophrenia had larger intrapair differences in dermatoglyphic ridge counts compared with normal controls (Bracha et al., 1992). Also germane to this question is the finding that siblings of schizophrenic patients had MPA scores that were significantly lower than those of patients and comparable to those of normal controls (Green et al., 1994b).

Some have speculated that atypical handedness in schizophrenia is part of a general failure to establish cerebral asymmetry which is under the control of genetic factors (Crow et al., 1989). However, other lines of evidence are suggesting that handedness is not part of the genetic predisposition to schizophrenia. For example, the first-degree relatives of schizophrenic patients did not demonstrate a shift in their handedness distribution (Clementz et al., 1994). In addition, another study reported a trend for mixed-handedness to be associated with a negative family history of schizophrenia (Cannon et al., 1995).

IS THERE A NEURODEVELOPMENTAL SUBTYPE OF SCHIZOPHRENIA?

We now have compelling evidence that neurodevelopmental factors are important, at least for some subgroups of schizophrenic patients. The nature of these neurodevelopmental factors is still obscure, but it appears that some of these factors are nongenetic. How then do we reconcile this possibility with the fact that schizophrenia has a substantial genetic component (see Chapter 4 for more discussion of this topic)?

Figure 1.5 includes diagrams of three possible models. One possibility is that there are two pathways to schizophrenia, one genetic and one neurodevelopmental. These pathways were previously captured in terms of "familial" and "sporadic" forms of schizophrenia (Lewis, Reveley, Reveley, Chitkara, & Murray, 1987; Murray, Lewis, & Reveley, 1985). Neurodevelopmental abnormalities can be viewed as etiologically relevant for a primarily nongenetic (e.g., sporadic) form of schizophrenia. In this model, some patients with schizophrenia have the genetic form of the disorder, but other patients have a "phenocopy" in which they have the same clinical presentation, but lack the genetic predisposition. One prediction from this model

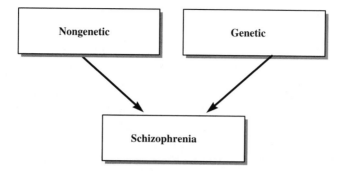

FIGURE 1.5a   **Physical Anomalies Reflect a Nongenetic (Sporadic) Form of Schizophrenia**

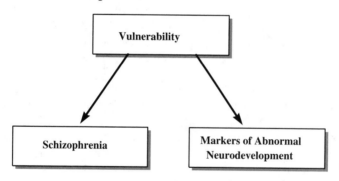

FIGURE 1.5b   **Physical Anomalies and Schizophrenia Are Separate Components of a Common Latent Trait**

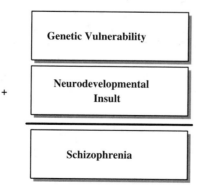

FIGURE 1.5c   **Physical Anomalies Reflect a Nongenetic Potentiator in a Person at Risk**

would be that patients without a family history (i.e., with a primarily non-genetic form of schizophrenia) would show more markers of abnormal neurodevelopment, a prediction that has not been supported by studies on MPAs and handedness. Indeed, the familial/sporadic distinction has evolved into a neurodevelopmental classification of schizophrenia (Murray, O'Callaghan, Castle, & Lewis, 1992) that does not make the same assumptions about etiology. In the reformulation, a neurodevelopmental form of the disorder (with associated markers of abnormal neurodevelopment) could arise either through genetic or environmental factors.

Could the neurodevelopmental factors be part of the genetic vulnerability for schizophrenia? This type of "latent trait" model has been used successfully by Matthysse, Holzman, and their colleagues (Matthysse, Holzman, & Lange, 1986) to explain the association between schizophrenic symptoms and abnormalities in smooth pursuit eye movements (see Chapter 4). However, this type of model would lead to the prediction that markers of abnormal neurodevelopment would be more frequent in the first-degree relatives of the patient than in the general population. As mentioned, this does not seem to occur with handedness and MPAs.

An alternative model is the general vulnerability/stress model of schizophrenia (Mirsky & Duncan, 1986; Zubin & Spring, 1977). In this model, the neurodevelopmental factors would be considered nongenetic stressors that interact with a genetic predisposition. We normally think of stressors in terms of job demands, interpersonal and social challenges, and personal tragedies such as the loss of a loved one. However, we can also view stressors more broadly to include neurodevelopmental challenges to a developing fetus. Certain neurodevelopmental factors may affect a relatively large percentage of the population (as in an influenza epidemic) but they would only increase risk for schizophrenia for a subgroup of individuals who have a genetic predisposition to schizophrenia. In essence, these individuals are carrying a double burden of genetic vulnerability and early neurodevelopmental insult.

Whatever model we choose, we are stuck with one perplexing problem: Why do the symptoms begin so much later than the underlying neural events? Although we currently do not have a complete answer to this question, Weinberger (1987; 1995) has speculated that the neural disruption remains silent until that region of the brain is called "on line." For example, we have evidence for cellular disruption in the prefrontal cortex of schizophrenic patients. This area is not fully myelinated (and therefore not fully mature) until late adolescence. Perhaps a disruption in cell migration occurs in the second trimester, but the effects of this problem are not completely appreciated until the prefrontal cortex is called on to perform cognitive operations some two decades later. Alternatively, the delay in onset of symptoms could involve an interaction between neurotransmitters (particularly the dopamine system) and neurohormonal indicators of stress responsivity. As part of an innovative neural model of schizophrenia, Walker and DiForio (in press) suggest that increases in cortisol release occurring in adolescence can have an augmenting effect on dopamine activity and lead to the onset of symptoms.

IMPLICATIONS FOR NEUROCOGNITION

We started our exploration of the neurocognition of schizophrenia at an early stage, namely the period of cell migration. There are several good reasons to believe that neurodevelopmental problems beginning as early as the second trimester increase an individual's risk for schizophrenia. How does this happen? It is highly unlikely that a failure of cell migration could lead to psychotic symptoms without first affecting more basic neurocognitive processes. Cell displacement does not lead to an absence of neural connectivity—it leads to non-optimal connectivity.

> The data do not suggest that there are dead or missing cortical regions, or that some or many cortical regions are completely out of touch with each other (i.e., disconnected). Rather, they suggest that neuronal connections and circuits are to some degree anomalous and that cortical laminae and regions may be "dysconnected."... It is likely to translate into inefficient or "noisy" processing rather than no processing, into cortical communication that is "misinformed" rather than uninformed. (Weinberger & Lipska, 1995, pp. 89–90)

Starting from the premise that schizophrenia involves misinformed rather than uninformed communication stemming from a problem in neural migration in multiple regions, we can make a number of predictions: (1) that information processing difficulties are core features of the illness; (2) that they will be relatively pervasive, at least compared with focal lesions; (3) that they will be relatively mild, at least compared with disorders of neural disconnection; and (4) that they will occur relatively early, at least compared with the onset of psychotic symptoms. All of these predictions have received considerable support. There may even be neurocognitive differences within a group of schizophrenic patients depending on the degree of neurodevelopmental involvement (Goldstein, Seidman, Santangelo, Knapp, & Tsuang, 1994).

Beyond these predictions, we can begin to speculate about the relationships of these neurocognitive problems with symptoms, course, and outcome. If neurocognitive deficits are core features of the illness, should they become a target of treatment? The neurocognitive perspective of schizophrenia that will emerge over the subsequent chapters should not be viewed as an insulated, modular content area. Instead it should be viewed as a means to integrate biological, genetic, and developmental aspects of the illness with symptoms, course, outcome, and treatment.

REFERENCES

Akbarian, S., Bunney, W. E., Potkin, S. G., Wigal, S. B., Hagman, J. O., Sandman, C. A., & Jones, E. G. (1993). Altered distribution of nicotinamide-adenine dinucleotide phosphate-diaphorase cells in frontal lobe of schizophrenics implies disturbances of cortical development. *Archives of General Psychiatry, 50,* 169–177.

Akbarian, S., Kim, J. J., Potkin, S. G., Hetrick, W. P., Bunney, W. E., & Jones, E. G. (1996). Maldistribution of interstitial neurons in prefrontal white matter of the brains of schizophrenic patients. *Archives of General Psychiatry, 53,* 425–436.

Arnold, S. E., Hyman, B. T., Van Hoesen, G. W., & Damasio, A. R. (1991). Some cytoarchitectural abnormalities of the entorhinal cortex in schizophrenia. *Archives of General Psychiatry, 48,* 625–632.

Barr, C. E., Mednick, S. A., & Munck–Jorgenson, P. (1990). Maternal influenza and schizophrenic births. *Archives of General Psychiatry, 47,* 869–874.

Bracha, H. S., Torrey, E. F., Bigelow, L. B., Lohr, J. B., & Linington, B. B. (1991). Subtle signs of prenatal maldevelopment of the hand ectoderm in schizophrenia: A preliminary monozygotic twin study. *Biological Psychiatry, 30,* 719–725.

Bracha, H. S., Torrey, E. F., Gottesman, I. I., Bigelow, L. B., & Cunniff, C. (1992). Second-trimester markers of fetal size in schizophrenia: A study of monozygotic twins. *American Journal of Psychiatry, 149,* 1355–1361.

Brodoff, A. S. (1988). First person account: Schizophrenia through a sister's eyes—The burden of invisible baggage. *Schizophrenia Bulletin, 14,* 113–116.

Cannon, M., Byrne, M., Cassidy, B., Larkin, C., Horgan, R., Sheppard, N. P., & O'Callaghan, E. (1995). Prevalence and correlates of mixed-handedness in schizophrenia. *Psychiatry Research, 59,* 119–125.

Clementz, B. A., Iacono, W. G., & Beiser, M. (1994). Handedness in first-episode patients and their first-degree biological relatives. *Journal of Abnormal Psychology, 103,* 400–403.

Conrad, A. J., Abebe, T., Austin, R., Forsythe, S., & Scheibel, A. (1991). Hippocampal pyramidal cell disarray in schizophrenia as a bilateral phenomenon. *Archives of General Psychiatry, 48,* 413–417.

Conrad, A. J., & Scheibel, A. B. (1987). Schizophrenia and the hippocampus: The embryological hypothesis extended. *Schizophrenia Bulletin, 13,* 577–587.

Crow, T. J. (1994). Prenatal exposure to influenza as a cause of schizophrenia. *British Journal of Psychiatry, 164,* 588–592.

Crow, T. J., Ball, J., Bloom, S. R., Brown, R., Bruton, C. J., Colter, N., Frith, C. D., Johnstone, E. C., Owens, D. G. C., & Roberts, G. W. (1989). Schizophrenia as an anomaly of development of cerebral asymmetry: A postmortem study and a proposal concerning the genetic basis of the disease. *Archives of General Psychiatry, 46,* 1145–1150.

David, A. S. (1994). Dysmodularity: A neurocognitive model for schizophrenia. *Schizophrenia Bulletin, 20,* 249–255.

Goldstein, J. M., Seidman, L. J., Santangelo, S., Knapp, P. H., & Tsuang, M. T. (1994). Are schizophrenic men at higher risk for developmental deficits than schizophrenic women? Implications for adult neuropsychological functions. *Journal of Psychiatry, 28,* 483–498.

Green, M. F., Bracha, S. H., Satz, P., & Christenson, C. (1994a). Preliminary evidence for an association between minor physical anomalies and second trimester neurodevelopment in schizophrenia. *Psychiatry Research, 53,* 119–127.

Green, M. F., Satz, P., & Christenson, C. (1994b). Minor physical anomalies in schizophrenia patients, bipolar patients, and their siblings. *Schizophrenia Bulletin, 20,* 433–440.

Green, M. F., Satz, P., Gaier, D. J., Ganzell, S., & Kharabi, F. (1989a). Minor physical anomalies in schizophrenia. *Schizophrenia Bulletin, 15,* 91–99.

Green, M. F., Satz, P., Smith, C., & Nelson, L. (1989b). Is there atypical handedness in schizophrenia? *Journal of Abnormal Psychology, 98,* 57–61.

Gualtieri, C. T., Adams, A., Shen, C. D., & Loiselle, D. (1982). Minor physical anomalies in alcoholic and schizophrenic adults and hyperactive and autistic children. *American Journal of Psychiatry, 139,* 640–643.

Guy, J. D., Majorski, L. V., Wallace, C. J., & Guy, M. P. (1983). The incidence of minor physical anomalies in adult male schizophrenics. *Schizophrenia Bulletin, 9,* 571–582.

Hoffman, R. E., & McGlashan, T. H. (1993). Parallel distributed processing and the emergence of schizophrenic symptoms. *Schizophrenia Bulletin, 19,* 119–140.

Hollister, J. M., Laing, P., & Mednick, S. A. (1996). Rhesus incompatibility as a risk factor for schizophrenia in male adults. *Archives of General Psychiatry, 53,* 19–24.

Huttunen, M. O., & Niskanen, P. (1978). Prenatal loss of father and psychiatric disorders. *Archives of General Psychiatry, 35,* 429–431.

Jakob, H., & Beckman, H. (1986). Prenatal developmental disturbances in the limbic allocortex in schizophrenics. *Journal of Neural Transmission, 65,* 303–326.

Kovelman, J. A., & Scheibel, A. B. (1984). A neurohistological correlate of schizophrenia. *Biological Psychiatry, 19,* 1602–1621.

Lam, C. W., & Berrios, G. E. (1992). Psychological concepts and psychiatric symptom-atology in some ancient Chinese medical texts. *History of Psychiatry, 3,* 117–128.

Lewis, S. W., Reveley, A. M., Reveley, M. A., Chitkara, B., & Murray, R. M. (1987). The familial/sporadic distinction as a strategy in schizophrenia research. *British Journal of Psychiatry, 151,* 306–313.

Markow, T. A., & Gottesman, I. I. (1989). Fluctuating dermatoglyphic asymmetry in psychotic twins. *Psychiatry Research, 29,* 37–43.

Markow, T. A., & Wandler, K. (1986). Fluctuating dermatoglyphic asymmetry and the genetics of liability to schizophrenia. *Psychiatry Research, 19,* 323–328.

Matthysse, S., Holzman, P. S., & Lange, K. (1986). The genetic transmission of schizophrenia: Application of Mendelian latent trait structure analysis to eye tracking dysfunctions in schizophrenia and affective disorder. *Journal of Psychiatric Research, 20,* 57–76.

Mednick, S. A., Machon, R. A., Huttunen, M. O., & Bonett, D. (1988). Adult schizophrenia following prenatal exposure to an influenza epidemic. *Archives of General Psychiatry, 45,* 189–192.

Mellor, C. S. (1992). Dermatoglyphic evidence of fluctuating asymmetry in schizophrenia. *British Journal of Psychiatry, 160,* 467–472.

Mirsky, A. F., & Duncan, C. C. (1986). Etiology and expression of schizophrenia: Neurobiological and psychosocial factors. *Annual Review of Psychology, 37,* 291–319.

Murray, R. M., & Jones, P. (1995). Back to the future in schizophrenia research. In J. Hafner & W. F. Gattaz (Eds.), *Search for the causes of schizophrenia* (Vol. 3, pp. 186–192). Berlin: Springer-Verlag, Berlin Heidelberg.

Murray, R. M., Lewis, S. W., & Reveley, A. M. (1985). Towards an aetiological classification of schizophrenia. *Lancet, 1,* 1023–1026.

Murray, R. M., O'Callaghan, E., Castle, D. J., & Lewis, S. W. (1992). A neurodevelopmental approach to the classification of schizophrenia. *Schizophrenia Bulletin, 18,* 319–332.

O'Callaghan, E., Larkin, C., Kinsella, A., & Waddington, J. L. (1991a). Familial, obstetric, and other clinical correlates of minor physical anomalies in schizophrenia. *American Journal of Psychiatry, 148,* 479–483.

O'Callaghan, E., Sham, P., Takei, N., Glover, G., & Murray, R. M. (1991b). Schizophrenia after prenatal exposure to 1957 A2 influenza epidemic. *Lancet, 337,* 1248–1250.

Selemon, L. D., Rajkowska, G., & Goldman-Rakic, P. S. (1995). Abnormally high neuronal density in the schizophrenic cortex. *Archives of General Psychiatry, 52,* 805–818.

Susser, E., Neugebauer, R., Hoek, H. W., Brown, A. S., Lin, S., Labovitz, D., & Gorman, J. M. (1996). Schizophrenia after prenatal famine. *Archives of General Psychiatry, 53,* 25–31.

Susser, E. S., & Lin, S. P. (1992). Schizophrenia after prenatal exposure to the Dutch Hunger Winter of 1944–1945. *Archives of General Psychiatry, 49,* 983–988.

Walker, E. F. (1994). Developmentally moderated expressions of the neuropathology underlying schizophrenia. *Schizophrenia Bulletin, 20,* 453–480.

Walker, E. F., & DiForio, D. (in press). Schizophrenia: A neural diathesis-stress model. *Psychological Review.*

Walker, E. F., Grimes, K. E., Davis, D. N., & Smith, A. J. (1993). Childhood precursors of schizophrenia: Facial expressions of emotion. *American Journal of Psychiatry, 150,* 1654–1660.

Walker, E. F., Savoie, T., & Davis, D. (1994). Neuromotor precursors of schizophrenia. *Schizophrenia Bulletin, 20,* 441–451.

Weinberger, D. R. (1987). Implications of normal brain development for the pathogenesis of schizophrenia. *Archives of General Psychiatry, 44,* 660–669.

Weinberger, D. R. (1995). From neuropathology to neurodevelopment. *Lancet, 346,* 552– 557.

Weinberger, D. R., & Lipska, B. K. (1995). Cortical maldevelopment, anti-psychotic drugs, and schizophrenia: A search for common ground. *Schizophrenia Research, 16,* 87–110.

Wyatt, R. J. (1996). Neurodevelopmental abnormalities and schizophrenia: A family affair. *Archives of General Psychiatry, 53,* 11–15.

Zubin, J., & Spring, B. (1977). Vulnerability: A new view of schizophrenia. *Journal of Abnormal Psychology, 86,* 103–126.

▶ 2

Neurocognition and Schizophrenia: General Approaches and Specific Models

My concentration is very poor. I jump from one thing to another. If I am talking to someone they only need to cross their legs or scratch their heads and I am distracted and forget what I was saying. I think I could concentrate better with my eyes shut. (McGhie & Chapman, 1961, p. 104)

My thoughts get all jumbled up. I start thinking or talking about something but I never get there. Instead, I wander off in the wrong direction and get caught up with all sorts of different things that may be connected with things I want to say but in a way I can't explain. People listening to me get more lost than I do. (McGhie & Chapman, 1961, p. 108)

EARLY FORMULATIONS OF ATTENTIONAL DYSFUNCTION IN SCHIZOPHRENIA

Initial clinical impressions of schizophrenia, even from a naive observer, sometimes can be quite insightful. Clinicians often state that schizophrenic patients seem to suffer from "attentional" problems. This impression stems from observations that patients seem to be easily distracted by environmental stimuli, and from descriptions of the patients themselves in which they complain of confusion and of being overwhelmed by stimuli. Aside from these subjective complaints and clinical observations, the more dramatic symptoms of schizophrenia (e.g., perceptions without external stimuli, loss of goal-directedness of speech) indicate a problem in the normal encoding and processing of information. Considering these factors, it comes as no surprise that problems in neurocognition have long been considered central to schizophrenia.

Emil Kraepelin is well-known for his influential classification of psychiatric disorders in the late 19th and early 20th century (Kraepelin, 1971). It is not as widely known that he also described a rather sophisticated subtyping of attentional dysfunctions in schizophrenia. Kraepelin's interest in attentional processing may have been sparked during his training with Wilhelm Wundt, the founder of the first laboratory of psychology in Leipzig. Kraepelin suggested that schizophrenic patients have two types of attentional abnormalities. One is a disorder in active attention (*aufmerksamkeit*) in which the patients "lose both inclination and ability on their own initiative to keep their attention fixed for any length of time" (pp. 5–6). This disorder in active attention, he suggested, was relatively consistent over time. Another disorder is in passive attention (*auffassung*) in which there is an "irresistible attraction of the attention to casual external impression" (pp. 6–7). He proposed that this disorder in passive attention was present only during the acute and terminal stages of the illness. The description of active attention is close to the modern definition of sustained attention, whereas passive attention is similar to selective attention. Kraepelin not only provided a rich characterization of types of attentional dysfunction in schizophrenia, but importantly, he also proposed a systematic relationship between the type of attentional dysfunction and the phase of illness (Nuechterlein & Asarnow, 1989).

In many ways, it is the contributions of Eugen Bleuler that shape current views of neurocognition in schizophrenia (Bleuler, 1950). He began by making a critical distinction between *fundamental* and *accessory* symptoms of schizophrenia. Fundamental symptoms were of two types. The *simple* fundamental symptoms included alterations in association, affectivity, and ambivalence. Disturbance in association was afforded a special status as the abnormality most closely linked to the disease process. These simple fundamental symptoms combined to form *compound* fundamental symptoms that included disturbances in attention. The term attention was used broadly in this formulation. Alteration in passive attention for Bleuler was much like a social withdrawal or lack of responsiveness to the environment: "... it is evident that the uninterested or autistically encapsulated patients pay very little attention to the outer world" (p. 68). Other descriptions of alterations in attention sound much like deficits in sustained attention: "The general tendency to fatigue in some cases also causes the rapid dwindling of attention" (p. 69).

Within Bleuler's framework, accessory symptoms derived from fundamental symptoms. Accessory symptoms included hallucinations, delusions, and a variety of behavioral and speech abnormalities. The fact that these symptoms were considered secondary made them no less important from a treatment perspective.

> It is not often that the fundamental symptoms are so markedly exhib-
> ited as to cause the patient to be hospitalized in a mental institution.
> It is primarily the accessory phenomena which make his retention at
> home impossible, or it is they which make the psychosis manifest and
> give occasion to require psychiatric help. These accessory symptoms
> may be present throughout the whole course of the disease, or only
> in entirely arbitrary periods of illness. (Bleuler, 1950, p. 94)

Bleuler introduced at least three essential concepts. First, in his distinction between simple and compound fundamental symptoms, he suggested
that certain basic dysfunctions can be assembled into composite symptoms,
including disordered attention. Bleuler's view, like Kraepelin's, may have
reflected the influence of Wilhelm Wundt and his structural school of psychology. Structuralism was an attempt to understand how elementary psychological units (e.g., the basic sensory qualities of an object) were combined
via certain principles of association into more complex experiences. The basic
psychological elements combined to form phenomena, which had properties
that could not have been predicted based on knowledge of the elements
alone. Wundt's approach to psychology was analogous to how a chemist
approaches the mixing of elements and was sometimes considered to be a
form of "mental chemistry." Wundt's notion of elementary and compound
normal psychological processes seem to have been mirrored in Bleuler's theory of simple and compound abnormal psychological processes.

A second contribution was Bleuler's view that psychotic symptoms such
as hallucinations and delusions were secondary to fundamental symptoms.
His view of a hierarchy of symptoms was both brilliant and counter-intuitive.
Bleuler proposed that features of the illness that were most noticeable and
dramatic, such as hallucinations and delusions, were relatively removed
from the disease process. To understand the nature of schizophrenia, we
should focus on core features of the illness even if it means de-emphasizing
more obvious defining features of the disorder. Bleuler (1950) argued that the
specific content of these symptoms are not predetermined, but instead are
based on chance: "Almost the totality of the heretofore described symptomatology of dementia praecox is a secondary, in a certain sense, an accidental
one" (p. 349).

A third and related contribution was his emphasis on the temporal
aspects of fundamental versus accessory symptoms. Features of the illness
that were enduring were considered more central to the disorder than features that were episodic.

The primary symptoms are the necessary partial phenomena of a disease; the secondary symptoms may be absent, at least potentially, or they may change without the disease process having to change at the same time. (Bleuler, 1950, p. 349)

Curiously, Bleuler's substantial impact on subsequent neurocognitive studies is not generally appreciated. Within his framework we have most of the conceptual building blocks for modern studies of neurocognitive vulnerability. Bleuler's uncoupling of the primary and secondary aspects of the disorder would have been a major conceptual advance by itself. However, he also proposed ways of testing his conceptualization by using different temporal courses of primary and secondary symptoms. In Chapter 4, we will see how modern studies of neurocognitive indicators of vulnerability to schizophrenia use exactly this approach to distinguish primary from secondary aspects of illness.

Since the seminal work of Kraepelin and Bleuler, studies of the neurocognition of schizophrenia have followed two quite different traditions. These different traditions are rarely explicitly stated by authors; instead they usually take the form of background assumptions that are nearly imperceptible to the reader. One tradition comes from *clinical neuropsychology*, the other from *experimental psychology*. The clinical neuropsychology approach started out by emphasizing assessment techniques to aid in differential diagnosis. In a typical study of this type, two groups of patients, one psychiatric and one neurological, were given a neuropsychological measure. Patients were then placed into one of two possible diagnostic categories (e.g., schizophrenia vs. brain damaged) based on their performance and this classification was compared to their actual diagnosis. As we will see shortly, the rationale for differential diagnosis was deeply flawed. More recent examples of the clinical neuropsychological approach to schizophrenia have gone beyond questions of strict differential diagnosis and have not suffered from the same conceptual flaws.

A second approach has grown from *experimental psychology* in which the goal is to characterize and understand the nature of cognitive deficits in psychotic disorders. A fundamental problem in studying neurocognition in schizophrenia is that a neurocognitive deficit could potentially arise from a number of sources. It could, in theory, be due to the symptoms of the illness, the medications that are used to treat the illness, or the effects of being institutionalized. The experimental psychological approach attempts to identify the nature of the deficits and to find deficits that are central to the illness (i.e., not a result of these other factors).

Different traditions generate their own lingo. The term "neuropsychology" connotes the clinical neuropsychology tradition and the term "cognition" is more common in the experimental psychology tradition. Although both of these terms will be used in this book, preference will be given to the term "neurocognition" because it cuts across the two traditions and because it reinforces the emphasis on underlying neural systems of higher mental processes.

CLINICAL NEUROPSYCHOLOGY AND DIFFERENTIAL DIAGNOSIS

Over the past century, neuropsychologists in clinical settings were asked to provide assessments to aid in differential diagnosis. A typical clinical neuropsychology referral question for schizophrenic patients was whether neurocognitive abnormalities were a result of schizophrenia or some type of brain dysfunction. The question was sometimes phrased as whether neurocognitive deficits were "organic" or "functional" in nature. While the question may seem simple on the surface, it is filled with conceptual and practical problems. This type of referral question generated studies that attempted to discriminate between schizophrenic and brain damaged patients on the basis of neurocognitive tests.

Differential Diagnosis

Heaton and his colleagues (Heaton, Baade, & Johnson, 1978) reviewed 94 studies published between 1960 and 1975 that compared neuropsychological performance of patients with brain injury to patients with various psychiatric disorders. The studies classified patients by selecting a cut-off score for a given test. Patients who scored better than the cut-off were classified as "schizophrenic" and those who scored worse were considered "brain damaged." Specificity of a neurological lesion was not a major concern because neurological patients were typically combined into a single brain damaged group regardless of the location or type of damage. Classification of patients based on neuropsychological tests was compared with their actual diagnosis to yield a "hit rate," which was the percentage of correct classifications. Hit rates from these studies are shown in Table 2.1. With only two groups (assuming equal size), arriving at a diagnosis by flipping a coin will yield 50% correct classification. The median hit rates are reasonably good for several of the diagnoses such as mixed psychiatric, affective, and mixed psychotic. But the hit rate for chronic schizophrenic patients was only 54%; not much better than flipping a coin.

The conclusion from this review is that neuropsychological tests cannot adequately discriminate chronic schizophrenic patients from brain damaged patients. Although the hit rates were better for patients with acute schizophrenia, most of these patients would not receive a diagnosis of schizophre-

TABLE 2.1   Classification Rates for Psychiatric Patients Versus
Brain Damaged Patients

Types of Psychiatric Patients	Number of Studies	Classification Rates (%)
Mixed Psychiatric	29	77
Affective	10	77
Mixed Psychotic	8	70
Acute Schizophrenic	14	77
Chronic Schizophrenic	34	54

nia with modern diagnostic criteria (e.g., DSM-III-R or DSM-IV) because
these systems require a six-month duration of symptoms. Overall, it does not
appear that neuropsychological tests can distinguish brain damaged from
schizophrenic patients when current diagnostic criteria are used.

Why were the classification rates so poor? One obvious explanation for
the poor classification rates is that the reason underlying group differences is
illusory: schizophrenic patients probably have a particular type of brain dysfunction. In the previous chapter we reviewed evidence that schizophrenia is
associated with abnormalities in neural migration and in a later chapter we
will consider additional evidence for structural and functional abnormalities
in the brains of schizophrenic patients. Once we view schizophrenia as a special type of brain disorder, the brain damaged (organic) versus schizophrenic
(functional) distinction becomes meaningless. We would not expect clinical
neuropsychological measures to have much success in differentiating
between these two groups.

Although there is ample reason to believe that schizophrenic patients
have some form of brain dysfunction, we cannot assume that the same performance from both groups on a clinical neuropsychological test indicates
the same underlying problem (Keefe, 1995; Levy, 1996). Clinical neuropsychological tests were designed to be sensitive to the type of dysfunction seen
with brain lesions (e.g., tumor or stroke). However, there are many pathways
to poor performance and schizophrenic patients may perform poorly for reasons that involve quite separate brain processes. Along these lines, it has
been suggested that brain damaged patients *cannot* perform better on neuropsychological measures due to structural damage whereas schizophrenic
patients *will not* perform better perhaps due to motivational factors
(reviewed in Goldstein, 1986). This distinction initially treated motivation as
something independent of neural structures, which clearly it is not. Hence,
the cannot/will not distinction is one way of saying that similar performance
can be explained by abnormalities in different underlying neural structures.

Another limitation of these earlier studies of differential diagnosis was the ill-advised practice of treating all forms of brain damage as a single entity. The approach of comparing schizophrenic patients with brain damaged patients has some merit *if* the brain damaged group is narrowly defined and well-characterized. Modern descendants of the differential diagnosis approach have compared schizophrenic patients to neurological patients with clearly-defined loci (e.g., left or right temporal lobe epilepsy) so that investigators can determine whether the performance of schizophrenic patients is consistent with (not necessarily caused by) the activity of a certain brain region (Gold et al., 1994). These more sophisticated studies have not strongly implicated a particular brain region for schizophrenia, suggesting instead the relevance of widely distributed brain circuits.

A Neuropsychological Profile for Schizophrenia

Assuming that schizophrenia is a particular type of brain disorder, it is still possible for schizophrenia and brain damaged patients to differ in the *pattern* of their neurocognitive performance. Neuropsychological batteries often yield profiles which graph patients' strengths and weaknesses across various neurocognitive abilities (e.g., language, memory, motor). Perhaps the type of brain damage that is associated with schizophrenia has its own neurocognitive profile.

The search for a characteristic neurocognitive profile in schizophrenia can be viewed as a search for a *differential deficit*. Compared to normal controls, schizophrenic patients, as a group, almost always have generally poor performance on tasks of higher mental abilities. Within the context of this suppressed performance, the question becomes whether patients are a little worse than controls on some neurocognitive measures and a lot worse on others. Although it may sound like an easy task, documenting differential neurocognitive deficits in the context of an overall deficit is surprisingly hard to do. If two groups appear to differ more on one test than another, it may reflect a true differential deficit, or it may reflect psychometric differences because one test has more power to discriminate between groups than the other (Chapman & Chapman, 1973).

Studies have used statistical techniques to roughly equate tests on discriminating power in an effort to identify true neurocognitive peaks and valleys. Using such techniques, some have suggested that schizophrenic patients have unusually large deficits in verbal memory (Saykin et al., 1991), whereas others found that retention of verbal material was relatively well-preserved in schizophrenia (Heaton et al., 1994). It has been suggested that deficits in schizophrenia are especially noticeable for abstraction, problem solving, and other prefrontal functions (Goldberg, Weinberger, Berman, Pliskin, & Podd, 1987). An alternative view is that neuropsychological deficits can be explained entirely as part of a generalized deficit—that it is unnecessary to look for particular areas of strength or weakness (Blanchard & Neale, 1994). An apparent generalized deficit could arise through an artifact. Perhaps there are several subgroups of schizophrenic patients, each with a different profile of neurocognitive performance depending on which brain system is most affected (Heinrichs & Awad, 1993). In this case, averaging the performance scores of the subgroups together would give the appearance of a generalized deficit.

Given these rather inconsistent results across studies, there is no agreed-upon, single neuropsychological profile for schizophrenia and, consequently, the role of clinical neuropsychology in psychiatric diagnosis is limited. The absence of a clear schizophrenia profile could be explained either by a global generalized deficit alone, by several subgroups of patients who have their own profile, or by a faint neurocognitive profile for schizophrenia that is hard to see against the background of a generalized deficit. To the extent that schizophrenia involves multiple brain regions and circuits, it may be unreasonable to expect a single consistent profile. Perhaps only a limited number of neural circuits are associated with schizophrenia, but the relevant circuits differ from patient to patient due to neurodevelopmental events, genetic risk factors, or learning history.

Cerebral Laterality of Schizophrenia

A separate, but somewhat related, question concerns whether schizophrenia can be linked to dysfunction in a particular cerebral hemisphere. Interest in a possible left hemisphere dysfunction in schizophrenia can be traced to observations of patients with epilepsy. Flor-Henry noticed that epilepsy patients with a left hemisphere focus sometimes had schizophrenia-like psychotic features, whereas patients with a right hemisphere focus had more mood-related symptoms (Flor-Henry, 1976). He concluded that it was "abnormal neuronal activity in the dominant temporal lobe and in its hippocampal-amygdaloid-cingular projections which is fundamentally responsible for the schizophrenic syndrome" (p. 390).

Flor-Henry essentially used a phenomenological approach in which he examined the symptoms of patients with documented, lateralized brain damage. Using a similar approach, Cutting (1994) examined the phenomenology of various neurological conditions and concluded that the evidence favored right hemisphere involvement in schizophrenia. Cutting argued that some patients with cerebrovascular accidents in the right hemisphere manifest classic schizophrenic symptoms such as disordered self-other boundaries, annihilation of will, and flattened affect. That two investigators used a similar approach and arrived at opposite sides of the brain probably indicates the limitations of a phenomenological approach for the question of laterality.

An alternative approach involves lateralized neurocognitive measures (Walker & McGuire, 1982).

Specialized neurocognitive procedures with lateralized presentation of stimuli have the advantage that subjects essentially serve as their own control. Hence, abnormalities in laterality are interpretable even if the patients have poorer overall performance than controls. The results of these neurocognitive studies are often generally consistent with the notion of a left hemisphere abnormality, possibly due to an overactivation of that hemisphere (Gur, 1978). Some functional neuroimaging studies have also supported the notion of a left hemisphere that is more active in patients than in controls (Gur et al., 1995). Schizophrenic patients might be using their left hemisphere to perform operations normally conducted more efficiently by the right hemisphere. Although the issue of laterality is an important question for schizophrenia research, it would be a profound oversimplification to describe schizophrenia strictly as a left hemisphere disorder. For one thing, it has been argued that the key neurocognitive deficit in schizophrenia is not intrinsic to any one hemisphere, but instead is an abnormality in the communication between the hemispheres (David, 1993). Further, it has been argued from neurocognitive and psychophysiological data that schizophrenia is not a uniformly lateralized disorder, but instead there are subgroups of schizophrenic patients who differ in hemispheric balance, some with left activity greater than right and others with right greater than left (Gruzelier, Seymour, Wilson, Jolley, & Hirsch, 1988).

To summarize, the clinical neuropsychological approach to schizophrenia may have initially bolted in the wrong direction with an emphasis on differential diagnosis. For the foreseeable future, the diagnostic process will continue to rely on structured clinical interviews, not neurocognitive assessments. Subsequent studies of differential deficit and laterality have been well-directed and informative. As we will see in later chapters, neuropsychological assessments of schizophrenic patients may provide valuable *prognostic* information, even if they provide poor *diagnostic* information.

EXPERIMENTAL PSYCHOLOGY OF SCHIZOPHRENIA

In contrast to the well-intended but misguided efforts to use neuropsychological assessments as a means of differential diagnosis, another approach, experimental psychology, has been used to explore the nature of neurocognitive impairments in schizophrenia. One goal of the experimental psychology approach has been to characterize neurocognitive impairment using the most current theoretical frameworks. A second and related goal is to use techniques from experimental psychology to search for neurocognitive indicators of vulnerability to schizophrenia. To understand the first goal, we need to review models of information processing. To appreciate the second goal, we need to consider a model of vulnerability/stress interactions.

Models of Information Processing

Many neurocognitive studies of schizophrenia in the 1970s and 1980s were influenced by two models of normal cognition: *capacity models* or *stage models*. Although the two models are partially overlapping, they have different emphases. With capacity models, the emphasis is on the overall processing capacity of the individual (Kahneman, 1973). Deficits in cognition can be attributed to a decrease in the overall amount of processing resources, or to an inefficient allocation of resources. Certain neurocognitive measures (e.g., the Continuous Performance Test, a measure of vigilance that will be discussed in the next chapter) are often viewed as indicators of overall attentional capacity, or attentional allocation priorities.

Alternatively, stage models emphasize a series of processing stages in which the output of one stage is fed to subsequent stages that transform and elaborate the information. When stage models are applied to schizophrenia, the goal is usually to identify the earliest stage at which a dysfunction occurs. The assumption is that a dysfunction at an early stage will have a cascading effect that will lead to disruptions in the quality of the information at later processing stages. Certain measures of early information processing, such as the backward masking procedure, are often viewed within a stage model.

A more integrative model of normal cognitive processing that has been developed by Cowan (1988) is shown in Figure 2.1. This model combines features of the other two and has heuristic value for understanding the types of attentional dysfunction that may be present in schizophrenia (Nuechterlein, Dawson, & Green, 1994). The Cowan model has several major components including a brief sensory store, memory components, and a central executive. The sensory store is very brief, lasting for a few hundred milliseconds and is experienced as the continuation of sensory input. Unlike many other models, there is no separate box for short-term memory. Instead, short-term memory (called activated memory) is a small portion of a long-term memory store that is activated at a given time. The focus of attention is a subset of the activated memory that is in conscious awareness. The central executive directs the process of voluntary attention by controlling which items are in the focus of attention.

Suppose that a stimulus from the environment enters the brief sensory store (the sound of a beeping car horn at a distance). The physical properties of the stimulus will be maintained briefly, perhaps a few hundred milliseconds (a mental representation of the tonal qualities of the horn). Whether or not that stimulus will enter awareness and become a focus of attention depends on two factors. First, it depends on whether the individual has habituated to the stimulus. If the current stimulus is similar to other recently encountered stimuli (your office is in Manhattan), habituation will occur and it will not enter the focus of attention. If, on the other hand, the stimulus is novel and different from other recent stimuli (the horn is particularly loud, or an unusual pitch), it will capture attention such as stimulus "D" in Figure 2.1. A second means for the stimulus to enter awareness shown with stimulus "A" is if the central executive decides that a stimulus is significant and selects it for further processing (you are expecting someone to pick you up in a car). This "top-down" processing, differs from "bottom-up" processing which is based on the sensory qualities of the stimulus.

The Cowan model allows for a complex set of interactions among its various components and subcomponents. We can take a particular neurocognitive deficit in schizophrenia and see how it is explained in terms of the model (Nuechterlein et al., 1994). For example, observed deficits in early visual and auditory processing could be explained by sensory/perceptual abnormalities that disrupt the operations of the brief sensory store. If the brief sensory store was disrupted, there could be a failure to activate the correct stimulus

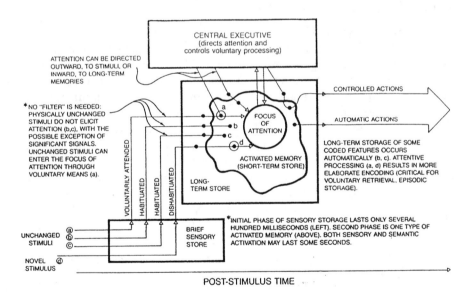

FIGURE 2.1

Source: From "Evolving Conceptions of Memory Storage, Selective Attention, and Their Mutual Constraints within the Human Information-Processing System" by N. Cowan, 1988, *Psychological Bulletin, 104*, p. 180. © 1988, American Psychological Association. Reprinted with permission.

code in long-term store. Deficits in frontal systems or selective attention could be viewed as a malfunction of the central executive's control of voluntary attention, which would interfere with the selection of certain stimuli for enhanced processing. The model could also explain well-documented psychophysiological abnormalities in orienting and habituation. Some patients are slow to habituate to stimuli, whereas others show fast and excessive habituation. For patients who are slow to habituate, stimuli that would normally be ignored by the central executive capture the focus of attention and pull the central executive off its primary task. For patients with excessive habituation, the process of dishabituation (orienting) is disrupted so that stimuli fail to capture the focus of attention when they normally should.

When such models are applied to schizophrenia research, neurocognitive deficits that initially appear unrelated can be viewed within a single framework. Within the framework of a cognitive model, it becomes possible to look for common links among different neurocognitive measures. Without such models, the long list of neurocognitive deficits in schizophrenia appears haphazard.

Vulnerability/Stress Formulations

The second major goal of the experimental psychology approach is to determine which aspects of neurocognition are linked to genetic vulnerability to schizophrenia. In its simplest form, the vulnerability/stress model of schizophrenia holds that some individuals are predisposed (not predetermined) to developing schizophrenia and that environmental factors influence the expression of the predisposition (Zubin & Spring, 1977).

One of the earliest examples of a vulnerability/stress model for schizophrenia comes from the famous Russian physiologist, I. P. Pavlov. In the early 1930s, after 30 years of groundbreaking research on conditioned reflexes, Pavlov moved his activities from the laboratory to the clinic. The switch in focus can be seen as an extension of his interest in brain/behavior interactions and his goal to develop theories that encompass both normal and abnormal activities (Windholz, 1993). Pavlov considered higher functions of the brain to involve a balance between spreading neural excitation (the basis of approach behavior) and spreading neural inhibition (the basis of avoidance behavior). In his view of schizophrenia, a weak genotype allows the brain to be swamped by neural excitation when faced with taxing environmental conditions. To save the brain from destruction, a self-protective inhibition spreads over the cortex. The result is schizophrenia. In 1935, three months before his death, Pavlov clearly articulated an early version of a vulnerability/stress model for schizophrenia during clinical rounds at the Balinskii Hospital Psychiatric Clinic in Leningrad. His statements reflect an appreciation of the interaction between the schizophrenic genotype and environmental events.

For the last two years I often saw sick people, and I asked myself many times this question: What would have happened if all these schizophrenics, of whom there are so many, just imagine this, if those schizophrenics would be, at the first sign of illness, put in a greenhouse to keep them away from the blows of life, of all the difficulties that life creates, well, would they then become real schizophrenics? The more I see, and the more I think about it, I come to the conclusion, that it is possible that they would not become ill, but remain healthy...(Bykov 1954; translated in Windholz, 1993, p. 519)

The vulnerability/stress model is now widely accepted. Because of the abundant evidence of a genetic component for schizophrenia, the predisposition is presumed to be genetic in origin, but additional early factors, such as prenatal and perinatal neurodevelopmental factors can potentiate the risk for the disorder. The interaction between predisposition and environmental stress is represented in Figure 2.2 (Mirsky & Duncan, 1986). The figure displays an inverse relationship between the extent of genetic predisposition and the amount of stress that is necessary to push someone across a "threshold" into the schizophrenia spectrum (e.g., Schizotypal Personality Disorder)

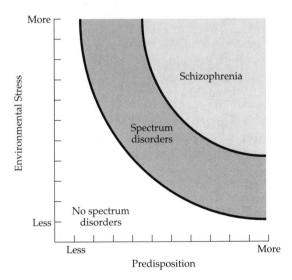

FIGURE 2.2

Source: Adapted from "Etiology and Expression of Schizophrenia: Neurobiological and Psychosocial Factors" by A. F. Mirsky and C. C. Duncan, 1986, *Annual Review of Psychology, 37,* p. 312.

or into schizophrenia itself. With more predisposition to schizophrenia, less stress is needed to cross the threshold.

The general nature of the vulnerability/stress model makes it more applicable, but also harder to experimentally test components of the model. The goal of research in this area is to isolate the particular vulnerability factors, early potentiating factors, and environmental stressors at a more specific level. Figure 2.3 shows efforts in this direction. The figure is a heuristic framework for the etiology of schizophrenia, which was developed by the members of the UCLA Clinical Research Center for the Study of Schizophrenia (Nuechterlein et al., 1992). This interactive framework presents several different categories of variables. Near the top of the figure is the category of Personal Vulnerability Factors including enduring neurocognitive abnormalities that are present at various levels of severity both in and out of psychotic episode. These vulnerability factors are believed to reflect a genetic predisposition. The model also includes both Personal and Environmental Protective Factors, which can reduce the likelihood that a person will develop schizophrenia. Knowledge of such factors is naturally important for the development of interventions. The different categories of variables interact to produce a Transient Intermediate State that immediately precedes the development of Prodromal Symptoms. The Prodromal Symptoms can be non-psychotic symptoms such as anxiety or low-level psychotic-like symptoms that, in turn, precede the development of psychotic symptoms. The various types of outcomes are shown on the right side of the figure. Note that psychotic symptoms are only one of three categories of outcome domains. The other two areas, work and social impairment, may be especially relevant for long-term rehabilitation.

The level of detail in this framework conveys the complexity of linkages in this area. Comprehensive theories for the etiology and course of schizophrenia need to take into account multiple domains ranging from basic biology to complex social interactions. It is difficult to imagine any other illness that depends on such a wide variety of variables for its expression. Despite the complexity of the UCLA model, the relationships among variables are clearly testable and the model is continually undergoing revision based on research findings. For example, in a recent revision neurodevelopmental factors have been added to the model and the types of neurochemical dysfunctions have been broadened. Based on recent findings, the model has been modified to include more specific aspects of neurocognition, such as early perceptual processes and working memory, in the panels for Personal Vulnerability Factors and Intermediate States. Essentially, neurocognitive processes are viewed as bridges between genetic vulnerability, protective factors, neurodevelopmental abnormalities, and neurochemical dysfunctions on the one hand, and outcome on the other. All roads to schizophrenia go through neurocognitive intersections.

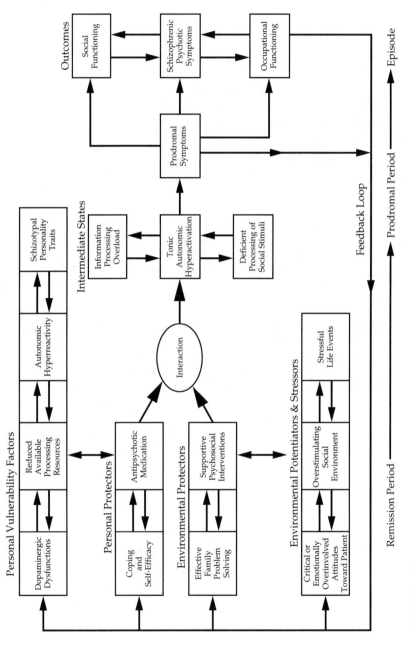

FIGURE 2.3

REFERENCES

Blanchard, J. J., & Neale, J. M. (1994). The neuropsychological signature of schizophrenia: Generalized or differential deficit? *American Journal of Psychiatry, 151,* 40–48.

Bleuler, E. (1950). *Dementia praecox or the group of schizophrenias.* New York: International Universities Press.

Chapman, L. J., & Chapman, J. P. (1973). Problems in the measurement of cognitive deficit. *Psychology Bulletin, 79,* 380–385.

Cowan, N. (1988). Evolving conceptions of memory storage, selective attention, and their mutual constraints within the human information-processing system. *Psychological Bulletin, 104,* 163–191.

Cutting, J. (1994). Evidence for right hemisphere dysfunction in schizophrenia. In A. S. David & J. C. Cutting (Eds.), *The neuropsychology of schizophrenia* (pp. 231–242). London: Lawrence Erlbaum.

David, A. S. (1993). Callosal transfer in schizophrenia: Too much or too little? *Journal of Abnormal Psychology, 102,* 573–579.

Flor-Henry, P. (1976). Lateralized temporal-limbic dysfunction and psychopathology. *Annals New York Academy of Science, 280,* 777–795.

Gold, J. M., Herman, B. P., Randolph, C., Wyler, A. R., Goldberg, T. E., & Weinberger, D. R. (1994). Schizophrenia and temporal lobe epilepsy. *Archives of General Psychiatry, 51,* 265–272.

Goldberg, T. E., Weinberger, D. R., Berman, K. F., Pliskin, N. H., & Podd, M. H. (1987). Further evidence for dementia of the prefrontal type in schizophrenia? A controlled study of teaching the Wisconsin Card Sorting Test. *Archives of General Psychiatry, 44,* 1008–1014.

Goldstein, G. (1986). The neuropsychology of schizophrenia. In I. Grant & K. M. Adams (Eds.), *Neuropsychological assessment of neuropsychiatric disorders.* New York: Oxford University Press.

Gruzelier, J., Seymour, K., Wilson, L., Jolley, A., & Hirsch, S. (1988). Impairments on neuropsychologic tests of temporohippocampal and frontohippocampal functions and word fluency in remitting schizophrenia and affective disorders. *Archives of General Psychiatry, 45,* 623–629.

Gur, R. E. (1978). Left hemisphere dysfunction and overactivation in schizophrenia. *Journal of Abnormal Psychology, 87,* 226–238.

Gur, R. E., Mozley, P. D., Resnick, S. M., Mozley, L. H., Shtasel, D. L., Gallacher, F., Arnold, S. E., Karp, J. S., Alavi, A., Reivich, M., & Gur, R. C. (1995). Resting cerebral glucose metabolism in first-episode and previously treated patients with schizophrenia relates to clinical features. *Archives of General Psychiatry, 52,* 657–667.

Heaton, R. K., Baade, L. E., & Johnson, K. L. (1978). Neuropsychological test results associated with psychiatric disorders in adults. *Psychology Bulletin, 85,* 141–162.

Heaton, R., Paulsen, J. S., McAdams, L. A., Kuck, J., Zisook, S., Braff, D., Harris, J., & Jeste, D. V. (1994). Neuropsychological deficits in schizophrenics. *Archives of General Psychiatry, 51,* 469–476.

Heinrichs, R. W., & Awad, A. G. (1993). Neurocognitive subtypes of chronic schizophrenia. *Schizophrenia Research, 9,* 49–58.

Kahneman, D. (1973). *Attention and effort.* Englewood Cliffs: Prentice-Hall.

Keefe, R. S. E. (1995). The contribution of neuropsychology to psychiatry. *American Journal of Psychiatry, 152,* 6–15.

Kraepelin, E. (1971). *Dementia praecox and paraphrenia.* Huntington, NY: Robert E. Krieger.

Levy, D. L. (1996). Location, location, location: The pathway from behavior to brain locus in schizophrenia. In S. W. Matthysse, D. L. Levy, F. Benes, & J. Kagan (Eds.), *Psychopathology: The evolving science of mental disorder* (pp. 100–126). New York: Cambridge University Press.

McGhie, A., & Chapman, J. (1961). Disorders of attention and perception in early schizophrenia. *British Journal of Medical Psychology, 34,* 103–116.

Mirsky, A. F., & Duncan, C. C. (1986). Etiology and expression of schizophrenia: Neurobiological and psychosocial factors. *Annual Review of Psychology, 37,* 291–319.

Nuechterlein, K. H., & Asarnow, R. F. (1989). Cognition and perception. In H. I. Kaplan & B. J. Sadock (Eds.), *Comprehensive textbook of psychiatry* (5th ed., Vol. 1). Baltimore, MD: Williams & Wilkins.

Nuechterlein, K. H., Dawson, M. E., Gitlin, M., Ventura, J., Goldstein, M. J., Snyder, K. S., Yee, C. M., & Mintz, J. (1992). Developmental processes in schizophrenic disorders: Longitudinal studies of vulnerability and stress. *Schizophrenia Bulletin, 18,* 387–425.

Nuechterlein, K. H., Dawson, M. E., & Green, M. F. (1994). Information-processing abnormalities as neuropsychological vulnerability indicators for schizophrenia. *Acta Psychiatrica Scandinavica, 90* (Suppl . 384), 71–79.

Saykin, A. J., Gur, R. C., Gur, R. E., Mozley, P. D., Mozley, L. H., Resnick, S. M., Kester, D. B., & Stafiniak, P. (1991). Neuropsychological function in schizophrenia: Selective impairment in memory and learning. *Archives of General Psychiatry, 48,* 618–624.

Walker, E., & McGuire, M. (1982). Intra- and interhemispheric information processing in schizophrenia. *Psychological Bulletin, 92,* 701–725.

Windholz, G. (1993). Pavlov's concept of schizophrenia as related to the theory of higher nervous activity. *History of Psychiatry, 4,* 511–526.

Zubin, J., & Spring, B. (1977). Vulnerability: A new view of schizophrenia. *Journal of Abnormal Psychology, 86,* 103–126.

► **3**

The Scope of Neurocognitive Deficits in Schizophrenia

The range of neurocognitive deficits in schizophrenia is extremely broad; a comprehensive review would be rather dense and would likely obscure the main points. Instead, illustrative types of deficits will be selected for discussion, with an emphasis on measures that will appear again in subsequent chapters. Cross-sectional comparisons of patients and controls, like many of the studies in this chapter, are only the first step. Fuller appreciation of the nature of the deficits will emerge over the following chapters when we see how neurocognitive measures are used in longitudinal designs, studies of first-degree relatives, and treatment studies.

TYPES OF NEUROCOGNITIVE DEFICITS IN SCHIZOPHRENIA

Early Visual Processing

In the mid 1800s, the Scottish philosopher Sir William Hamilton raised a central question: How many items can the mind perceive and attend to (i.e., apprehend) at one time?

> If you throw a handful of marbles on the floor, you will find it difficult to view at once more than six or seven at most, without confusion; but if you group them into twos or threes, you can comprehend as many groups as you can units because the mind considers these groups as units. (cited in Asarnow, Granholm, & Sherman, 1991)

In this quote, Hamilton not only suggested a limitation of our ability to attend to multiple items (six or seven at most), he also anticipated the process of cognitive "chunking" by which items are combined to facilitate encoding. In the later part of the 1800s, Hamilton's observation received experimental testing. Jevons (1871) conducted a clever experiment in which he served as both subject and experimenter. He chose to investigate the observations of Hamilton empirically because "it is one of the very few points in psychology which can, as far as we yet see, be submitted to experiment" (p. 281). He set a box lined with white paper on a black tray. After grabbing a handful of black beans, he threw the beans toward the box so that an undetermined number would fall into it. At the exact moment when the beans came to rest, he made an estimate of the number of beans in the box and then compared his estimate to the actual number of beans in the box. He repeated this procedure over 1,000 times and was able to calculate accuracy rates across a wide range of values. In accordance with the statement from Hamilton, the estimates were highly accurate with only 4 beans, dropped to 82% correct with 6 beans, and only 43% correct with 10 beans.

The introduction of the tachistoscope and computerized presentations has provided much better control over stimulus presentations for modern Span of Apprehension Tests (Span; Asarnow et al., 1991). In a commonly used version of the Span, subjects are told that letters will be flashed on a screen, and that either the letter "T" or "F" will be in each array of letters. Non-target letters are presented in other positions and the difficulty of the task can be modified by altering the number of non-target letters. The letters are presented briefly (usually less than 100 ms), so most of the cognitive processing occurs *after* the letters have disappeared from the screen. This is accomplished by scanning an internal representation of the screen, called the icon.

Another measure of early visual processing is backward masking. Imagine looking at a screen when a simple target stimulus (e.g., a single letter) is presented. The duration of the target is extremely brief (perhaps 5–20 ms), but you are able to identify it with absolute accuracy nonetheless. Now imagine that, after the presentation of the target, the screen goes blank for a brief period, and then another stimulus (overlapping Xs) is presented (see Figure 3.1). Your instructions are to ignore the Xs and to continue to identify the target. If the interval between the two stimuli is short (e.g., less than 100 ms) you may discover that you are unable to identify the stimulus. You may not even be aware that a target was presented at all. The Xs effectively masked the target. Because the Xs were presented after the target, this procedure is called backward masking.

Backward masking effects occur for everyone, but schizophrenic patients consistently exhibit *deficits* in backward masking tasks, meaning that the mask interferes even more with visual processing of the target for schizophrenic patients than for normal individuals (Braff, 1981; Knight, 1992; Saccuzzo & Braff, 1981). The exact reasons for this deficit are not known, but

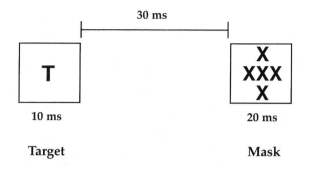

FIGURE 3.1   Backward Masking

may be related to the process by which the internal representation of the target (the *icon*) is formed. The masking effect is believed to occur because the mask prevents the full formation of the icon of the target. This inability to form a complete icon could be either because the target icon in schizophrenia is especially susceptible to disruption, or because the mask is especially powerful (Green, Nuechterlein, & Mintz, 1994b). Because the backward masking effect is determined by interactions of specific visual pathways, masking procedures can help isolate the pathways involved with the performance deficit in schizophrenia. Backward masking depends on the interactions between the transient (magnocellular) and sustained (parvocellular) visual pathways (Breitmeyer, 1984; Breitmeyer & Ganz, 1976). It has been suggested that the deficit in schizophrenia may stem from a dysfunction in which the transient channels are overactive (Green, Nuechterlein, & Mintz, 1994a; Green et al., 1994b; Schwartz et al., 1994).

Both the Span of Apprehension and Backward Masking tasks are designed to explore how patients create an internal representation of a brief visual display and how they scan it to extract relevant information. These measures will be discussed in more detail in the next chapter because they are putative indicators of genetic vulnerability to schizophrenia. While these tasks can present difficult momentary perceptual judgments, they do not require the same ongoing expenditure of effort compared with tasks of sustained attention such as the Continuous Performance Test (CPT).

Sustained Attention

During World War II, airborne radar operators of the Royal Air Force flew over the English Channel searching for German U-boats. The U-boats appeared as small blips on a radar screen that was already noisy (i.e., the screen had lines, streaks, and other blips that were a result of imperfections in the equipment, or were generated by objects other than U-boats). Consider the task of the radar operator. First of all, the discrimination between a U-boat (a target) and every other visual image on the screen (noise) was quite difficult. In addition, the risks of making a mistake are enormous. If the operator says that there is a U-boat when there is none, it may cause a costly unnecessary mobilization of defense forces. If a blip is really a U-boat, but the operator decides that it is only noise, the costs are even greater. The situation presented a practical question for the Royal Air Force: How long can someone perform such a task at their optimal level? A way to assess sustained attention, or vigilance, was developed. This test, called the Continuous Performance Test (CPT), assessed the ability of a subject to discriminate targets from non-targets under various conditions and over various lengths of time. The CPT became a standard measure in experimental psychology and now is commonly used in the study of schizophrenia. Many laboratories internationally are now using modern computerized procedures that approximate the perceptual characteristics of World War II radar screens.

In a typical CPT, stimuli are briefly presented on a computer screen one at a time over a period of several minutes (see Figure 3.2). The subject is expected to focus attention on the stimuli and to respond by pressing a button each time the target stimulus appears. Stimuli are usually presented at a rate of one per second at durations of less than 100 ms. The CPT yields an index of the subject's ability to press to targets (signal) and not press to non-targets (noise), an ability called *sensitivity*. Sensitivity across an entire test is called vigilance level, and the change in sensitivity from the beginning to the end of a test is called vigilance decrement.

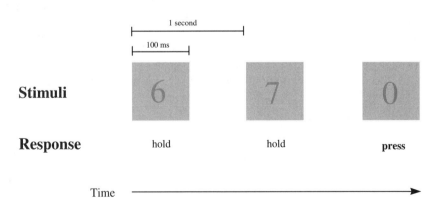

FIGURE 3.2   Continuous Performance Test—Single Target

Schizophrenic patients show deficits on the CPT compared with controls (Nuechterlein, 1991). The deficits are found in multiple studies that have used CPT versions with a single target (Orzack & Kornetsky, 1966), a target sequence that imposes a slight memory load (Cornblatt, Lenzenweger, & Erlenmeyer-Kimling, 1989), or in a version of the CPT that imposes a perceptual burden by using visually degraded stimuli (Nuechterlein et al., 1992). Although the presence of a deficit on the CPT is well-established, the exact nature of the deficit is not clear. If we intuit that patients have a deficit in sustained attention, then we would expect them to show a relatively sharp drop in performance over the duration of the test (i.e., a greater vigilance decrement). However, schizophrenic patients generally do not differ from normal controls in vigilance decrement (Cornblatt et al., 1989). Instead they differ most reliably on overall sensitivity (vigilance level). Hence, it appears that the CPT taps an ability related to schizophrenia (we will see later that it is also a promising indicator of vulnerability to the disorder), but the critical deficit may not be sustained attention per se.

Sustained attention can be distinguished from selective attention. Selective attention is demonstrated by the real life example of a cocktail party. The listener is able to follow one conversation (usually with a little bit of difficulty), while simultaneously ignoring a host of other conversations. In this manner, the listener is able to selectively attend. Laboratory measures of selective attention approximate this "cocktail party phenomenon" by presenting multiple stimuli to the subject, some of which are to be ignored. Consistent with clinical observations, schizophrenic patients are more distractible than controls on experimental measures of selective attention (Oltmanns & Neale, 1975). Latent inhibition has served as an alternative means of assessing selective attention in schizophrenia (Lubow & Gewirtz, 1995). In latent inhibition, one group of subjects is preexposed to a stimulus that has no particular consequence at that time. On later trials, the stimulus is given significance, but it takes longer for preexposed subjects to learn these new associations. Schizophrenic patients in the acute phase of illness fail to display the typical latent inhibition effect (Baruch, Hemsley, & Gray, 1988), a finding that has been viewed as indicating a deficit in selective attention.

Memory

Bleuler (see Chapter 2), whose observations were so astute when it came to attentional deficits, completely missed the presence of memory deficits. He believed that memory functions were intact in schizophrenia. In his defense, documenting memory deficits in schizophrenia has been tricky for several reasons. Most importantly, there are different types of "memory" such as verbal and nonverbal. Within verbal memory tasks, a key distinction is made between recall (e.g., generating a list of words or a story from memory) versus recognition (e.g., deciding whether or not a word was previously presented). Some earlier investigations proposed that schizophrenic patients have deficits in recall, but that their recognition was intact (e.g., Nachmani & Cohen, 1969). Subsequent studies suggested that recognition deficits are present in schizophrenia, but they may be relatively less severe than recall deficits (Calev, 1984).

A clearer understanding of memory deficits in schizophrenia may come from the distinction between *explicit* (or declarative) versus *implicit* (or non-declarative) forms of learning and memory (Squire, 1992; Squire & Zola-Morgan, 1988). Explicit forms of memory include tasks that rely on conscious recollection of specific, previous events and can be articulated. Recalling a list of words or a story is an explicit memory task. In contrast, implicit forms of memory occur outside of conscious awareness. Procedural learning is a type of implicit learning in which subjects learn how to perform a task. They demonstrate learning through improved performance on a task over a series of trials (Squire & Zola-Morgan, 1988). The distinction between explicit and implicit (specifically procedural) learning is of interest in clinical neuropsychology because amnesic patients have severe deficits in explicit learning, but have intact implicit learning (Cohen & Squire, 1980; Corkin, 1968). Could the same pattern be true for schizophrenic patients?

Procedural learning in schizophrenia is often measured with the Pursuit Rotor Test. In this test, the subject tries to maintain contact between the tip of a light-sensitive wand and a small, lit target area that moves in a circular path at a constant speed. The critical measure is not how well someone does at the beginning of the task, it is how much better they perform with practice. Hence, motor learning can be assessed over several blocks of trials. Some, but not all, studies have reported that schizophrenic patients have normal rates of improvement (Granholm, Bartzokis, Asarnow, & Marder, 1993; Kern, Green, & Wallace, 1997), on the Pursuit Rotor Test, suggesting that procedural learning is relatively intact in schizophrenia.

Another form of memory that has received increased attention is *working* memory. Sometimes described as our "mental blackboard," the concept of working memory is similar to the notion of short-term memory in which a memory representation is temporarily maintained. Measures of working memory include delayed matching-to-sample tests. In these tests, a stimulus is presented briefly to the subject, followed by a delay period during which the subject cannot see the stimulus. After the delay period, the subject selects the stimulus out of two or more possibilities. Working memory tests can be divided into verbal and spatial forms depending on whether the subject is asked to identify or locate the stimulus. Measures of spatial working memory are entirely appropriate for studies with non-human primates. As a result of careful studies of single cell recordings in animals, the neural underpinnings of spatial working memory have been mapped out with a fair amount of precision (Fuster, 1989; Goldman-Rakic, 1991; Goldman-Rakic, 1993). Certain neurons in the prefrontal cortex fire selectively in the delay periods of delayed matching-to-sample tasks. Hence, it appears that these neurons are responsible for maintaining an "on line" representation of the stimulus when the stimulus is no longer in the visual field and before any motor response is made. Because the neural circuits for spatial working memory tasks were known and included the prefrontal region, it was reasonable to apply these measures to the study of schizophrenia (Park & Holzman, 1992). Schizophrenic patients showed deficits compared with controls on tasks with a spatial working memory load, but not during control tasks without the delay period.

Overall, it appears that schizophrenic patients have well-documented deficits in several types of memory including explicit and working memory. For explicit verbal memory, the difficulties are especially obvious for recall, but are also present for recognition tasks. Some investigators have suggested that the deficits in verbal memory are disproportionately large compared with other neurocognitive deficits (Saykin et al., 1991, 1994), but not all agree with this notion. Deficits in procedural learning may be present also, but if so, they are less obvious than deficits in explicit memory.

Executive Functions ⟋

It is fairly common for schizophrenic patients to have difficulty with solving problems and planning sequences in daily situations. For this reason, there has been a long-standing interest in patients' performance on tests of *executive* functioning. Executive functioning refers to a host of neurocognitive activities that are associated with the prefrontal cortex such as planning, problem solving, shifting cognitive set, and alternating between two or more tasks.

Earlier incarnations of research on executive functioning in schizophrenia included studies of "abstraction." Kurt Goldstein (1959) proposed that the central problem in schizophrenia is an impairment in abstraction that leads to concrete responses. Support for an abnormality in abstraction came from card sorting tests in which patients looked at particular examples of items on cards and then tried to infer (abstract) common properties (Goldstein & Scheerer, 1941). Abstraction as an experimental construct was difficult to study empirically because it was, well, abstract. Nonetheless, this line of investigation evolved into a substantial and productive literature on executive functioning in schizophrenia.

The Wisconsin Card Sorting Test (WCST) has emerged as the most commonly used measure of executive functioning in schizophrenia research. On the WCST, subjects match a deck of cards to one of four target cards, on the basis of three rules (color, shape, or number). The trick is that the subjects are not told how to match the cards; they are only told if their match was right or wrong. From this feedback, they are supposed to work out the correct sorting rule. If subjects make 10 consecutive correct responses, the sorting rule changes, but they are not informed of the change. Subjects then need to determine the new sorting rule, again based only on feedback about which responses are right or wrong. To successfully complete the WCST, subjects need to *attain* a concept (sorting rule), *maintain* this concept for 10 consecutive responses, and *switch* the concept when the rule changes. Figure 3.3 shows examples of the stimulus cards in the WCST (Heaton, 1981).

Schizophrenic patients have difficulty on the WCST and other tests of executive functioning and some have suggested that their deficits on these measures may be greater than on other neurocognitive measures (Goldberg, Weinberger, Berman, Pliskin, & Podd, 1987). Although the amount of emphasis on the WCST defies complete explanation, heightened interest in this test comes in large part from a finding that normal controls activate the prefrontal cortex when performing the test, but schizophrenic patients do not (Weinberger, Berman, & Zec, 1986). This finding provides a neurophysiological explanation for the performance deficit (see Chapter 7). Interest in the WCST continues to be reflected by its frequent use in neuroimaging projects and studies of cognitive rehabilitation techniques (see Chapter 9).

General Intelligence

Intellectual ability can be considered a global neurocognitive function. Intellectual quotient (IQ) scales are designed to be multifactorial and are not

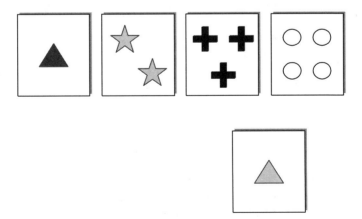

FIGURE 3.3   Wisconsin Card Sorting Test

well-suited for isolating particular neurocognitive functions or implicating particular brain regions. In addition, IQ scales do not assess some of the neurocognitive domains that are relevant to schizophrenia such as early visual processing and memory. Nonetheless, IQ measures are familiar to practitioners and large data bases are available because IQ tests are frequently administered in schools and hospitals.

In general, schizophrenic patients show lower IQs than would be expected based on their family and environmental factors (Aylward, Walker, & Bettes, 1984). The reduced IQ is true for pre-schizophrenic children and the difference may increase at the onset of illness and then remain fairly stable (Goldberg, Hyde, Kleinman, & Weinberg, 1993). An intriguing finding across studies is that schizophrenic patients tend to have higher verbal than performance IQ scores. This pattern, which is not consistent with a left-hemisphere dysfunction, may be explained by the fact that several of the verbal subtests (e.g., vocabulary and information) are relatively insensitive to injury and may be less influenced than other subtests by the onset of illness.

The relationship between schizophrenia and lower IQ could be viewed in a couple of ways (Aylward et al., 1984). First, IQ might be a mediating factor for schizophrenia that is independent of the predisposition to the disorder. Let us take a person who is at risk for schizophrenia because of their genetic predisposition. If that person happens to have a high IQ, it could increase the individual's capacity to cope with stressors and reduce the likelihood of developing schizophrenia. Alternatively, lower IQ could be viewed as part of the genetic predisposition to schizophrenia. In this case, lower IQ would be a marker, not a mediator, of the predisposition.

Psychophysiology: Startle-Blink and Eye Tracking

The psychophysiological literature in schizophrenia is vast, technical, and beyond the scope of this book. Nonetheless, we will briefly consider how two representative procedures, the pre-pulse inhibition of startle-blink and eye tracking, have informed neurocognitive research in schizophrenia.

Let us say that you are sitting in a quiet room when suddenly there is a sharp, loud noise. The natural reaction is to be startled; you will involuntarily flinch. As part of this startle response, you will also blink and the amplitude of the eye blink can serve as a measure of the magnitude of the startle. Now imagine that you hear a quiet, non-startling tone shortly before the loud noise. For most people, this pre-pulse reduces the amplitude of the blink (see Figure 3.4). However, for schizophrenic patients the blink is not attenuated as much as with normal controls (Braff et al., 1978). The patients appear less able to "dampen" the second stimulus. In essence, the second stimulus makes a larger physiological impression for patients than it should. Other studies have reported that the problem in pre-pulse inhibition with schizophrenic patients

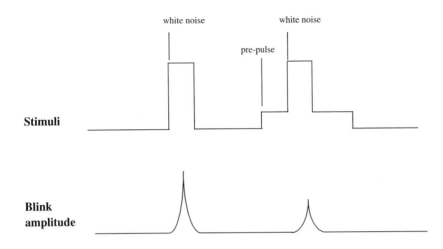

FIGURE 3.4   Pre-Pulse Inhibition of Startle-Eye Blink

is not lack of attenuation per se, but instead, the lack of the normal ability to modify the degree of attenuation when instructed to attend to or ignore certain tones (Dawson, Hazlett, Filion, Nuechterlein, & Schell, 1993).

This type of attenuation in which an initial stimulus reduces the physiological response to a subsequent stimulus is called *sensory gating*. One interpretation is that schizophrenic patients have a failure of sensory gating. At a neurophysiological level, Graham (1975) has suggested that the inhibition of the startle-blink involves interactions between two distinct groups of neurons that process sensory information. One population of neurons has a rapid rise time and a low detection threshold, whereas the other has a slower rise time and a higher threshold. These pathways are similar to the transient and sustained channels that were discussed in reference to backward masking (Braff, Saccuzzo, & Geyer, 1991). The notion that patients have a failure in sensory gating may provide insight into some of their subjective experiences. Patients sometimes indicate that they feel "bombarded" by sensory input and are unable to effectively filter out extraneous stimuli. Sensory gating methods offer a physiological explanation of this experience. The stimuli that are not effectively gated would probably be perceived more strongly than usual and might be experienced as more intrusive.

Another psychophysiological method is the recording of eye movements. In 1908, Diefendorf and Dodge coined the term "praecox pursuit" to describe the types of ocular motor deficits found in schizophrenia (cited in Levy, Holzman, Matthysse, & Mendell, 1993). Eye tracking dysfunction was studied sporadically over the next half century, and a comprehensive series of modern studies began in 1973 (Holzman, Proctor, & Hughes, 1973).

Abnormalities in eye tracking have been one of the most replicated findings in the schizophrenia literature.

In most eye tracking tasks, subjects are instructed to watch a moving target. Eye tracking involves two types of eye movements: smooth pursuit and saccades. The smooth pursuit system matches the velocity of the eye to the velocity of the target so that the image of the target is always stabilized on the fovea. If the eye is moving too fast or too slow for the target, saccades are needed to catch up to, or back up to, the target (Levy et al., 1993). Other types of saccades, which do not serve this corrective function, are normally inhibited during smooth pursuit. The primary disturbance in eye tracking in schizophrenia seems to involve an abnormality in the smooth pursuit system. There are also increases in the frequency of saccades, but these seem mainly a way to compensate for abnormal pursuit and not a primary disturbance.

Interest in eye tracking in schizophrenia stems partially from its established relationship to basic neurophysiological mechanisms. As we will see in the next chapter, eye tracking is especially valuable as a marker of genetic vulnerability to schizophrenia. Deviant eye tracking has been found in a relatively high proportion of first-degree relatives of patients.

HETEROGENEITY OF NEUROCOGNITIVE DEFICITS

Schizophrenia is frequently considered to be a heterogeneous disorder. In fact, the title of Bleuler's classic text refers to "The Group of Schizophrenias." Do all patients have neurocognitive deficits? On any given test, only a subgroup of patients will perform in the deficit range. The proportion of patients in this range depends on the severity of the patient sample and the selection of the cut-off score, but is often around 50%. In most samples, there is substantial variability in test performance and considerable overlap with a control sample. This observation has led investigators to wonder whether only a subgroup of patients actually demonstrate neurocognitive deficits, whereas others do not. An alternative view of heterogeneity, discussed in the previous chapter, is that there are multiple subgroups of schizophrenic patients, each with their own characteristic pattern of neurocognitive deficits.

However, a series of studies from the National Institute of Mental Health has raised questions about reliance on subgroups and presumed neurocognitive heterogeneity. For these studies, a rare and highly informative sample was assembled: monozygotic twins discordant for schizophrenia. These are pairs of genetically identical twins in which one developed schizophrenia and one did not. Most of the affected twins were living outside of a hospital. When given a battery of neurocognitive tests, the affected twin consistently performed worse than the unaffected twin across a wide range of measures

(Goldberg et al., 1990). This study did not support the notion that there were subgroups of affected twins. Instead, it suggested that almost all of the affected twins were somewhat below where they *should* have been. The estimate of their expected performance comes from the performance of their unaffected identical twin who serves as the ideal control subject. This study, as well as others from the same series, suggests that the presence of the disorder might consistently lead to a downward shift in performance. However, patients with high capabilities (e.g., advantageous genetic endowment) are likely to perform in the normal range even after the downward shift.

INTEGRATIVE EXPLANATIONS

An itemized listing of neurocognitive deficits in schizophrenia leaves one yearning for parsimony. It is natural to wonder if there are some unifying principles or some fundamental deficits that can explain the range of deficits. We will consider several.

Generalized Neurocognitive Deficit

The most parsimonious explanation for the range of deficits in schizophrenia would be that schizophrenic patients have a generalized neurocognitive deficit and perform poorly on all tests. If so, attempts to identify specific areas of deficit would be pointless. However, the findings do not support such a simple explanation. Patients undoubtedly have deficits in rather global areas such as overall IQ and deficits can be found across sensory modalities. Despite these global deficits, patients do not perform equally poorly on all measures. Tests that have been carefully matched on difficulty and reliability show that patients have more deficits in some conditions than in others. For example, patients have relatively greater deficits in immediate memory under a condition of distraction (Oltmanns & Neale, 1975) and relatively larger problems with recall versus recognition (Calev, 1984). Within a sample of schizophrenic patients, some of the deficits are not correlated, hence, they cannot be explained by a single cognitive factor. If the performance of schizophrenic patients was due to a single, global deficit, we might expect performance to be associated with IQ. But many neurocognitive measures used in schizophrenia research such as the CPT and the Span of Apprehension do not correlate well with IQ. For measures such as backward masking, the pattern of performance with schizophrenic patients is qualitatively different from that of normal aging and hence, do not appear to be associated with a general slowing of processing (Brody, Saccuzzo, & Braff, 1980). It is not obvious how a generalized neurocognitive deficit could explain performance abnormalities on some psychophysiological tests that seem largely reflexive such as the pre-pulse inhibition of startle-blink and eye tracking. Importantly, the notion of a generalized performance deficit does not account for the findings (discussed in the next chapter) of selected performance deficits in the first-degree relatives of schizophrenic patients who do not have the disorder. Overall, a reasonable conclusion is that schizophrenic patients have deficits in multiple domains, but a single generalized deficit fails to account for the range and pattern of findings. Nonetheless, a generalized deficit forms the background against which we squint to see neurocognitive trends.

Attentional Resources

Nuechterlein and Dawson proposed that a wide range of deficits in schizophrenia could be viewed in terms of reduced availability of attentional or processing resources (Nuechterlein & Dawson, 1984). Attention can be viewed as a pool of nonspecific resources that can be allocated voluntarily to particular information processing tasks (Kahneman, 1973). Limitations in resource allocation could arise for several reasons including a smaller than normal pool of attentional resources or an inefficient allocation strategy. If schizophrenic patients have problems with momentary allocation of resources, deficits would be expected on tasks that require substantial allocation of these attentional resources, but not necessarily on tasks that do not. The proposal has considerable explanatory power, especially for the pattern of deficits that are observed on tests like the CPT in which patients and relatives show more prominent and consistent deficits on versions of the task that have heavy processing loads. However, other models may be better suited for explaining deficits on tests of early perceptual processing such as pre-pulse inhibition of the startle-blink or the early components of backward masking. These paradigms are more naturally viewed within a model of sensory gating.

Sensory Gating

On the surface, backward masking and pre-pulse inhibition of the startle-blink do not appear to have much in common. However, Braff et al. (1991) have deftly shown that a common deficit may account for deficits on both paradigms. Both paradigms are interpreted in terms of the interactions of two types of neural pathways. One pathway (transient/fast) is characterized as having rapid onset and brief duration; the other pathway (sus-tained/slow) has a longer latency and longer duration. Both paradigms involve rapid, sequential processing of stimuli, which is thought to be dopaminergically modulated. Hence, these procedures provide a link with a possible underlying dopamine dysregulation.

> At this point, we do not know that the neural substrate of these two phenomena is equivalent....But if the two (fast and slow) neural populations are so pervasive and important, perhaps the common theme of the loss of an aminergically mediated, inhibitory tone overrides paradigmatic differences and highlights a critical Achilles heel in the attentional/information processing of schizophrenic patients. This vulnerability to deviant information processing would span multiple paradigms through the common theme of disrupted information processing of rapidly presented sequential stimuli. (Braff et al., 1991, p. 329)

Viewing backward masking and pre-pulse inhibition of startle-blink within this general sensory gating framework is useful in a number of respects. First, the model can be tested in a converging fashion with multiple methods. Second, the components of the model are testable at both the behavioral and neurochemical level. Third, in this model the basic abnormalities occur quite early in information processing and may account for deficits on other measures, including certain versions of the CPT that place demands on perceptual processes (Nuechterlein, Dawson, & Green, 1994). Fourth, a failure in sensory gating may be related to particular aspects of phenomenology. Although backward masking performance deficits are not associated with severity of psychotic symptoms, a breakdown in sensory gating could be linked to subjective experiences of distractibility and confusion, which are sometimes experienced as prodromal signs.

Maintenance of Context

During the 1980s several influential computational models of information processing were developed. Unlike previous efforts to design computers that can perform tasks with multiple serial operations, the goal of computational models was to design computer programs that took into account basic features of neural processing. For example, we know that neural transmission is relatively slow, that the brain relies on parallel (as opposed to serial) processing, that regions of the brain tend to have reciprocal connections, and that learning occurs through adjustment of synaptic strengths between neurons (Cohen & Servan-Schreiber, 1992). Computer models that have included these features have been useful for understanding how the normal brain may process information, as well as how neural networks might break down.

Some investigators have turned to computational models as a means to specify the neurocognitive processes that underlie the performance of schizophrenic patients over a wide range of tasks (Hoffman, 1987; Servan-Schreiber, Cohen, & Steingard, 1996). In this approach, one first develops a computer simulation model of the cognitive operations that are believed to be relevant for successfully completing a task. For example, Figure 3.5 shows a model adapted from Servan-Schreiber et al. (1996) that has applications to several tasks including the CPT and tests of behavioral inhibition (e.g., perseverative errors on the WCST). The input module represents externally presented stimuli, the output module represents the response, the associative module relates stimuli to particular responses, and the context module regulates the flow of information through the associative module. The bi-directional connections between the associative and context modules allow stimuli presented to the network to help establish the context. Once a context is established, it can influence the processing of subsequent stimuli.

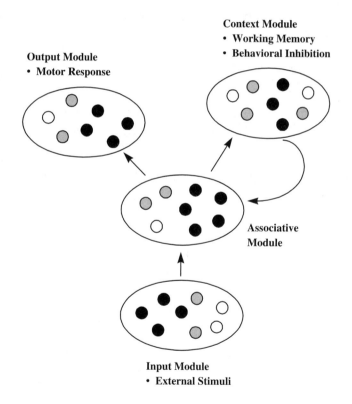

FIGURE 3.5

Source: From "Schizophrenic Deficits in the Processing Context: A Test of a Theoretical Model" by Servan-Schreiber, Cohen, and Steingard, 1996, *Archives of General Psychiatry, 53*, p. 1108. Copyright 1996, American Medical Association. Reprinted with permission.

According to this model both working memory and behavioral inhibition reflect the operation of the context module. The link between context and working memory is fairly obvious—the context module maintains a representation "on line." The link with behavioral inhibition is less obvious. Essentially, subjects need to maintain a notion of what they should not do. These investigators suggest that a basic failure to represent and maintain context can account for the deficits shown by schizophrenic patients on a variety of cognitive tasks. Tasks that have working memory and behavioral inhibition components include delayed matching-to-sample tests, certain versions of the CPT, and the WCST. Computer models can predict the consequences of an underlying abnormality in the establishment of context, and the predicted performance can then be compared with actual patient performance on tests of working memory and behavioral inhibition. Cohen, Servan-Schreiber, and their colleagues have shown that a single disturbance in the context module produces changes in computer models that both quantitatively and qualitatively matched those observed in schizophrenic patients.

Coming from a completely different perspective, Hemsley arrived at a similar conclusion about the role of context. Based on laboratory studies of normal cognition he proposed that "a weakening of the influence of stored memories of regularities of previous input on current perception" (Hemsley, 1987, p. 182) constitutes the basic deficit in schizophrenia.

> It is important to note that it is not claimed that the "memories of past regularities" are not stored, nor that they are inaccessible. They may indeed be accessed by consciously controlled processing. Rather, the suggestion is that it is the rapid and automatic assessment of the significance or lack of significance of aspects of sensory input (and their implications for actions) that is impaired as a result of a weakening of the influence of stored past regularities. (Hemsley, 1994, p. 101)

Hemsley's view grew out of his work in experimental psychology and the apparent failure for schizophrenic patients to take advantage of spatial and temporal redundancy of information. Despite the different origins, his proposal sounds very much like the failure in context described by Cohen and Servan-Schreiber based on computer simulations.

In summary, there is no shortage of documented neurocognitive deficits in schizophrenia. The challenge is not simply to identify more deficits. The challenge will be to identify a smaller set of integrating principles or brain systems that can explain a highly diverse range of problems.

In the next few chapters we will see that potential artifacts such as clinical state, medications, or institutionalization fail to account for the deficits.

Many of the deficits are so central to schizophrenia that, paradoxically, they are not associated with symptoms of the illness.

REFERENCES

Asarnow, R. F., Granholm, E., & Sherman, T. (1991). Span of apprehension in schizophrenia. In S. R. Steinhauer, J. H. Gruzelier, & J. Zubin (Eds.), *Handbook of schizophrenia: Neuropsychology, psychophysiology, and information processing* (Vol. 5, pp. 335–370). Amsterdam: Elsevier.

Aylward, E., Walker, E., & Bettes, B. (1984). Intelligence in schizophrenia: Meta-analysis of the research. *Schizophrenia Bulletin, 10,* 430–459.

Baruch, I., Hemsley, D. R., & Gray, J. A. (1988). Differential performance of acute and chronic schizophrenics in a latent inhibition task. *Journal of Nervous and Mental Disease, 176,* 598–606.

Braff, D., Stone, C., Callaway, E., Geyer, M., Glick, I., & Bali, L. (1978). Prestimulus effects on human startle reflex in normals and schizophrenics. *Psychophysiology, 15,* 339–343.

Braff, D. L. (1981). Impaired speed of information processing in nonmedicated schizotypal patients. *Schizophrenia Bulletin, 7,* 499–508.

Braff, D. L., Saccuzzo, D. P., & Geyer, M. A. (1991). Information processing dysfunctions in schizophrenia: Studies of visual backward masking, sensorimotor gating, and habituation. In S. R. Steinhauer, J. H. Gruzelier, & J. Zubin (Eds.), *Handbook of schizophrenia* (Vol. 5, pp. 303–334). Amsterdam: Elsevier.

Breitmeyer, B. G. (1984). *Visual masking: An integrative approach.* New York: Oxford University Press.

Breitmeyer, B. G., & Ganz, L. (1976). Implications of sustained and transient channels for theories of visual pattern masking, saccadic suppression, and information processing. *Psychological Review, 83,* 1–36.

Brody, D., Saccuzzo, D. P., & Braff, D. L. (1980). Information processing for masked and unmasked stimuli in schizophrenia and old age. *Journal of Abnormal Psychology, 89,* 617–622.

Calev, A. (1984). Recall and recognition in chronic nondemented schizophrenics: The use of matched tasks. *Journal of Abnormal Psychology, 93,* 172–177.

Cohen, J. D., & Servan-Schreiber, D. (1992). Context, cortex, and dopamine: A connectionist approach to behavior and biology in schizophrenia. *Psychological Review, 99,* 45–77.

Cohen, N. J., & Squire, L. R. (1980). Preserved learning and retention of pattern-analyzing skill in amnesia: Dissociation of knowing how and knowing that. *Science, 210,* 207–210.

Corkin, S. (1968). Acquisition of motor skill after bilateral medial temporal-lobe excision. *Neuropsychologia, 6,* 255–265.

Cornblatt, B. A., Lenzenweger, M. F., & Erlenmeyer-Kimling, L. (1989). The continuous performance test, identical pairs version: II. Contrasting attentional profiles in schizophrenic and depressed patients. *Psychiatric Research, 29,* 65.

Dawson, M. E., Hazlett, E. A., Filion, D. L., Nuechterlein, K. H., & Schell, A. M.

(1993). Attention and schizophrenia: Impaired modulation of the startle reflex. *Journal of Abnormal Psychology, 102,* 633–641.

Fuster, J. M. (1989). *The prefrontal cortex: Anatomy, physiology, and neuropsychology of the frontal lobe.* (2nd ed.). New York: Raven Press.

Goldberg, T. E., Hyde, T. M., Kleinman, J. E., & Weinberg, D. R. (1993). Course of schizophrenia: Neuropsychological evidence for a static encephalopathy. *Schizophrenia Bulletin, 19,* 797–804.

Goldberg, T. E., Ragland, J. D., Torrey, E. F., Gold, J. M., Bigelow, L. B., & Weinberger, D. R. (1990). Neuropsychological assessment of monozygotic twins discordant for schizophrenia. *Archives of General Psychiatry, 47,* 1066–1072.

Goldberg, T. E., Weinberger, D. R., Berman, K. F., Pliskin, N. H., & Podd, M. H. (1987). Further evidence for dementia of the prefrontal type in schizophrenia? A controlled study of teaching the Wisconsin Card Sorting Test. *Archives of General Psychiatry, 44,* 1008–1014.

Goldman-Rakic, P. S. (1991). Prefrontal cortical dysfunction in schizophrenia: The relevance of working memory. In B. J. Carroll & J. E. Barrett (Eds.), *Psychopathology and the brain* (pp. 1–23). New York: Raven Press.

Goldman-Rakic, P. S. (1993). Working memory and the mind. *Mind and brain: Readings from Scientific American magazine* (pp. 67–77). New York: W.H. Freeman & Co.

Goldstein, K. (1959). Concerning the concreteness in schizophrenia. *Journal of Abnormal and Social Psychology, 59,* 146–148.

Goldstein, K., & Scheerer, M. (1941). Abstract and concrete behavior: An experimental study with special tests. *Psychological Monographs, 53,* 239.

Graham, F. K. (1975). The more or less startling effects of weak prestimulation. *Psychophysiology, 12,* 238–248.

Granholm, E., Bartzokis, G., Asarnow, R. F., & Marder, S. R. (1993). Preliminary associations between motor procedural learning, basal ganglia T2 relaxation times, and tardive dyskinesia. *Psychiatry Research: Neuroimaging, 50,* 33–44.

Green, M. F., Nuechterlein, K. H., & Mintz, J. (1994a). Backward masking in schizophrenia and mania: Specifying a mechanism. *Archives of General Psychiatry, 51,* 939–944.

Green, M. F., Nuechterlein, K. H., & Mintz, J. (1994b). Backward masking in schizophrenia and mania: Specifying the visual channels. *Archives of General Psychiatry, 51,* 945–951.

Heaton, R. K. (1981). *Wisconsin Card Sorting Test Manual.* Odessa, FL: Psychological Assessment Resources.

Hemsley, D. R. (1987). An experimental psychological model for schizophrenia. In H. Hafner, W. F. Gattaz, & A. Janzarik (Eds.), *Search for the causes of schizophrenia* (pp. 179–188). Heidelberg, Germany: Springer-Verlag.

Hemsley, D. R. (1994). Perceptual and cognitive abnormalities as the bases for schizophrenic symptoms. In D. S. Anthony & J. C. Cutting (Eds.), *The neuropsychology of schizophrenia* (pp. 97–116). Hove, UK: Lawrence Erlbaum.

Hoffman, R. E. (1987). Computer simulations of neural information processing and the schizophrenia-mania dichotomy. *Archives of General Psychiatry, 44,* 178–188.

Holzman, P. S., Proctor, L. R., & Hughes, D. W. (1973). Eye-tracking patterns in schizophrenia. *Science, 181,* 179–181.

Jevons, W. S. (1871). The power of numerical discrimination. *Nature, 3,* 281–282.

Kahneman, D. (1973). *Attention and effort.* Englewood Cliffs, NJ: Prentice-Hall.

Kern, R. S., Green, M. F., & Wallace, C. J. (1997). Declarative and procedural learning in schizophrenia: A test of the integrity of divergent memory systems. *Cognitive Neuropsychiatry, 2,* 39–50.

Knight, R. (1992). Specifying cognitive deficiencies in premorbid schizophrenics. *Progress in Experimental Personality and Psychopathology Research, 15,* 252–289.

Levy, D. L., Holzman, P. S., Matthysse, S., & Mendell, N. (1993). Eye-tracking dysfunction and schizophrenia: A critical perspective. *Schizophrenia Bulletin, 19,* 461–536.

Lubow, R. E., & Gewirtz, J. C. (1995). Latent inhibition in humans: Data, theory, and implications for schizophrenia. *Psychological Bulletin, 117,* 87–103.

Nachmani, G., & Cohen, B. D. (1969). Recall and recognition free learning in schizophrenics. *Journal of Abnormal Psychology, 74,* 511–516.

Nuechterlein, K. H. (1991). Vigilance in schizophrenia and related disorders. In S. R. Steinhauer, J. H. Gruzelier, & J. Zubin (Eds.), *Handbook of schizophrenia* (Vol. 5, pp. 397–433). Amsterdam: Elsevier.

Nuechterlein, K. H., & Dawson, M. E. (1984). Information processing and attentional functioning in the developmental course of schizophrenia disorders. *Schizophrenia Bulletin, 10,* 160–203.

Nuechterlein, K. H., Dawson, M. E., Gitlin, M., Ventura, J., Goldstein, M. J., Snyder, K. S., Yee, C. M., & Mintz, J. (1992). Developmental processes in schizophrenic disorders: Longitudinal studies of vulnerability and stress. *Schizophrenia Bulletin, 18,* 387–425.

Nuechterlein, K. H., Dawson, M. E., & Green, M. F. (1994). Information-processing abnormalities as neuropsychological vulnerability indicators for schizophrenia. *Acta Psychiatrica Scandinavica, 90* (Suppl. 384), 71–79.

Oltmanns, T. F., & Neale, J. M. (1975). Schizophrenic performance when distractors are present: Attentional deficit or differential task difficulty? *Journal of Abnormal Psychology, 84,* 205–209.

Orzack, M. H., & Kornetsky, C. (1966). Attention dysfunction in chronic schizophrenia. *Archives of General Psychiatry, 14,* 323–326.

Park, S., & Holzman, P. S. (1992). Schizophrenics show spatial working memory deficits. *Archives of General Psychiatry, 49,* 975–982.

Saccuzzo, D. P., & Braff, D. L. (1981). Early information processing deficit in schizophrenia. *Archives of General Psychiatry, 38,* 175–179.

Saykin, A. J., Gur, R. C., Gur, R. E., Mozley, P. D., Mozley, L. H., Resnick, S. M., Kester, D. B., & Stafiniak, P. (1991). Neuropsychological function in schizophrenia: Selective impairment in memory and learning. *Archives of General Psychiatry, 48,* 618–624.

Saykin, A. J., Shtasel, D. L., Gur, R. E., Kester, D. B., Mozley, L. H., Stafiniak, P., & Gur, R. C. (1994). Neuropsychological deficits in neuroleptic naive patients with first-episode schizophrenia. *Archives of General Psychiatry, 51,* 124–131.

Schwartz, B. D., Evans, W. J., Pena, J. M., & Winstead, D. K. (1994). Visible persistence decay rates for schizophrenics and substance abusers. *Biological Psychiatry, 36,* 662–669.

Servan-Schreiber, D., Cohen, J. D., & Steingard, S. (1996). Schizophrenic deficits in the processing of context: A test of neural network simulations of cognitive functioning in schizophrenia. *Archives of General Psychiatry, 53,* 1105–1112.

Squire, L. R. (1992). Declarative and nondeclarative memory: Multiple brain systems supporting learning and memory. *Journal of Cognitive Neuroscience, 4,* 232–243.

Squire, L. R., & Zola-Morgan, S. (1988). Memory: Brain systems and behavior. *Trends in Neuroscience, 11,* 170–175.

Weinberger, D. R., Berman, K. F., & Zec, R. F. (1986). Physiologic dysfunction of dorsolateral prefrontal cortex in schizophrenia. *Archives of General Psychiatry, 43,* 114–124.

▶ 4

Neurocognitive Indicators of Vulnerability to Schizophrenia

The mere mention of a neurocognitive deficit in schizophrenia frequently leaves colleagues and students unimpressed, perhaps because many people have their own explanations for why neurocognitive deficits occur in schizophrenia. An example of an *empathic* response would be "If I was hearing voices (or concerned that the CIA was trying to kill me), I would not perform well on those tests either." This response assumes that impaired performance on neurocognitive measures is a by-product of psychotic symptoms. A *socially aware* response would be "If I was institutionalized (stigmatized, marginalized), I would not perform well on those tests either." Here the assumption is that demoralization or social isolation from long years of illness can explain deficits. Lastly, a *pharmacological* response would be "If I was taking all of those drugs, I would not perform well on those tests either." In this case the concern is that the performance deficits are artifacts of the medications that patients are given. These responses are understandable, intuitive, reasonable,—and wrong.

Over the next several chapters, we will begin to identify neurocognitive deficits that are so central to the disorder that they can occur in the absence of symptoms. Strong evidence for the centrality of neurocognitive deficits in schizophrenia comes from studies of relatives of schizophrenic patients who presumably have a vulnerability to the disorder, but not the disorder itself, as well as studies of schizophrenic patients who are in symptomatic remission.

There is no doubt that schizophrenia has a genetic component (Gottesman, 1991; Kendler & Diehl, 1993). Evidence for the genetics of schizophrenia has come from studies of family aggregations, twin concordance, and adoption methods. Family studies show mean risks of about 8% to siblings and 5% to parents of schizophrenic patients, compared to roughly 1% in the general population (Holzman & Matthysse, 1990). The relatively lower risk of the parents compared with siblings is most likely explained by selection factors; only a subgroup of patients with schizophrenia become parents. Risk to the children of parents with schizophrenia is about 12%. Family studies suggest a genetic contribution, but they are not definitive because first-degree relatives share environmental factors as well as 50% of their genes. Other methods are needed as well.

The twin method takes advantage of the fact that monozygotic (MZ) twins share 100% of their genes, whereas dizygotic (DZ) twins share 50%. The genetic contribution of a disorder can be assessed by comparing concordance rates for MZ and DZ twins. Concordance rates are usually calculated as the percentage of twin pairs in which both members have the illness divided by the number of twin pairs in which at least one member has the illness. In a disorder that is fully genetically determined, the concordance rates for MZ twins should be 100% (i.e., whenever one twin has the disorder, so does the other). In disorders that are not completely under genetic control, higher concordance rates for MZ twins than for DZ twins constitute evidence of a genetic component. In schizophrenia, despite some variability across studies, the concordance rates are consistently higher in MZ twins. Roughly 45% of MZ and 9% DZ twin pairs are concordant for schizophrenia (Holzman & Matthysse, 1990).

Perhaps the best method for the separation of genetic and environmental factors has been adoption studies. The probands in adoption studies are patients with schizophrenia who were adopted at a young age. Adoption studies compare the rates of schizophrenia in the biological and adoptive relatives of schizophrenic probands. Studies of this type are often conducted in Scandinavian countries where excellent records are maintained and the populations are mainly geographically stable. The adoption studies show that the rates of schizophrenia and schizophrenia spectrum disorders are clearly higher in the biological relatives of the probands compared with the adoptive relatives. This difference in rates is viewed as evidence for increased genetic risk to biological relatives.

All of the studies indicate that the liability (i.e., vulnerability) for schizophrenia is largely, but not entirely, due to genetic factors. The next challenge is to identify markers of this liability. It is estimated that roughly 60–70% of the liability to schizophrenia is likely to be genetic (Gottesman, 1991; McGuffin, 1991). Hence, indicators of liability would be expected to have a substantial genetic component. In this chapter, we will expand on a topic that was introduced in Chapter 2, the relationship of neurocognition to the vulnerability to schizophrenia.

VULNERABILITY THEORY

In its general form, a vulnerability theory of schizophrenia postulates that certain individuals are predisposed, but not predetermined, to having the illness (Cromwell & Spaulding, 1978; Nuechterlein & Dawson, 1984; Zubin & Spring, 1977). Within a general vulnerability framework, a person's predisposition (i.e., vulnerability) is enduring and largely attributable to genetic and/or neurodevelopmental factors. The greater the vulnerability, the higher the risk for developing schizophrenia. The final expression of this predisposition depends on a host of other personal and environmental factors, some of which are noxious and others protective (see Figures 2.2 and 2.3). A complex interaction of vulnerability, stressors, and protective factors would influence both the onset (e.g., whether or not a vulnerable person develops schizophrenia) and the course of the disorder (e.g., relapses).

The major components of the vulnerability/stress model are usually viewed along a continuum, or probably more accurately, as a bell-shaped distribution. Within a polygenic model of schizophrenia, the degree of vulnerability might depend on the total number of schizophrenia-relevant genes that a person has. Individuals with greater vulnerability may become ill with relatively little environmental stress. Stressors would also be on a severity continuum such that some stressors have greater impact and are more likely to precipitate an episode than others.

In this chapter, we will consider methods that have been used to identify subtle indicators of underlying vulnerability to schizophrenia. Smooth pursuit eye tracking is a psychophysiological procedure that is not generally considered to be a neurocognitive measure, but it provides an excellent illustration of how to approach the question of vulnerability (Levy, Holzman, Matthysse, & Mendell, 1993).

Normally, when people follow a moving target with their eyes, the visual pursuit system is turned on and the saccadic eye movement system is turned off. About 65% of schizophrenic patients show saccadic intrusions into their smooth pursuit, compared with only 8% of normal controls (Holzman & Matthysse, 1990). Figure 4.1 shows an example of normal and abnormal pursuits. Abnormalities in eye tracking cannot be explained as part of the symptomatic aspects of the disorder or as side effects of neuroleptic medications because they are found in healthy relatives. About 40% of the first-degree relatives of patients show such eye tracking abnormalities. Abnormalities in smooth pursuit may have some specificity to schizophrenia because first-degree relatives of patients with affective disorder have much lower rates of eye tracking abnormalities (about 14%). One of the more intriguing findings in the eye tracking literature is that some schizophrenic

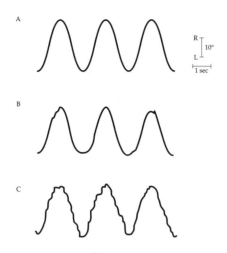

FIGURE 4.1   Normal and Abnormal Eye Tracking

A: 0.4 hertz (Hz) sinusoidal target. B: Qualitatively normal eye tracking of the target in
A. C: Qualitatively abnormal eye tracking of the target in A. From Levy et.al, 1993.

patients with normal pursuit have healthy relatives with impaired pursuit.
We will discuss the implications of this finding later in the chapter.

Abnormal eye tracking is considered an indicator of vulnerability to
schizophrenia because it occurs in unaffected first-degree relatives. Patients
with abnormal pursuit tend to have at least one parent with abnormal pursuit. This pattern strongly suggests that abnormalities in eye tracking are
genetically transmitted. These abnormalities most likely reflect the disruption
of a relatively basic neural system that is associated with genetic predisposition to schizophrenia. Based on these results, it appears that abnormal eye
tracking is a highly promising indicator of vulnerability to schizophrenia.

Are any neurocognitive measures promising indicators of vulnerability,
similar to eye tracking? A deficit on a neurocognitive measure can be considered a likely indicator of vulnerability to schizophrenia under certain conditions. First, it should be present to a larger extent in schizophrenic patients
than in the general population. Second, it should be present when the
patients are in symptomatic remission as well as when they are in psychotic
episode. Third, it should be disproportionately present in biological first-
degree relatives of the patients, even if the relatives do not have the illness.
These criteria for an indicator of vulnerability to schizophrenia lead directly
to two primary experimental designs, and indirectly to a third type of design.
One design involves assessing the performance of patients in symptomatic
(or at least psychotic) remission to determine whether the deficits endure
after the symptoms have gone away. A second design involves the study of
first-degree relatives of patients to determine whether there are performance

deficits in individuals who are vulnerable to the disorder but not ill. Sometimes a third design is used in which performance is assessed for individuals who do not have frank psychotic symptoms, but are believed to be in the schizophrenia spectrum because of subtle clinical symptoms (e.g., Schizotypal Personality Disorder or high scores on psychometric tests).

We will review three neurocognitive measures (introduced in the previous chapter) that are promising indicators of vulnerability to schizophrenia: The Continuous Performance Test (CPT), the Span of Apprehension (Span), and backward masking. Other measures could have been selected but the goal was to be illustrative, not comprehensive.

NEUROCOGNITIVE DEFICITS THAT ENDURE INTO REMISSION

Remitted patients provide a valuable means to test vulnerability indicators. If a measure indicates vulnerability to the disorder, performance should be stable as the person moves from psychotic episode to remission because the individual's vulnerability has not changed. A deficit that normalizes with remission is indicating the presence of illness (although it remains ambiguous whether the onset of the deficit leads or lags the onset of symptoms). Most studies of neurocognitive performance in remission have been cross-sectional comparisons of remitted patients with normal controls. A rigorous test of vulnerability is offered by longitudinal studies in which patients are assessed across different clinical states. Longitudinal studies are highly informative, but they are also more difficult to conduct.

Continuous Performance Test (CPT)

The CPT is a standard measure of vigilance, or sustained attention. In the CPT, the subject views a series of stimuli on a screen and is instructed to press a response button whenever a "target" stimulus appears. The target could be a single stimulus (the number "0") or a sequence (a "3" followed by a "7"). Stimuli are typically presented briefly, usually less than one tenth of a second, and follow at a rate of about one every second. The test yields a measure of "sensitivity," which is the ability to discriminate signal (i.e., targets) from noise (i.e., nontargets).

Several cross-sectional studies have considered the performance of remitted (Asarnow & MacCrimmon, 1978; Wohlberg & Kornetsky, 1973) or stabilized patients (Steinhauer et al., 1991) on the CPT. Results from these studies have been consistent; schizophrenic patients, even when in clinical remission, show deficits in detecting targets for moderately difficult versions of the CPT. A rigorous longitudinal study was conducted with recent-onset schizophrenic patients using two versions of the CPT (Nuechterlein et al., 1992). One version used stimuli that were perceptually degraded to appear blurry to the subjects and imposed a burden for initial perceptual discrimination. The other used clear stimuli, but involved a target sequence of stimuli (a "3" followed by a "7"). Versions of the CPT with a target sequence involve active, working memory because the mental representation of one stimulus needs to be maintained long enough to compare with the subsequent stimulus, and then the representation needs to be updated. Patients were tested while in psychotic episode and again when they were in symptomatic remission. Controls were individually matched to the patients and tested at the same points in time. The performance for the two groups on both versions of the CPT are shown in Figure 4.2. Both versions follow patterns that we would expect from indicators of vulnerability, but they differ from each other. Scores from the degraded-stimulus version change very little between clinical states and fit the pattern of a "Stable" Vulnerability Indicator. In contrast, performance on the memory-load CPT shows a difference between patients and controls when the patients are in remission, and this difference becomes more pronounced when the patients are in psychotic episode. This pattern fits a "Mediating" Vulnerability Indicator. We may be able to explain the differences in performance pattern between these two versions of the CPT by considering the neurocognitive components of each version. The degraded-stimulus CPT relies on early perceptual processing and deficits in this component of information processing may be stable across state. However, the memory-load version of the CPT involves an additional neurocognitive component (active working memory), and deficits in this ability may change with state.

Span of Apprehension (Span)

The Span is a measure of relatively early visual processing. In the Span, subjects see an array of letters that are presented very briefly on a screen (usually less than one tenth of a second). In the forced-choice version of the Span, subjects decide which of two letters (e.g., a "T" or an "F") was in the array. The task is made more or less difficult by the number of distractor letters that are presented. Because each array of letters is presented very briefly, the visual display disappears from the screen before subjects have completed a visual search for the letter. So, instead of scanning the screen, subjects need to scan a mental representation of the array called the "icon." Hence, the Span is sometimes considered to be a measure of iconic read-out.

Two studies have considered performance on the Span in groups of remitted patients (Asarnow & MacCrimmon, 1978; Asarnow & MacCrimmon, 1981). Similar to findings with the CPT, performance on the Span was impaired during remission for the versions of the Span that were at least of

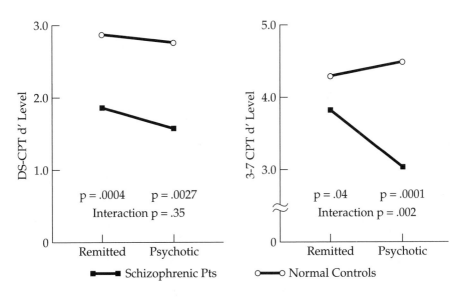

FIGURE 4.2   Clinical State of Patients

Source: Reprinted with permission from Nuechterlein et al., 1991, p. 188. Copyright © Springer-Verlag, 1991.

Note: *n* = 17 patients, 17 matched controls. DS-CPT = Degraded-stimulus CPT, (Nuechterlein et al. 1983).

moderate difficulty. A longitudinal study assessed recent-onset patients on the Span when they were in full remission and again when in a psychotic episode (Nuechterlein et al., 1992). Normal controls were matched to the patients and were tested at the same points in time. The results shown in Figure 4.3 reveal remarkable stability in Span performance across clinical state. Performance on the Span appears insensitive to changes in psychotic symptoms and fits the pattern of a Stable Vulnerability Indicator.

Backward Masking

Like the Span, backward masking is a measure of visual processing, but it involves very early visual processes. In backward masking, the subject is shown a target stimulus (e.g., a letter or a word) on the screen. The target is presented for a brief duration, perhaps as short as 5 or 10 ms. Despite the brief duration of the target, subjects can accurately identify it when it is presented alone. A visual mask is presented after the target. The mask is usually a complex stimulus such as overlapping letters and, in schizophrenia research, it usually occupies the area on the screen where the target

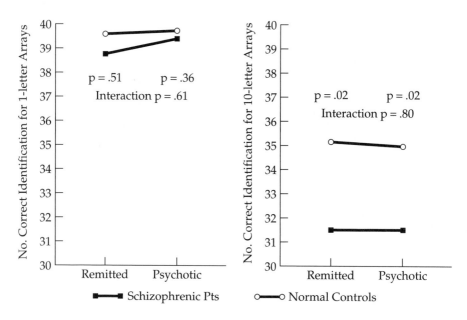

FIGURE 4.3   Clinical State of Patients

Source: Reprinted with permission from Nuechterlein et al., 1991, p. 187. Copyright ©
Springer-Verlag, 1991.

Note: n = 13 patients, 13 matched controls.

appeared. When the interval between the target and mask is brief, subjects
are not able to identify the target. They report seeing the mask, but might not
even be aware that the target was presented at all. This interference in target
identification is the masking effect.

Backward masking procedures have rarely been applied to remitted
schizophrenic patients. One study (Miller, Saccuzzo & Braff, 1979) reported
deficits in remitted patients compared with matched controls, suggesting that
masking performance might be an indicator of vulnerability to schizophrenia.
However, the remitted patients in this study were medicated and had poor
social functioning, so the degree of remission is not clear. In an unpublished
study from our laboratory, several backward masking procedures were
administered to recent-onset patients and matched controls. The remitted
patients had achieved psychotic remission and were in a period of no medications. Masking deficits were found in these remitted, unmedicated patients
across the test conditions, indicating that a masking performance deficit is
present after the psychotic symptoms have disappeared. The findings from

these two cross-sectional studies strongly suggest that visual masking deficits are vulnerability indicators. The field is awaiting rigorous longitudinal studies in which masking performance is assessed across clinical states.

VULNERABILITY IN FIRST-DEGREE RELATIVES

First-degree biological relatives of schizophrenic patients have a risk of developing schizophrenia about 10 times that of the general population (Kendler & Diehl, 1993). This increased risk for schizophrenia means that the relatives, as a group, have a greater liability or predisposition for the illness than the general population. Figure 4.4 shows a bell-shaped distribution of liability that is shifted upward for the relatives of schizophrenic patients. An accurate indicator of vulnerability to schizophrenia should reflect this predisposition in a disproportionate number of first-degree relatives.

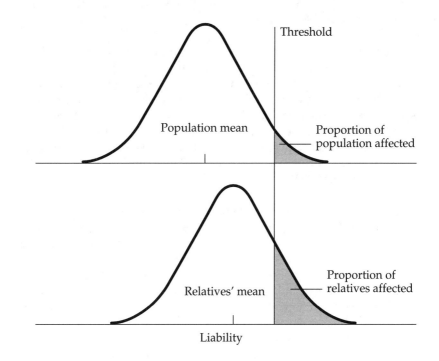

FIGURE 4.4

Source: Adapted from "Genetic Models of Madness" by P. McGuffin, 1991. In P. McGuffin and R. Murray (Eds.), *The new genetics of mental illness* (p. 32). Oxford: Butterworth-Heinemann Ltd. Reproduced with permission.

Two complimentary methods have been used to examine first-degree relatives. One is the high-risk method, which identifies children who are considered to be at increased risk for schizophrenia because they have mothers with schizophrenia. The high-risk method starts with children who are younger than the typical age of onset for schizophrenia. The other method selects adult siblings or parents of patients who are mainly through their age of risk and are unlikely to later develop the disorder.

HIGH-RISK SAMPLES

The high-risk method was employed to address a very basic problem in schizophrenia research: once the onset of the disorder has occurred, it is exceedingly difficult to determine which factors caused the disorder and which factors are the result of having the disorder. Perhaps the best known example of the high-risk method is the Copenhagen High-Risk Project, which was started in 1962 by Mednick and his colleagues.

> In the late 1950s and 1960s, we became acutely aware of the pitfalls involved in studying the etiology of schizophrenia by comparing schizophrenic patients with normal controls (Mednick & Higgins, 1960). In such designs it is difficult to disentangle the *consequences* of schizophrenia from possible etiological agents. It became clear to us that it was necessary to study schizophrenics within a longitudinal, prospective framework, before the life-long concomitants of schizophrenia made it difficult to isolate and examine causal factors. (Mednick, Parnas, & Schulsinger, 1987, p. 485)

In a typical design, the high-risk sample consists of the children of schizophrenic mothers. Controls are the children of psychiatrically healthy mothers, or the children of mothers with other conditions (e.g., mood disorder). The age of the children at first contact varies across studies from infancy to adolescence. The high-risk design offers several advantages (Mednick et al., 1987). When a study begins, no one knows which children will develop schizophrenia, so the data collection is relatively objective. The data are not subject to any distortions that may occur with retrospective reporting. Outcome is based on diagnostic interviews and the information can be fairly comprehensive. Finally, high-risk studies are extremely well-suited to evaluate the interactions of vulnerability with environmental conditions and stressors. For example, the Israeli High-Risk study (Mirsky, Ingraham, & Kugelmass, 1995) explored vulnerability/environmental interactions by comparing high-risk and control offspring in two dramatically different rearing environments: One group was raised on a kibbutz in a communal setting, the other was raised in towns by the family.

High-risk studies are similar in many respects to studies with siblings and parents of patients because they examine first-degree relatives, but they have certain advantages. If the investigator is reasonably patient (and reasonably young), it is possible to follow offspring individually through their age of risk to learn if neurocognitive deviations early in life predict subsequent development of psychiatric problems. High-risk studies provide a rare opportunity to test whether potential indicators of vulnerability are present before the onset of illness.

CPT

Various versions of the CPT have been administered to children at risk for schizophrenia. The findings differ depending on the type of CPT. If the CPT is relatively easy (e.g., responding to a single, clearly focused, target) there tends to be little difference in performance between high-risk and control children (Nuechterlein, 1991). However, the situation is quite different when the CPT is made more difficult either by the addition of a short-term memory load or by visually degrading the stimuli. Two separate samples from the New York High-Risk Project were evaluated with versions of the CPT that imposed additional processing burdens, including a short-term memory load (Cornblatt, Lenzenweger, Dworkin, & Erlenmeyer-Kimling, 1992; Cornblatt, Winters, & Erlenmeyer-Kimling, 1989; Rutschmann, Cornblatt, & Erlenmeyer-Kimling, 1977; 1986). In both samples, the children of schizophrenic mothers showed deficits on the CPT compared with the children of parents without a psychiatric disorder. The later study by this group included the children of parents with affective disorder as an additional control group. Children of mothers with schizophrenia differed from both control groups, suggesting some diagnostic specificity of the CPT deficits.

Similar to the New York study, a high-risk study in Minnesota administered a version of the CPT that imposed a burden for perceptual processing by using visually degraded stimuli (Nuechterlein, 1983). This project revealed deficits in the high-risk sample compared with children of nonpsychiatric parents and children of parents with disorders other than schizophrenia (mainly depression).

In contrast to these studies, the Israeli High-Risk study found that the CPT performance of high-risk offspring was intermediate between schizophrenic patients and control offspring, and that the difference between the two groups of offspring was not striking. The Israeli study used versions of the CPT that were less demanding than the versions used in the previous studies. Taken together, the findings suggest that versions of the CPT that are moderately difficult indicate vulnerability to schizophrenia. The vulnerability reflected by CPT performance may be somewhat specific to schizophrenia and not a general vulnerability to other major psychiatric disorders.

Span

Two studies have been conducted with high-risk children using the Span of Apprehension. In one of these studies, the high-risk children showed deficits on the Span compared with controls (Asarnow, Steffy, MacCrimmon, & Cleghorn, 1977), whereas the other study failed to reveal deficits in high-risk children (Harvey, Weintraub, & Neale, 1985). The versions of the Span in these studies differed in a key parameter: the visual angle of the screen display. The study with positive effects used wide, visual angle display and the study with negative effects used a narrow, visual angle display. The deficits in Span performance during clinical remission that were described in the previous section were obtained with a wide angle version of the Span. For this reason, it has been suggested (Asarnow, Granholm, & Sherman, 1991) that deficits on the wide angle versions of the Span indicate vulnerability to schizophrenia.

Overall, we can conclude that certain (but not all) versions of the CPT and the Span reveal deficits in groups of high-risk children compared with controls, a pattern that would be expected from indicators of vulnerability to schizophrenia. Perhaps deficits on these measures only serve as *markers* of vulnerability much like abnormalities in eye tracking. Alternatively, deficits in vigilance or early visual processing could also be *causally* related to the onset of disorder. We will consider this rather perplexing issue in the next chapter.

SIBLINGS AND PARENTS OF SCHIZOPHRENIC PATIENTS

Siblings and parents of schizophrenic patients, like high-risk children, have increased liability for the disorder. Because of this increased liability, a neurocognitive indicator of vulnerability should reflect the predisposition, at least for a subgroup of these first-degree relatives. As mentioned, a major difference between studies of siblings/parents and the high-risk studies concerns the period of risk. High-risk studies assess subjects before they enter the period of risk. Siblings and parents are largely through their period of risk for schizophrenia (depending on their age) and are unlikely to develop the disorder if they have not already done so. Hence, an advantage of studying siblings and parents is that the psychiatric status of the relatives (i.e., affected or unaffected by illness) can be determined with a fair amount of confidence. This feature of sibling/parent studies enables us to determine to what extent a neurocognitive indicator of vulnerability is separate from the signs and symptoms of the disorder.

CPT

Several studies have used CPT performance to compare relatives of patients to controls (Grove et al., 1991; Mirsky et al., 1992; Steinhauer et al., 1991). The studies have all found differences between relatives (siblings and parents) and controls when using versions of the CPT that were moderately difficult. In one study, the CPT deficits were limited to those relatives who had a disorder in the schizophrenia spectrum (Steinhauer et al., 1991). In contrast, the presence of psychiatric disorders in the relatives did not account for the pattern of CPT deficits in another study (Mirsky et al., 1992). At this point, it appears that CPT deficits are present in relatives of patients, but we do not know if these deficits are limited to an especially vulnerable subgroup who have clinical signs of schizophrenia spectrum disorder, or if they are also present in completely unaffected relatives.

Backward Masking

One study has considered backward masking performance in siblings of schizophrenic patients (Green, Nuechterlein, & Breitmeyer, 1997). Backward masking procedures have an advantage in that they are well-suited for isolating basic components of visual perception. This ability to parse visual processing into subcomponents (a process of experimental reductivism) can help us to determine which specific aspects of neurocognition are linked to vulnerability. In the study of siblings of schizophrenic patients, masking performance was partitioned into two components: a very early sensory/perceptual component, and a slightly later attentional disengage component. Overall, the siblings of patients had poorer performance than controls, consistent with the notion that masking is an indicator of vulnerability. More specifically, the siblings differed from controls on the early, sensory perceptual component, but not the later, attentional disengage component. The results were the same even when only unaffected siblings (e.g., no disorders in the schizophrenia spectrum, no major mood disorder, no substance dependence) were compared to controls, suggesting that masking performance deficits are quite separate from phenomenology. Masking procedures provide one example of how studies of vulnerability can move to a level of greater specificity. These results strongly suggest that a very early sensory/perceptual component is associated with vulnerability to schizophrenia.

SCHIZOTYPAL PERSONALITY DISORDER AND PSYCHOSIS-PRONENESS

The boundaries of schizophrenia are blurry (Siever, Kalus, & Keefe, 1993). Modern diagnostic criteria enable a clinician to make reliable decisions about who should and should not receive a diagnosis of schizophrenia. However, schizophrenia is only the extreme end of a continuum that ranges from mild to severe. The milder versions of this continuum include individuals who are unmedicated, fully functioning, and have no psychotic symptoms. Well-functioning college freshman have provided a rich source for exploring the mildest regions of the schizophrenia spectrum. In a typical

TABLE 4.1   Items from Psychosis-Proneness Scales

		Magical Ideation
T	F	I have had the momentary feeling that I might not be human.
T	F	Things seem to be in different places when I get home, even though no one has been there.
T	F	I have occasionally had the silly feeling that a TV or radio broadcaster knew I was listening to him.
T	F	I have sometimes had the thought that strangers are in love with me.
		Perceptual Aberration
T	F	Parts of my body occasionally seem dead or unreal.
T	F	Sometimes I have felt that I could not distinguish my body from other objects around me.
T	F	Occasionally it has seemed as if my body had taken on the appearance of another person's body.
T	F	Sometimes people whom I know well begin to look like strangers.
		Physical Anhedonia
T	F	I have had very little fun from physical activities like walking, swimming, or sports.
T	F	Sex is okay, but not as much fun as most people claim it is.
T	F	I have never found a thunderstorm exhilarating.
T	F	I don't understand why people enjoy looking at the stars at night.

study, a large number of undergraduates are given a scale of psychosis-proneness. Table 4.1 includes examples of items from such scales (Chapman, Chapman, & Miller, 1982). Groups of subjects scoring unusually high or low on the psychosis-proneness scales would be considered high or low on schizotypy and could be compared on neurocognitive performance.

Studies with college students have the advantage that the subjects are truly non-clinical and they have not received any diagnosis or treatment. These studies make an assumption that the scales are picking up personality tendencies on the same continuum as schizophrenia. Partly in an effort to bypass this assumption, some studies have opted to use clinical samples of patients with a diagnosis of schizotypal personality disorder (SPD). Patients with SPD have a watered-down version of the symptoms of schizophrenia. Family studies of schizophrenia show elevated rates of SPD in family members, suggesting a genetic connection. To the extent that these milder psychometrically and clinically defined schizotypic groups share a common genetic vulnerability to schizophrenia, we may find converging evidence for neurocognitive indicators of vulnerability.

CPT

CPT performance was compared between two groups of university students who were defined as having high or low schizotypy based on a psychosis-proneness scale (see Table 4.1) (Lenzenweger, Cornblatt, & Putnick, 1991). High schizotypic subjects had poorer performance on the CPT, adding further support to its role as an indicator of vulnerability. The groups also differed in terms of anxiety and depression, but these did not account for the results. The findings suggest some specificity for an association between mild, psychotic-like symptoms and CPT performance. Studies of first-degree relatives provided additional support for the notion that CPT deficits are characteristic of schizotypy. In a study of siblings of schizophrenic patients, a small subgroup of siblings who met criteria for SPD performed similarly to stabilized patients on the CPT, whereas unaffected siblings performed comparably to normal controls (Steinhauer et al., 1991). Similarly, CPT errors of omission were correlated with ratings of schizotypal symptoms in a sample of non-psychotic first-degree relatives (Keefe et al., 1997).

Span

In a clever design, subjects from a temporary employment agency with no history of psychiatric disorder were first divided into good versus poor performers based on a wide angle version of the Span and then compared on a measure of schizotypy (Asarnow, Nuechterlein, & Marder, 1983). The poor Span performers scored significantly higher than the good performers on various indices of schizotypy including the schizophrenia scale on the MMPI and a scale of magical ideation, which is one of the psychosis-proneness scales (Eckblad & Chapman, 1983). The poor Span performers did not have generally elevated MMPI scores, suggesting some specificity for a relationship between psychotic-like experiences and Span performance.

Backward Masking

University students who scored high on a schizotypy index from the MMPI or psychosis-proneness scales have shown masking performance deficits compared with controls who scored low on these indices (Balogh & Merritt, 1985; Steronko & Woods, 1978). Two additional studies considered masking performance in hospitalized patients with SPD, including medicated adolescents (Saccuzzo & Schubert, 1981) and unmedicated adults (Braff, 1981). In these studies, patients with SPD (but not borderline personality disorder) showed masking performance deficits, and the deficits were roughly comparable in degree to those of schizophrenic patients. In general, backward masking deficits are apparent in schizotypy whether it is defined psychometrically or clinically by SPD. Relationships between schizotypy and specific components of masking (e.g., early sensory/perceptual vs. later attentional disengage) are not known because backward masking studies with schizotypic samples have not yet isolated performance on particular masking components.

THE NATURE OF VULNERABILITY TO SCHIZOPHRENIA

Our selective review included three neurocognitive measures which have been used in studies of patients in remission, studies of biological first-degree relatives, and studies of individuals who are considered to be in the schizophrenia spectrum. Data across the various designs indicate that these three measures are promising indicators of vulnerability (see Table 4.2). Do these results reflect three different types of vulnerability to schizophrenia, or are they reflections of a single vulnerability? Results from backward masking studies indicate that very early sensory/perceptual processes may be associated with vulnerability to schizophrenia. Span performance also relies on early visual sensory/perceptual processes, so the results from these two measures are compatible and very possibly derived from a single type of vulnerability. But how do we view these findings in relation to those of the CPT?

The CPT is described as a measure of vigilance or sustained attention. Findings of CPT deficits in remitted patients or in first-degree relatives of schizophrenic patients have been interpreted to mean that sustained attention deficits reflect vulnerability to schizophrenia. However, at least some CPT deficits may rely on early sensory/perceptual processes (Nuechterlein,

Table 4.2 **Findings for Three Promising Indicators of Vulnerability to Schizophrenia**

Measure	Deficits Present in Symptomatic Remission?	Deficits Present in Samples at High-Risk for Schizophrenia?	Deficits Present in Siblings or Parents of Patients?	Deficits Present in Schizotypal Subjects?
Continuous Performance Test	Yes*	Yes*	Yes*	Yes
Span of Apprehension	Yes	Yes**	?	Yes
Backward Masking	Yes	?	Yes	Yes

* for versions with moderate or high processing loads
** for versions with wide view angles

Dawson, & Green, 1994). Because the CPT involves a series of very brief presentations, the stimuli are relatively poor perceptual images (a feature that has been further emphasized in CPT versions with degraded stimuli). Perhaps one vulnerability factor for schizophrenia revealed by the CPT is not sustained attention per se, but instead a sensory/perceptual process—a process that is also relevant to backward masking and the Span.

Indirect evidence supports such a reformulation. The CPT yields two key measures of sensitivity: "vigilance level," which is the ability to separate signal stimuli from noise stimuli, and "vigilance decrement," which is the change in vigilance level over the course of the test. Vigilance decrement is a measure of the ability to maintain attention over the length of a dull task and it is the better index of sustained attention (Davies & Parasuraman, 1982). However, first-degree relatives do not generally show abnormalities on vigilance *decrement* on the CPT. Instead, they differ on vigilance *level,* which is more dependent on sensory/perceptual processes.

CONTRIBUTIONS OF NEUROCOGNITION TO THE GENETICS OF SCHIZOPHRENIA

Studies of classical genetics (family studies, twin method, adoption method) may have taken the genetics of schizophrenia about as far as they can. Hopes for the next phase of genetic studies are pinned on studies of molecular genetics using techniques such as restriction fragment length polymorphisms (RFLPs). Exciting results of the molecular genetics of schizophrenia have been produced, but in several instances, enthusiasm for a particular chromosomal marker has given way to disappointment following failures to replicate.

Molecular genetic techniques have been extremely successful with other disorders such as Huntington's disease, so why is schizophrenia presenting such a challenge? One weakness in applying molecular genetic techniques to schizophrenia stems from the reliance on a psychiatric diagnosis to define the phenotype. The problem is that diagnoses such as schizophrenia are based on phenomenology, not on biological markers. Psychiatric diagnoses can change over time as certain criteria are added or deleted from diagnostic systems. It is hard for genetic linkage studies to hit a moving diagnostic target. An additional problem is that a diagnosis of schizophrenia is a relatively rare event, even in the families of schizophrenic patients. The scarcity of the disorder yields low statistical power for the linkage analyses. Holzman, Matthysse and their colleagues have argued that as long as we limit the phenotype of schizophrenia to the diagnosis of schizophrenia, linkage studies will be fighting an uphill battle. The solution, they argue, lies in reformulating the notion of a schizophrenia phenotype.

> It seems to us that psychology, psychophysiology, and related disciplines have the task of uncovering the underlying psychopathological processes of mental diseases in order to explore the hidden nature of the phenotype. (Holzman & Matthysse, 1990, p. 282)

The genotype of schizophrenia appears to be reluctant to announce its presence. Painstaking steps will be needed to reveal a carefully hidden phenotype. Consider the example of eye tracking, which was discussed in the beginning of this chapter. Recall a curious observation that some patients with normal eye tracking have relatives with abnormal eye tracking. Along these lines, in some sets of DZ twins who are discordant for schizophrenia, the affected twin had normal eye tracking, but the unaffected twin had abnormal eye tracking. To account for these seemingly paradoxical observations, Holzman, Matthysse, and colleagues proposed that schizophrenia involves a partially hidden trait, called a *latent trait*, which is genetically transmitted. This trait can be expressed as schizophrenia (rare form), or eye tracking dysfunction (more common form), or both. The consideration of this latent trait goes a long way in helping with two problems mentioned above. First, compared with psychiatric diagnoses, eye tracking is more closely based on underlying biology and is less subject to shifting tides of opinion. Second, with the addition of eye tracking dysfunction, the phenotype becomes considerably more frequent in families than if it is limited to the disorder alone. The combination of markers yields a much more feasible distribution for genetic analyses.

Neurocognitive deficits on measures such as the CPT, Span, and backward masking procedures offer similar possibilities. As indicators of vulnerability to schizophrenia, they may serve as alternative versions of a schizophrenia-related phenotype that could be used for genetic linkage studies.

Considering the diversity of the methods, one may legitimately wonder if there is really a common process that is assessed with eye tracking, the CPT, the Span, and backward masking. Assuming a single latent trait, we could use a type of "triangulation" in which we search for areas of overlap in neurochemistry, neuroanatomy, and neurocognitive mechanisms. An excellent example of such triangulation comes from Freedman and colleagues who used an electrophysiological procedure, the P50 auditory evoked potential (Freedman et al., 1997). Normal controls typically demonstrate a reduced P50 response to the second of two paired auditory stimuli, but schizophrenic patients and many non-psychotic relatives fail to show a reduction. The P50 procedure was used to identify genetic mechanisms in two ways. First, basic studies of neurobiology showed that inhibition of response on the P50 procedure involved the nicotinic cholinergic receptor. In doing so, these studies helped to identify candidate genes for the neurobiological mechanisms. Second, deficits on the P50 procedure were used as an alternative phenotype for linkage analyses. The result is a linkage study with more direction and statistical power.

The varied expression of the schizophrenia genotype could turn out to be an advantage, not a limitation, for models of etiology.

> In our view, the apparent incomparability of the manifest traits that seem to cosegregate within families is not an obstacle to genetic research, but a powerful heuristic clue that should be pursued. As in navigation, fixing on several landmarks helps to triangulate one's position, so in the search for causes the attempt to make sense of divergent manifestations may point us toward an etiological process. A cell type in the brain common to the several manifestations; a shared neurotransmitter; a common developmental epoch; vascular supply from the same arterial bed: any of these, and more could be explanations suggested by pondering the diverse manifestations of a latent trait. Finding other traits associated with the gene for schizophrenia might do more than facilitate linkage analysis; it might give us clues about etiology. (Holzman & Matthysse, 1990, p. 285)

In summary, the search for indicators of vulnerability has, at a minimum, offered compelling evidence that some neurocognitive deficits are central to schizophrenia and not merely the reflection of psychotic symptoms, medications, or institutionalization. Neurocognitive indicators of vulnerability are likely to aid studies of molecular genetics by revealing alternative manifestations of the schizophrenic gene. In addition, they could provide clues about etiological processes by directing us toward affected brain regions and neurochemical systems.

REFERENCES

Asarnow, R. F., Granholm, E., & Sherman, T. (1991). Span of apprehension in schizophrenia. In S. R. Steinhauer, J. H. Gruzelier, & J. Zubin (Eds.), *Handbook of schizophrenia: Neuropsychology, psychophysiology, and information processing* (Vol. 5, pp. 335–370). Amsterdam: Elsevier.

Asarnow, R. F., & MacCrimmon, D. J. (1978). Residual performance deficit in clinically remitted schizophrenics: A marker of schizophrenia? *Journal of Abnormal Psychology, 87,* 597– 608.

Asarnow, R. F., & MacCrimmon, D. J. (1981). Span of apprehension deficits during the postpsychotic stages of schizophrenia. *Archives of General Psychiatry, 38,* 1006–1011.

Asarnow, R. F., Nuechterlein, K. H., & Marder, S. R. (1983). Span of apprehension performance, neuropsychological functioning, and indices of psychosis-proneness. *The Journal of Nervous and Mental Disease, 171,* 662–669.

Asarnow, R. F., Steffy, R. A., MacCrimmon, D. J., & Cleghorn, J. M. (1977). An attentional assessment of foster children at risk for schizophrenia. *Journal of Abnormal Psychology, 86,* 267–275.

Balogh, D. W., & Merritt, R. D. (1985). Susceptibility to type A backward pattern masking among hypothetically psychosis-prone college students. *Journal of Abnormal Psychology, 94,* 377–383.

Braff, D. L. (1981). Impaired speed of information processing in nonmedicated schizotypal patients. *Schizophrenia Bulletin, 7,* 499–508.

Chapman, L. J., Chapman, J. P., & Miller, E. N. (1982). Reliabilities and intercorrelations of eight measures of proneness to psychosis. *Journal of Consulting and Clinical Psychology, 50,* 187–195.

Cromwell, R. L., & Spaulding, W. (1978). How schizophrenics handle information. In W. E. Fann, I. Karacan, A. D. Pokorny, & R. L. Williams (Eds.), *Phenomenology and treatment of schizophrenia.* New York: Spectrum.

Cornblatt, B., Lenzenweger, M. F., Dworkin, R., & Erlenmeyer-Kimling, L. (1992). Childhood attentional dysfunction predicts social deficits in unaffected adults at risk for schizophrenia. *British Journal of Psychiatry, 161* (Suppl. 18), 59–64.

Cornblatt, B. A., Winters, L., & Erlenmeyer-Kimling, L. (1989). Attentional markers of schizophrenia: Evidence from the New York High Risk Study. In S. C. Schultz & C. A. Tamminga (Eds.), *Schizophrenia: Scientific progress.* New York: Oxford University Press.

Davies, D. R., & Parasuraman, R. (1982). *The psychology of vigilance.* London: Academic Press.

Eckblad, M., & Chapman, L. J. (1983). Magical ideation as an indicator of schizotypy. *Journal of Consulting and Clinical Psychology, 51,* 215–225.

Freedman, R., Coon, H., Myles-Worsley, M., Orr-Urtreger, A., Olincy, A., Davis, A., Polymeropoulos, M., Holik, J., Hopkins, J., Hoff, M., Rosenthal, J., Waldo, M. C., Reimherr, F., Wender, P., Yaw, J., Young, D. A., Breese, C. R., Adams, C., Patterson, D., Adler, L. E., Kruglyak, L., Leonard, S., & Byerley, W. (1997). Linkage of a neurophysiologcal deficit in schizophrenia to a chromosome 15 locus. *Proceedings of the National Academy of Sciences of the United States of America, 94,* 587–592.

Gottesman, I. I. (1991). *Schizophrenia genesis: The origins of madness.* New York: Freeman.

Green, M. F., Nuechterlein, K. H., & Breitmeyer, B. (1997). Backward masking performance in unaffected siblings of schizophrenia patients: Evidence for a vulnerability indicator. *Archives of General Psychiatry, 54,* 465–472.

Grove, W. M., Lebow, B. S., Clementz, B. A., Cerri, A., Medus, C., & Iacono, W. G. (1991). Familial prevalence and coaggregation of schizotypy indicators: A multitrait family study. *Journal of Abnormal Psychology, 100,* 115–121.

Harvey, P. D., Weintraub, S., & Neale, J. M. (1985). Span of apprehension deficits in children vulnerable to psychopathology: A failure to replicate. *Journal of Abnormal Psychology, 94,* 410–413.

Holzman, P. S., & Matthysse, S. (1990). The genetics of schizophrenia: A review. *Psychological Science, 1,* 279–286.

Keefe, R. S. E., Silverman, J. M., Mohs, R. C., Siever, L. J., Harvey, P. D., Friedman, L., Lees Roitman, S. E., DuPre, R. L., Smith, C. J., Schmeidler, J., & Davis, K. L. (1997). Eye tracking, attention, and schizotypal symptoms in nonpsychotic relatives of patients with schizophrenia. *Archives of General Psychiatry, 54,* 169–176.

Kendler, K. S., & Diehl, S. R. (1993). The genetics of schizophrenia: A current, genetic-epidemiologic perspective. *Schizophrenia Bulletin, 19,* 261–285.

Lenzenweger, M. F., Cornblatt, B. A., & Putnick, M. (1991). Schizotypy and sustained attention. *Journal of Abnormal Psychology, 100,* 84–89.

Levy, D. L., Holzman, P. S., Matthysse, S., & Mendell, N. (1993). Eye-tracking dysfunction and schizophrenia: A critical perspective. *Schizophrenia Bulletin, 19,* 461–536.

McGuffin, P. (1991). Genetic models of madness. In P. McGuffin & R. Murray (Eds.), *The new genetics of mental illness* (pp. 27–43). Oxford: Butterworth-Heinemann.

Mednick, S. A., & Higgins, S. (1960). *Current research in schizophrenia.* Ann Arbor, MI: Edwards Brothers.

Mednick, S. A., Parnas, J., & Schulsinger, F. (1987). The Copenhagen high-risk project, 1962–86. *Schizophrenia Bulletin, 13,* 485–495.

Miller, S., Saccuzzo, D., & Braff, D. (1979). Information processing deficits in remitted schizophrenics. *Journal of Abnormal Psychology, 88,* 446–449.

Mirsky, A. F., Ingraham, L. J., & Kugelmass, S. (1995). Neuropsychological assessment of attention and its pathology in the Israeli cohort. *Schizophrenia Bulletin, 21,* 193–204.

Mirsky, A. F., Lockhead, S. J., Jones, B. P., Kugelmass, S., Walsh, D., & Kendler, K. S. (1992). On familial factors in the attentional deficit in schizophrenia: A review and report of two new subject samples. *Journal of Psychiatric Research, 26,* 383–403.

Nuechterlein, K. H. (1983). Signal detection in vigilance tasks and behavioral attributes among offspring of schizophrenic mothers and among hyperactive children. *Journal of Abnormal Psychology, 92,* 4–28.

Nuechterlein, K. H. (1991). Vigilance in schizophrenia and related disorders. In S. R. Steinhauer, J. H. Gruzelier, & J. Zubin (Eds.), *Handbook of schizophrenia* (Vol. 5, pp. 397–433). Amsterdam: Elsevier.

Nuechterlein, K. H., & Dawson, M. E. (1984). A heuristic vulnerability/stress model of schizophrenic episodes. *Schizophrenia Bulletin, 10,* 300–312.

Nuechterlein, K. H., Dawson, M. E., Gitlin, M., Ventura, J., Goldstein, M. J., Snyder, K. S., Yee, C. M., & Mintz, J. (1992). Developmental processes in schizophrenic disorders: Longitudinal studies of vulnerability and stress. *Schizophrenia Bulletin, 18,* 387–425.

Nuechterlein, K. H., Dawson, M. E., & Green, M. F. (1994). Information-processing abnormalities as neuropsychological vulnerability indicators for schizophrenia. *Acta Psychiatrica Scandinavica, 90* (Suppl. 384), 71–79.

Rutschmann, J., Cornblatt, B., & Erlenmeyer-Kimling, L. (1977). Sustained attention in children at risk for schizophrenia: Report on a continuous performance test. *Archives of General Psychiatry, 34,* 571–576.

Rutschmann, J., Cornblatt, B., & Erlenmeyer-Kimling, L. (1986). Sustained attention in children at risk for schizophrenia: Findings with two visual continuous performance tests in a new sample. *Journal of Abnormal Child Psychology, 14,* 365–385.

Saccuzzo, D. P., & Schubert, D. L. (1981). Backward masking as a measure of slow processing in schizophrenia spectrum disorders. *Journal of Abnormal Psychology, 90,* 305–312.

Siever, L. J., Kalus, O. F., & Keefe, R. S. E. (1993). The boundaries of schizophrenia. *Psychiatric Clinics of North America, 16,* 217–244.

Steinhauer, S. R., Zubin, J., Condray, R., Shaw, D. B., Peters, J. L., & Van Kammen, D. P. (1991). Electrophysiological and behavioral signs of attentional disturbance in schizophrenics and their siblings. In C. A. Tamminga & S. C. Schulz (Eds.), *Advances in neuropsychiatry and psychopharmacology, volume 1: Schizophrenia research* (Vol. 1, pp. 169–178). New York: Raven Press.

Steronko, R. J., & Woods, D. J. (1978). Impairment in early stages of visual information processing in nonpsychotic schizotypic individuals. *Journal of Abnormal Psychology, 87,* 481–490.

Wohlberg, G. W., & Kornetsky, C. (1973). Sustained attention in remitted schizophrenics. *Archives of General Psychiatry, 28,* 533–537.

Zubin, J., & Spring, B. (1977). Vulnerability: A new view of schizophrenia. *Journal of Abnormal Psychology, 86,* 103–126.

▶ 5

Symptoms and Neurocognition

After visiting a treatment unit for symptomatic schizophrenic patients, one can get the impression that the only thing the patients have in common is a chart diagnosis. The variety of symptoms in schizophrenia is both impressive and perplexing. The diversity of symptoms and signs is so striking that it is natural to wonder if all patients with a diagnosis of schizophrenia are suffering from the same disorder. Recall that Bleuler thought that schizophrenia was comprised of multiple disorders, which he referred to as the "Group of Schizophrenias."

Diversity in schizophrenia is not limited to symptoms but is also the hallmark of performance measures. One experimental finding emerges with the reliability of a Swiss watch—schizophrenic patients show increased variability of performance on almost any type of measure. Can individual differences in neurocognitive abilities explain some of the variability in clinical presentation? As we will see, the answer depends on the type of neurocognitive deficit, and on the type of symptom.

As shown in Figure 5.1, performance across clinical states can fit one of three types of indicators (Nuechterlein & Dawson, 1984). The figure depicts hypothetical performance patterns for schizophrenic patients when they are in psychotic episode and in remission. Of course, the normal controls never enter a psychotic episode; values for controls represent repeated testings time-linked to those of the patients. The top panel shows the pattern for an Episode Indicator in which the deficit is present when patients are psychotic, but normalizes when patients are in remission. When psychotic symptoms are temporally linked to performance deficits, we can speculate that performance and symptoms are causally linked. The direction of the causality, however, is ambiguous. It is possible that the presence of symptoms led

Episode Indicator

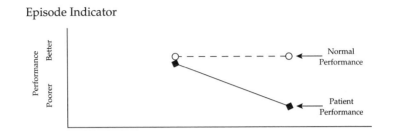

Mediating Vulnerability Indicator

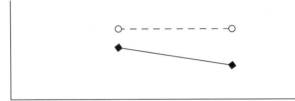

Stable Vulnerability Indicator

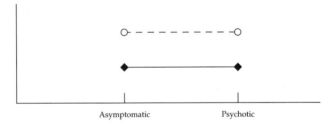

FIGURE 5.1

to poor performance (e.g., hearing voices distracted the patient). Alternatively, it is equally possible that a particular neurocognitive deficit caused the symptoms to occur (e.g., cognitive disinhibition led to a hallucinatory experience).

The bottom panel shows the expected pattern for a test that is a Stable Vulnerability Indicator. Deficits on this test endure through periods of symptomatic remission and cannot be explained as part of the symptom picture of the disorder. We saw a similar pattern for the degraded-stimulus CPT and the Span of Apprehension in Figures 4.2 and 4.3. The pattern is expected for measures that are closely linked to vulnerability to the disorder and are insensitive to clinical state.

The middle panel shows the pattern for a Mediating Vulnerability Indicator. Here, patients perform more poorly than controls both in episode and in remission, as in a Stable Vulnerability Indicator. The difference is that the patients' performance is worse in episode than in remission, suggesting that the indicator is reflecting vulnerability to schizophrenia and also somewhat sensitive to changes in symptoms. Tests that fit this pattern (e.g., versions of the CPT with a memory load) may have multiple components and thereby be a composite vulnerability and episode indicator.

With these characteristic patterns of performance in mind, what type of relationship would one expect to find between performance and symptoms longitudinally? Figure 5.2 depicts the temporal relationships that may be involved between the three types of neurocognitive indicators and psychotic

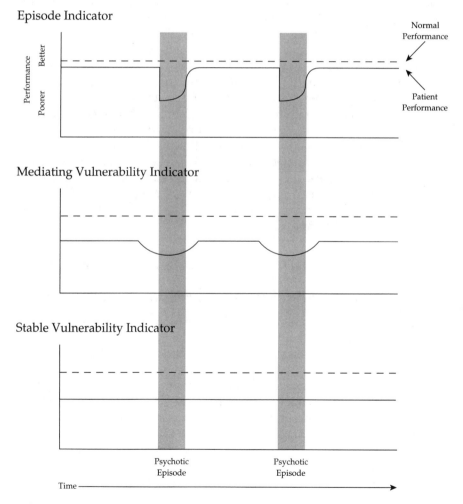

FIGURE 5.2

episodes. For an Episode Indicator, we expect a temporal relationship between the indicator and symptoms because the deficit is present only when the patient has psychotic symptoms. However, this temporal relationship does not necessarily mean that, at any given time, the level of psychotic symptoms correlates with the degree of neurocognitive deficit. In other words, the relationship is not necessarily "dose-dependent." For a Stable Vulnerability Indicator, both the temporal and cross-sectional relationships between neurocognitive performance and psychotic symptoms should be fairly weak or absent because this indicator is insensitive to psychotic symptoms. Nonetheless, this type of indicator may be related to other types of psychiatric symptoms, such as negative symptoms. The pattern for the Mediating Vulnerability Indicator is intermediate between the Episode and Stable Vulnerability Indicators, and the cross-sectional relationships between psychotic symptoms and neurocognition for this type of indicator should still be relatively weak.

Approaches to studying the relationship between neurocognition and symptoms have followed two diametrically opposite paths. One approach is to find deficits in neurocognition that can explain the phenomenology of the disorder. In this approach, one tries to find neurocognitive deficits that are closely linked to psychotic symptoms (most likely Episode Indicators). The other approach has been to find neurocognitive deficits believed to be central to schizophrenia because they are *not* closely linked to psychotic symptoms. This approach has focused on measures thought to be Stable Vulnerability Indicators. We will begin our discussion with the approach that tries to link neurocognition and symptoms.

ATTEMPTS TO LINK NEUROCOGNITION AND SYMPTOMS

Neurocognition and Psychotic Versus Negative Symptoms

During the 1980s the phenomenology of schizophrenia was modified by a growing awareness of negative symptoms. When Crow (1980) proposed the highly influential distinction between Type I and Type II schizophrenia, he hypothesized that Type I schizophrenia was characterized by positive symptoms and generally intact neurocognition. In contrast, he suggested that Type II schizophrenia was characterized by negative symptoms, structural brain abnormalities, and neurocognitive dysfunction. Along with the development of several scales to measure psychotic (positive) and negative symptoms (Andreasen, 1984a; 1984b), Crow's hypotheses stimulated a small cottage industry of studies on the association between symptom dimensions and neurocognition. As is often the case, the story is more complicated than it initially appeared.

The literature on psychotic versus negative symptoms and neurocognition has been reviewed previously (Strauss, 1993; Walker & Lewine, 1988). Most of the studies have been cross-sectional. In some studies, symptoms were treated categorically and patients were divided into subgroups (e.g., positive vs. negative vs. mixed symptoms). These groups were then compared on their neurocognitive performance. Alternatively, symptoms were sometimes treated as continuous variables and correlational analyses were used. While both approaches continue to be used, correlational studies offer two advantages over a categorical approach: they make more thorough use of the data and they do not require an assumption that the symptoms reflect subgroups or syndromes that are etiologically distinct.

Negative symptoms tend to be associated with deficits on measures of visual processing (e.g., backward masking, the CPT, the Span of Apprehension) and motor speed and dexterity (Braff, Callaway, & Naylor, 1989; Green & Walker, 1985; 1986; Nuechterlein, Edell, Norris, & Dawson, 1986). In contrast, psychotic symptoms tend to be associated, although weakly and not as consistently, with auditory-processing deficits as reflected by tests of verbal memory, and auditory distractibility (Cornblatt, Lenzenweger, Dworkin, & Erlenmeyer-Kimling, 1985; Green & Walker, 1985; Walker & Harvey, 1986). It is intriguing that the patterns of association appear to depend on the sensory modality of the stimulus (e.g., visual processing for negative symptoms, auditory processing for psychotic symptoms). This formulation, however, does not inform us about the underlying processes that connect symptoms with performance (Strauss, 1993). Besides, the story is becoming more complex as finer lines of division are drawn within the symptom dimensions.

Many studies initially emphasized two dimensions of symptoms (psychotic vs. negative), reflecting the influence of Crow's typology and early studies from Andreasen and colleagues (Andreasen & Olsen, 1982). Subsequent studies have considered three symptom dimensions instead of two. Factor analytic studies across several samples have revealed that the structure of psychotic symptoms is often better captured when they are subdivided into two factors: one for delusions and hallucinations and one for symptoms of "disorganization" such as formal thought disorder and bizarre behavior (Andreasen, Arndt, Aliger, Miller, & Flaum, 1995; Lenzenweger, Dworkin, & Wethington, 1989; Liddle, 1987). Few studies have evaluated relationships between neurocognition and these three factors (negative, disorganized, hallucinations/delusions). The results suggest that of the three factors, the disorganized factor correlates most strongly with neurocognitive dysfunction, especially for measures of language and memory (Bilder, Mukherjee, Rieder, & Pandurangi, 1985) and possibly visuo-spatial tasks (Addington, Addington, & Maticka-Tyndale, 1991). Gruzelier and colleagues have proposed a similar three factor model, which includes active (behavioral over-arousal), negative (withdrawal), and unreality (hallucinations and delusions) subtypes (Gruzelier & Raine, 1994; Gruzelier, 1994). According to this model, neurocognitive deficits are not limited to one subtype. Instead, each clinical subtype has a characteristic pattern of lateral asymmetry on neurocognitive and psychophysiological procedures. The active group has left > right asymmetry, the negative group has right > left asymmetry, and the unreality group has inconsistent asymmetry.

Even in studies that used two symptom dimensions, it appears that among the psychotic symptoms, it is thought disorder that correlates most consistently with performance (Walker & Harvey, 1986). In fact, the disorganized factor has sometimes been referred to as a "cognitive" factor (Lindenmayer, Bernstein-Hyman, & Grochowski, 1994). The term reflects an assumption that clinically observed disorganization is closely related to measurable neurocognitive deficits. Although it is understandable why such an assumption would be made, labeling a symptom factor as "cognitive" is potentially confusing. The clinical presentation of disorganized symptoms is better viewed as a separate construct that might be associated with, but not identical to, underlying neurocognition.

Negative symptoms have been divided into separate subtypes of primary and secondary negative symptoms. The distinction between primary and secondary negative symptoms has been based largely on presumed etiology (Carpenter, Heinrichs, & Wagman, 1988). Secondary negative symptoms are transitory and thought to be associated with factors extrinsic to schizophrenia such as depressed mood, medication side effects, or an understimulating environment. Negative symptoms can also be due to psychotic symptoms, for example, if a person's ability to interact with others is restricted because of suspiciousness. Primary negative symptoms, also called the "deficit syndrome," are considered the purer form of negative symptoms and a relatively enduring, core feature of the illness. The determination of primary negative symptoms depends on longitudinal observations. Similar to Crow's formulation of Type II schizophrenia, Carpenter et al. proposed that primary negative symptoms, not negative symptoms in general, are associated with neurocognitive impairment. This prediction has received some support from a study in which deficit syndrome patients performed more poorly on selected neuropsychological measures of frontal and parietal functioning (Buchanan et al., 1994).

To summarize, there have been significant relationships reported between negative symptoms and certain neurocognitive deficits that rely on visual processing and speeded response. Among the negative symptoms, relationships may be strongest with primary negative symptoms that are relatively enduring. Psychotic symptoms are related, but not very consistently, to measures of verbal memory and auditory processing and this relationship may apply particularly to disorganized symptoms.

There are at least two major considerations regarding this line of research. One is that the research in this area has been mainly descriptive, as opposed to explanatory (Strauss, 1993). The studies have explored correlations between symptom dimensions and performance, but the reasons for the correlations are not apparent. Another consideration is that neurocognitive performance can account for only a small amount of variability in symptoms. The relationships between symptoms and neurocognition, while significant, are usually quite modest in strength. In a typical study, neurocognition explains less than about 10% of the variance of symptoms. Clearly, even for Episode Indicators, most of the variance would have to be attributed to other factors. Perhaps the composite nature of the symptom dimensions obscures specific linkages that may be present for individual symptoms. An alternative approach has been to try to understand a particular symptom, such as hallucinations or delusions, instead of an entire symptom dimension.

Neurocognitive Models of Delusions

> I began to misinterpret the everyday world, finding enormous significance in apparent trifles. I knew I was evil, Satan's spawn, and to this day am not sure that I was not in fact responsible for JFK's assassination as well as other international catastrophes. (Wagner, 1996, p. 400)

> My delusional system leads me to believe that I am *not* schizophrenic; I believe that I am a psychic, that I "broadcast" my thoughts to anyone who is—what? In my immediate vicinity? Mentally focused on me? Maybe even anywhere on Earth? I don't know. I have believed all of these possibilities and more, but presently I believe that people can "read my mind" only if they are in my immediate vicinity.... My belief has withstood attack from anyone I've shared it with. (Bowden, 1993, p. 165)

In many ways, what is most striking about delusions is the way that patients maintain them despite what an outsider would consider to be compelling evidence to the contrary. Where does this fixed quality come from? Maher (1988) proposed that delusional thinking is not aberrant, but instead could be viewed as the by-product of theories generated to provide order for a set of observations. According to this theory, delusions arise when the individual is confronted with confusing or ambiguous observations. The puzzlement that arises from this situation creates some tension for the observer who in turn starts to search for an explanation. Once an explanation has been generated, the observer experiences a reduction in tension; the process is essentially reinforcing. Subsequent observations that are consistent with the explanation continue to reduce tension and are given higher priority than observations that are not. Note that the thinking processes described are not much different from those used by a scientist who encounters a puzzling experimental finding and then generates a theory to explain it. Further parallels could be drawn between Maher's theory of delusions and the understandable tendency to sometimes emphasize evidence that supports a favored theory, while de-emphasizing data that do not.

According to this model, the delusional processes depend on the perceptual processes. When first exposed to a stimulus (e.g., the sound of someone talking), people form various hypotheses about what it may be. The interpretation of that stimulus is dependent on the clarity of the perception. If there is a dysfunction in a sensory/perceptual process or a defect in the selection of sensory information, the interpretation may be wrong. Maher's theory suggests that disrupted sensory/perceptual processes in patients can generate delusional experiences. Such a process occurs to a limited extent when a normal person with a partial hearing loss generates a reasonable, but inaccurate, interpretation of what he/she thought someone said. For hallucinating patients, voices talking about them may lead to the belief of a plot against them. Maher's theory seems especially relevant for delusions of persecution and reference; perhaps less so for bizarre delusions. The theory has some difficulty explaining why normal people with hearing losses can revise their mistaken beliefs easily with additional information, but delusional patients cannot. This influential theory emphasized normal reasoning that leads to a mistaken conclusion, or a misattribution. We will see that misattribution is a central feature of several theories of symptom formation.

Chapman and Chapman (1988) started with Maher's theory and then extended it. They have conducted a series of landmark studies with university students defined as psychosis-prone based on psychometric scales of unusual beliefs and anomalous perceptual experiences (see Table 4.1). The Chapmans noted that some subjects with unusual thoughts, such as magical thinking, over time developed delusions related in content to their unusual beliefs. However, most subjects with unusual beliefs and perceptions did not develop full delusions during the follow-up period. What accounts for the individual differences? Chapman and Chapman suggested that a delusion originates from the interaction of impaired sensory perception with two types of cognitive abnormalities. One abnormality is cognitive slippage, a milder version of formal thought disorder in which the individual becomes vague, tangential, and has difficulty in verbal expression. They noticed that several subjects started to demonstrate cognitive slippage when discussing their symptoms, but not when discussing other types of anxiety-laden experiences. The second abnormality is the tendency to process information in a biased manner. The bias leads to selecting certain features of stimuli to attend to (e.g., those related to the subject's emotional responses to the stimuli) without the ability to evaluate and weigh information in a fashion needed to accurately interpret environmental events. Depending on whether cognitive abnormalities are present, some people with abnormal sensory experiences, but not others, will develop delusions.

Neurocognitive Models of Hallucinations

> One effect of the illness was that I heard voices—numerous voices—chatting, arguing, and quarreling with me telling me I should hurt myself or kill myself. I felt as if I was being put on a heavenly trial for misdeeds that I had done and was being held accountable by God. Other times I felt as if I was being pursued by the government for acts of disloyalty.
>
> I thought the voices I heard were being transmitted through the walls of my apartment and through the washer and dryer and that these machines were talking and telling me things. I felt that the government agencies had planted transmitters and receivers in my apartment so that I could hear what they were saying and they could hear what I was saying. (Anonymous, 1996, p. 183)

Hallucinations are perhaps the most dramatic and perplexing of the symptoms of schizophrenia. Jaspers (1962) suggested that psychotic symptoms are distinguished from other psychiatric symptoms in that they are impossible to "understand." Most of us have very little personal experience that allows us to "understand" what patients experience when they hear clear and complex non-existent voices. Does a neurocognitive approach provide any insight into this puzzling phenomenon?

One possible explanation for hallucinations, first raised in the 1940s, is that patients were talking quietly to themselves. This possibility has been revisited by Kinsbourne and colleagues (Bick & Kinsbourne, 1987; Green & Kinsbourne, 1990). The hypothesis is that patients are *subvocalizing* during auditory hallucinations, meaning that they are activating their speech musculature. Subvocal activity can be observed in children when they are learning to read, and sometimes even in adults when they are reading difficult material. Suppose patients have a lack of cortical inhibition of the speech musculature resulting in the initiation of subvocal activity, even when they do not intend to do so. Because the patients did not intend to initiate the activity, it would not be recognized as their own, but instead would be attributed to an external source.

The subvocal theory of hallucinations was tested by instructing hallucinating patients to perform maneuvers that should interfere with subvocal activity, as well as control maneuvers (Bick & Kinsbourne, 1987; Green & Kinsbourne, 1990). If auditory hallucinations result from unintended subvocal activity, then interfering with this activity should reduce the self-report of hallucinations. Alternatively, if the subvocal activity is a response to the voices (e.g., patients are talking back to their voices), then interfering with subvocal activity should not affect the hallucinatory experience. The results have been inconclusive. In support of the subvocalization theory, activities that interfered with subvocal activity (e.g., opening the mouth wide, or humming a single note quietly) reduced the frequency of reported hallucinations. The beneficial effect of disrupting subvocal activity did not appear merely to be the result of distraction, otherwise any effortful maneuver should reduce hallucinations. However, one premise of the theory was not supported because it was not possible to show a consistent temporal association between subvocal activity and self-report of hallucinations (Green & Kinsbourne, 1990).

Suppose that the underlying problem with auditory hallucinations does not involve output or expressive components of language, but instead involves auditory input and speech reception. This possibility has been studied with a measure of basic speech reception, the dichotic listening test (Bruder et al., 1995; Green, Hugdahl, & Mitchell, 1994). The dichotic listening test involves simultaneous presentation of different stimuli (e.g., "ba" and "ka") to each ear. Instead of hearing two stimuli, the subject typically perceives a single fused stimulus. More times than not, it is identified as the stimulus presented to the right ear. This "right-ear-advantage" is due to a combination of two factors: First, neural pathways from the right ear project primarily to the left temporal lobe. Second, in the vast majority of people (even most left-handers), the left hemisphere is especially suited for processing linguistic stimuli.

In a study that compared non-hallucinating to hallucinating schizophrenic patients, non-hallucinating patients showed the normal right-ear-advantage (Green et al., 1994). However, hallucinating patients, as a group, showed no ear advantage. Similarly, in another sample, the magnitude of the right-ear-advantage was inversely correlated with ratings of hallucinations (Bruder et al., 1995). These findings suggest that auditory hallucinations are linked to a fundamental defect in a speech receptive mechanism. One possible explanation is that hallucinations activate speech receptive mechanisms like real voices and prevent the normal establishment of a right-ear-advantage. In this case, the left hemisphere would be much like a switchboard that is already busy with an existing call (i.e., a hallucination) and cannot assign normal priority to signals from the right ear. This possibility explains why hallucinating patients lack an ear advantage, but not the origin of the hallucination. Alternatively, patients may have a relatively enduring abnormality in the left temporal lobe that renders them susceptible to hallucinations. Both of these explanations for hallucinations emphasize specific neural structures involved with speech processing.

Other theories have emphasized deficits in higher level processes such as attribution. Hoffman (1986) proposed that misattribution was central to the generation of auditory hallucinations in schizophrenia. According to this theory, hallucinations occur when there is a dysfunction in discourse planning. Normally, when individuals plan to say something, they generate a verbal image that is accompanied by a feeling of intentionality. If the verbal image of the discourse planning did not carry the feeling of intentionality, it could be experienced as foreign and have the "otherness" quality of a hallucination. The underlying problem is executive, or metacognitive in nature; a failure in discourse planning results in a failure to experience intentionality. The end result is a misattribution (e.g., the image must have come from an outside source). Hoffman has used this type of theory to explain other phenomena such as incoherent speech.

Comprehensive Models

In contrast to the focused efforts to understand particular psychotic symptoms, some theorists have tried to account for the entire range of schizophrenic phenomenology with a limited number of dysfunctional processes. The British, more than others, have generated innovative and rather comprehensive theories to explain phenomenology in terms of neurocognition. Some of the most influential theorists in this area have been Gray (Gray, Feldon, Rawlins, Hemsley, & Smith, 1991), Hemsley (1987), and Frith (1992). As an example to illustrate the scope of the models, we will review Frith's model.

In Frith's model, a deficit in "self-monitoring" is central to the symptoms of schizophrenia. The problem lies in a defect in a central monitoring system, and is essentially executive in nature. To grasp the idea of self-monitoring, let us turn to an example from physiology, namely, "corollary discharge" (Teuber, 1972). Each time we move our eyes, the image of the outside world moves across the retina, but our subjective experience is that the world remains stable and it is our eyes that are moving. To achieve this sense of stability, a corollary discharge is sent to a monitoring system at the same time as the message is sent to initiate the eye movement. The corollary discharge informs a monitor of the *intention* to make an eye movement so that it can compensate for the anticipated movement. As a result, we can distinguish between a moving retinal image caused by us versus one caused by moving objects in the outside world. To experience eye movements without corollary discharge, simply close one eye and poke the other with your finger (gently, please). Notice that the world no longer appears stationary. The central defect in schizophrenia, according to Frith, is the neurocognitive equivalent of a breakdown in corollary discharge.

Figure 5.3 shows the key components of Frith's model. The model includes an action component that leads to a response. Factors that determine decisions of the action component include two types of intentions: willed and stimulus. Willed intentions are internally generated and stimulus intentions are generated in response to signals from the external environment. The key components of this model include the monitoring of action, the monitoring of intention to act, and the ability to distinguish between the two types of intentions.

> I believe, however, that it is not only monitoring of action that is impaired in schizophrenia. In addition, it is the monitoring of the intentions to act. I am essentially describing two steps in a central monitoring system. First, the relationship between actions and external events are monitored in order to distinguish between events caused by our actions and by external agencies. This enables us to know the causes of events. Second, intentions are monitored in order to distinguish between actions caused by our own goals and plans (willed actions) and actions that are in response to external events (stimulus-driven actions). Such monitoring is essential if we are to have some awareness of the causes of our actions. (Frith, 1992, p. 81)

Frith attempts to explain a wide range of psychopathology with this model. Hallucinations are viewed in terms of the patient's own inner speech, which because of a defect in monitoring, is attributed to an external source. Note that this explanation for hallucinations is compatible with that of Hoffman's. It is also similar to Bentall's (1990) formulation that hallucinations stem from a problem in reality discrimination in which patients mistake their internal events for external events. Delusional experiences are similarly explained by Frith's model. Thought processes normally involve a sense of effort that reflects central monitoring. Without this sense of intention, the thoughts could be experienced as alien or as inserted by an external agent. Delusions of control might accompany this type of experience. A disorder in the ability to monitor the intention of *others* would also lead to other types of phenomena such as delusions of reference and paranoid delusions.

An impressive feature of the model is that it also attempts to account for negative symptoms. Unlike psychotic symptoms, these symptoms are not attributed to a problem in monitoring. Instead, they are viewed as an indica-

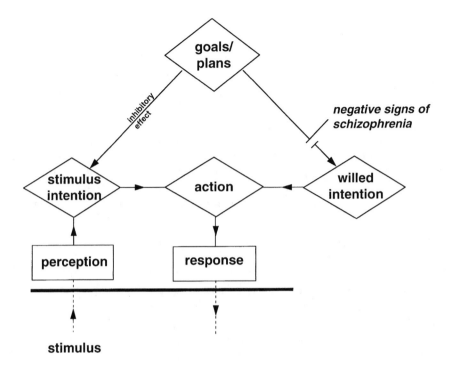

FIGURE 5.3

Source: Adapted from C. D. Frith, 1992, p. 46. *The Cognitive Neuropsychology of Schizophrenia.* United Kingdom: Lawrence Erlbaum. Reprinted by permission of Erlbaum (UK) Taylor & Francis, Hove, UK.

tion that the willed intention component itself is dysfunctional. As a result, the patient may have difficulty in producing spontaneous behavior in the absence of external stimuli and show a poverty of action.

> Positive symptoms occur because the brain structures responsible for willed actions no longer send corollary discharges to the posterior parts of the brain concerned with perception. This could be caused by disconnections between these brain regions. In consequence self-generated changes in perception are misinterpreted as having an external cause. If the structures responsible for action are more severely damaged then messages are no longer sent to the brain structures concerned with response generation either. This results in a lack of willed action and hence the negative features of schizophrenia. (Frith 1992, p. 93)

In essence, Frith's model attempts to explain the entire breadth of schizophrenic symptoms in terms of three types of deficits. A dysfunction of willed intentions leads to negative symptoms, a failure to monitor the intentions of self leads to some psychotic symptoms, and a failure to monitor the intentions of others leads to a different set of psychotic experiences. Frith attempts to trace all three of these types of dysfunction to a common underlying abnormality in metarepresentation (e.g., self-awareness). His model accounts well for many symptoms of schizophrenia such as motor retardation, some types of auditory hallucinations, thought insertion, and delusions of alien control. The model is not as easily applied to third person auditory hallucinations in which a patient hears voices talking to each other about the patient. Nor does it obviously explain some common types of symptoms, such as grandiose delusions.

WHEN NEUROCOGNITIVE DEFICITS PRECEDE SYMPTOMATOLOGY

No matter how we approach symptom/neurocognition relations in schizophrenia, we will encounter an obstacle. An attempt to explain psychotic symptoms through neurocognitive mechanisms will need to account for the fact that some neurocognitive deficits endure through non-symptomatic periods. Likewise, it will need to account for the fact that some neurocognitive deficits that are stable and present in childhood lead to symptoms years later in adulthood. The distinction between Episode Indicators and Vulnerability Indicators is helpful to some extent, but still does not provide an adequate neurocognitive explanation of how a vulnerable person develops psychosis. Some intermediate steps are missing.

High-risk studies, which were discussed in the previous chapter, provide guidance in this matter. These studies evaluate the offspring of mothers with schizophrenia because a relatively high proportion (about 10–15%) of the offspring are expected to develop schizophrenia. High-risk children show higher rates of neurocognitive dysfunction (often measured with the Span or CPT) compared with controls. The high-risk studies can be used to address several questions that are relevant to the origin of psychotic symptoms: Are the high-risk subjects with neurocognitive dysfunction the same ones who eventually develop psychiatric problems? Are the neurocognitive deficits simply markers of predisposition to the illness, or are they involved with the development of the disorder? If they are causally involved with the genesis of the illness, what is a plausible mechanism?

Neurocognitive Antecedents of Illness

Neurocognitive deficits characterize high-risk samples as a group, but do they identify individuals who will eventually develop psychiatric problems?

There are data from several sources indicating that neurocognitive deficits predate clinical symptoms within individuals. Deficits in groups at high risk for schizophrenia appear as early as they can be measured and seem stable throughout development. Cornblatt, Erlenmeyer-Kimling, and colleagues (Cornblatt, Lenzenweger, Dworkin, & Erlenmeyer-Kimling, 1992; Cornblatt & Erlenmeyer-Kimling, 1985) found that deviant attentional performance in childhood had excellent specificity and moderate sensitivity for later behavioral problems. Ninety-one percent of the subjects without adult behavioral disturbances had a normal childhood attentional index, and 36% of the subjects with adult behavioral disturbances had a deviant childhood attentional index (Cornblatt & Erlenmeyer-Kimling, 1985). Likewise, data from the Israeli High-Risk study indicate that poor scores on a task that required focused attention (digit cancellation under distraction) at age 11 predicted the presence of schizophrenia spectrum diagnoses at age 32 (Mirsky, Ingraham, & Kugelmass, 1995).

Neurocognitive Deficits: Causal Agents Versus Markers

Neurocognitive deficits are associated with subsequent illness, but are they *causally* involved? It is possible that the deficits are merely markers of vulnerability and do not contribute to onset of illness. Eye tracking abnormalities, which do not have obvious functional consequences, may fit this pattern. On the other hand, neurocognitive abnormalities may be directly involved with the genesis of the illness. One challenging aspect of this explanation is that neurocognitive deficits are stable throughout development, so an additional factor must be involved with the onset of illness. Cornblatt et al. (1992) have suggested that development of illness is mediated through social factors. They found that neurocognitive abnormalities in childhood predicted reduced social sensitivity, increased social indifference, and increased social isolation in adulthood. These relationships held for children at risk for schizophrenia, but not for children at risk for affective disorders or for controls. Figure 5.4 shows an innovative and speculative model that attempts to account for these relationships.

In this model, vulnerability to schizophrenia is associated with neurocognitive deficits. The neurocognitive deficit in this model is called a "Chronic Attentional Deficit" because the investigators used a broad attentional battery that included measures of sustained attention, selective attention, and immediate memory. The model requires two critical assumptions. First, it assumes that the neurocognitive deficit results in an inability to process information in the environment. The second assumption concerns the nature of the information to be processed:

> It is further postulated that interpersonal cues and communications are among the most subtle and complicated of the information that

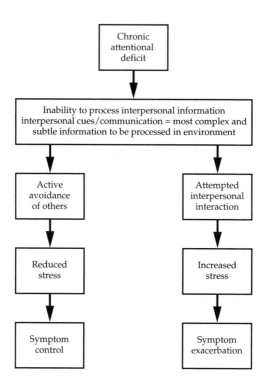

FIGURE 5.4

Source: Adapted from "Childhood Attentional Dysfunctions Predict Social Deficits in Unaffected Adults at Risk for Schizophrenia" by B. A. Cornblatt, M. F. Lenzenweger, R. H. Dworkin, and L. Erlenmeyer-Kimling, 1992, *British Journal of Psychiatry, 161* (Suppl. 18), p. 63. Reproduced with permission.

needs to be processed. Thus, an attentional difficulty is likely to be particularly disruptive to the processing of social/interpersonal information. (Cornblatt et al., 1992, p. 62)

As subjects move through adolescence, social interactions and relationships become more complex and more subtle. The functional limitations caused by the neurocognitive deficit would become more debilitating as the individual enters young adulthood. Stress from repeated social/interpersonal failures could serve as a trigger for the onset of the disease (for possible mechanisms see Walker and DiForio, in press).

Yet certainly not all individuals with neurocognitive impairment and social deficits go on to develop schizophrenia. What is protecting them? These at-risk individuals may protect themselves by avoiding the stressful situations that could lead to the onset of illness. They become socially isolated (see the left side of Figure 5.4). Although most people might consider social isolation to be generally maladaptive, it may be adaptive for such vulnerable individuals.

The model of Cornblatt et al., while providing a major step forward, has at least two limitations. First, it considers social isolation as the sole protective mechanism. However, not all social interactions are stressful and negative. An alternative protective route would be through positive and supportive interactions of family, friends, and spouses that might help to buffer the individual against stress.

A second limitation is that the model does not fully explain how social/interpersonal difficulties lead to the onset of psychotic symptoms. This problem is especially thorny. The neurocognitive deficits have been present and stable for many years. The stress of repeated unsuccessful social interactions must interact with the stable deficit (perhaps via neurohormonal mediation) to produce a temporary, intermediate, neurocognitive state that immediately precedes the onset of a prodrome and psychotic symptoms. This intermediate state or "leading edge" of a psychotic episode was discussed in Chapter 2 in reference to the UCLA comprehensive model for schizophrenia. The revised model suggests that the intermediate state may involve reduced working memory, autonomic hyperactivation, and deficient processing of social stimuli. Considering the hypotheses of Cornblatt et al., we could speculate that the increased stress of social interactions results in autonomic hyperactivation, which in turn, further destabilizes working memory and disrupts the processing of social information, which was not optimal to begin with. The situation spirals into prodromal and then psychotic phases.

Admittedly, these hypotheses are speculative. The models predict the existence of a neurocognitive leading edge, but so far data are lacking. In this situation, psychopathology resembles natural sciences in which theoretical models predict the existence of certain elements or particles long before empirical support is garnered. In fact, results from longitudinal studies are beginning to provide support for the notion that psychophysiological and neurocognitive changes anticipate and predict clinical changes (Hazlett, Dawson, Schell, & Nuechterlein, 1997; Serper, Davidson, & Harvey, 1994). In a preliminary study (Hazlett et al., 1997), a psychophysiological measure, electrodermal activity, was recorded in a control period (subjects were in remission and did not exacerbate for at least seven months) and a prodromal period (subjects were in remission but exacerbated within three weeks). The electrodermal variables were higher during the prodromal period compared with the control period, consistent with the notion that electrodermal hyperactivity is part of a leading edge. More definitive empirical support for these hypotheses will not come easily. To obtain meaningful data on short-term prediction of clinical change, a wide range of tests will need to be given at brief retest intervals, for a large number of patients, over a long period of time.

In summary, the links between neurocognition and symptoms in schizophrenia are filled with paradox and complexity. The heart of the paradox lies in the different time frames; many neurocognitive deficits begin long before the onset of psychotic symptoms and linger long after symptom remission. Complexity is inherent in the diversity of neurocognitive deficits, some of which are insensitive to symptom changes (vulnerability indicators) whereas others are temporally linked to symptom presence (episode indicators). A fundamental question is whether neurocognitive deficits in the premorbid period are merely markers of risk for schizophrenia, or if they are part of the causal pathway leading to onset of illness. There is reason to place the neurocognitive deficits on the causal pathway. Hence, the next major challenge in this area is to determine how stable neurocognitive deficits lead to episodic symptoms. The transition to psychotic episode requires some intermediate steps, perhaps in the form of a neurocognitive leading edge. Great clinical and theoretical challenges for psychopathologists lie in the grey zone between remission and relapse.

REFERENCES

Addington, J., Addington, D., & Maticka-Tyndale, E. (1991). Cognitive functioning and positive and negative symptoms in schizophrenia. *Schizophrenia Research, 5,* 123–134.

Andreasen, N. C. (1984a). *The scale for the assessment of negative symptoms (SANS).* Iowa City, IA: The University of Iowa.

Andreasen, N. C. (1984b). *The scale for the assessment of positive symptoms (SAPS).* Iowa City, IA: The University of Iowa.

Andreasen, N. C., Arndt, S., Aliger, R., Miller, D., & Flaum, M. (1995). Symptoms of schizophrenia. *Archives of General Psychiatry, 52,* 341–351.

Andreasen, N. C., & Olsen, S. A. (1982). Negative versus positive schizophrenia: Definition and validation. *Archives of General Psychiatry, 39,* 789–794.

Anonymous. (1996). First person account: Social, economic and medical effects of schizophrenia. *Schizophrenia Bulletin, 22,* 183–185.

Bentall, R. P. (1990). The illusion of reality: A review and integration of psychological research on hallucinations. *Psychological Bulletin, 107,* 82–95.

Bick, P. A., & Kinsbourne, M. (1987). Auditory hallucinations through occlusion of monaural auditory input. *American Journal of Psychiatry, 144,* 222–225.

Bilder, R. M., Mukherjee, S., Rieder, R. O., & Pandurangi, A. K. (1985). Symptomatic and neuropsychological components of defect states. *Schizophrenia Bulletin, 11,* 409–419.

Bowden, W. D. (1993). First person account: The onset of paranoia. *Schizophrenia Bulletin, 19,* 165–167.

Braff, D. L., Callaway, E., & Naylor, H. (1989). Sensory input deficits and negative symptoms in schizophrenic patients. *American Journal of Psychiatry, 146,* 1006–1011.

Bruder, G., Rabinowicz, E., Towey, J., Brown, A., Kaufmann, C. A., Amador, X., Malaspina, D., & Gorman, J. M. (1995). Smaller right ear (left hemisphere) advantage for dichotic fused words in patients with schizophrenia. *American Journal of Psychiatry, 152,* 932– 935.

Buchanan, R. W., Strauss, M. E., Kirkpatrick, B., Holstein, C., Breier, A., & Carpenter, W. T. (1994). Neuropsychological impairments in deficit versus nondeficit forms of schizophrenia. *Archives of General Psychiatry, 51,* 804–811.

Carpenter, W. T., Heinrichs, D. W., & Wagman, A. M. I. (1988). Deficit and nondeficit forms of schizophrenia: The concept. *American Journal of Psychiatry, 145,* 578–583.

Chapman, L. J., & Chapman, J. P. (1988). The genesis of delusions. In T. F. Oltmanns & B. A. Maher (Eds.), *Delusional beliefs* (pp. 167–183). New York: Wiley.

Cornblatt, B., Lenzenweger, M. F., Dworkin, R., & Erlenmeyer-Kimling, L. (1992). Childhood attentional dysfunction predicts social deficits in unaffected adults at risk for schizophrenia. *British Journal of Psychiatry, 161* (Suppl. 18), 59–64.

Cornblatt, B. A., & Erlenmeyer-Kimling, L. (1985). Global attentional deviance as a marker of risk for schizophrenia: Specificity and predictive validity. *Journal of Abnormal Psychology, 94,* 470–486.

Cornblatt, B. A., Lenzenweger, M. F., Dworkin, R. H., & Erlenmeyer-Kimling, L. (1985). Positive and negative schizophrenic symptoms, attention, and information processing. *Schizophrenia Bulletin, 11,* 397–408.

Crow, T. J. (1980). Molecular pathology of schizophrenia: More than one dimension of pathology? *British Medical Journal, 280,* 66–68.

Frith, C. D. (1992). *The cognitive neuropsychology of schizophrenia.* Hove, UK: Lawrence Erlbaum.

Gray, J. A., Feldon, J., Rawlins, J. N. P., Hemsley, D. R., & Smith, A. D. (1991). The neuropsychology of schizophrenia. *Behavioral and Brain Sciences, 14,* 1–84.

Green, M. F., Hugdahl, K., & Mitchell, S. (1994). Dichotic listening during auditory hallucinations in schizophrenia. *American Journal of Psychiatry, 151,* 357–362.

Green, M. F., & Kinsbourne, M. (1990). Subvocal activity in auditory hallucinations: Clues for behavioral treatments? *Schizophrenia Bulletin, 16,* 617–625.

Green, M. F., & Walker, E. (1985). Neuropsychological performance and positive and negative symptoms in schizophrenia. *Journal of Abnormal Psychology, 94,* 460–469.

Green, M. F., & Walker, E. (1986). Symptom correlates of vulnerability to backward masking in schizophrenia. *American Journal of Psychiatry, 143,* 181–186.

Gruzelier, J. H. (1994). Syndromes of schizophrenia and schizotypy, hemispheric imbalance and sex differences: Implications for developmental psychopathology. *International Journal of Psychophysiology, 18,* 167–178.

Gruzelier, J., & Raine, A. (1994). Bilateral electrodermal activity and cerebral mechanisms in syndromes of schizophrenia and the schizotypal personality. *International Journal of Psychophysiology, 16,* 1–16.

Hazlett, H., Dawson, M. E., Schell, A. M., & Nuechterlein, K. H. (1997). Electrodermal activity as a prodromal sign in schizophrenia. *Biological Psychiatry, 41,* 111–113.

Hemsley, D. R. (1987). An experimental psychological model for schizophrenia. In H. Hafner, W. F. Gattaz, & A. Janzarik (Eds.), *Search for the causes of schizophrenia* (pp. 179–188). Heidelberg, Germany: Springer-Verlag.

Hoffman, R. E. (1986). Verbal hallucinations and language production processes in schizophrenia. *Behavioral and Brain Sciences, 9,* 503–548.

Jaspers, K. (1962). *General psychopathology* (7th ed.). Manchester, UK: Manchester University Press.

Lenzenweger, M. F., Dworkin, R. H., & Wethington, E. (1989). Models of positive and negative symptoms in schizophrenia: An empirical evaluation of latent structures. *Journal of Abnormal Psychology, 98,* 62–70.

Liddle, P. F. (1987). The symptoms of chronic schizophrenia: A re-examination of the positive and negative dichotomy. *British Journal of Psychiatry, 151,* 145–151.

Lindenmayer, J. P., Bernstein-Hyman, R., & Grochowski, S. (1994). Five-factor model of schizophrenia. *The Journal of Nervous and Mental Disease, 182,* 631–638.

Maher, B. A. (1988). Anomalous experience and delusional thinking: The logic of explanations. In T. F. Oltmanns & B. A. Maher (Eds.), *Delusional beliefs* (pp. 15–33). New York: Wiley.

Mirsky, A. F., Ingraham, L. J., & Kugelmass, S. (1995). Neuropsychological assessment of attention and its pathology in the Israeli cohort. *Schizophrenia Bulletin, 21,* 193–204.

Nuechterlein, K. H., & Dawson, M. E. (1984). A heuristic vulnerability/stress model of schizophrenic episodes. *Schizophrenia Bulletin, 10,* 300–312.

Nuechterlein, K. H., Edell, W. S., Norris, M., & Dawson, M. E. (1986). Attentional vulnerability indicators, thought disorder, and negative symptoms. *Schizophrenia Bulletin, 12,* 408–426.

Serper, M. R., Davidson, M., & Harvey, P. D. (1994). Attentional predictors of clinical change during neuroleptic treatment in schizophrenia. *Schizophrenia Research, 13,* 65–71.

Strauss, M. E. (1993). Relations of symptoms to cognitive deficits in schizophrenia. *Schizophrenia Bulletin, 19,* 215–231.

Teuber, H. L. (1972). Unity and diversity of frontal lobe function. *Acta Neurobiologiae Experimentalis, 32,* 615–656.

Wagner, P. S. (1996). First person account: A voice from another closet. *Schizophrenia Bulletin, 22,* 399–401.

Walker, E., & Harvey, P. (1986). Positive and negative symptoms in schizophrenia: Attentional performance correlates. *Psychopathology, 19,* 294–302.

Walker, E., & Lewine, R. J. (1988). Negative symptom distinction in schizophrenia: Validity and etiological relevance. *Schizophrenia Research, 1,* 315–328.

Walker, E. F., & DiForio, D. (in press). Schizophrenia: A neural diathesis-stress model. *Psychological Review.*

▶ 6

Medications and Neurocognition

In *The Odyssey*, guests had gathered for a festive wedding feast at the home of Helen and Menelaus, but the conversation turned maudlin. The guests started talking about Odysseus who had been missing for 10 years. As the men told stories of brave Odysseus and his uncertain fate, they became sad and unable to enjoy the occasion. Then Helen came up with an idea.

> Then Zeus's daughter Helen thought of something else.
> Into the mixing-bowl from which they drank their wine
> she slipped a drug, heart's ease, dissolving anger,
> magic to make us all forget our pains ...
> No one who drank it deeply, mulled in wine,
> could let a tear roll down his cheeks all day,
> not even if his mother should die, his father die,
> not even if right before his eyes some enemy brought down
> a brother or darling son with a sharp bronze blade.
> So cunning the drugs that Zeus's daughter plied,

—HOMER: ODYSSEY 4:243–252

What kind of drug could this be? It has been suggested that the core function of this drug was neither to cause sedation nor to ease physical pain, but instead to cause an emotional separation and a reduced reactivity to one's surroundings (Caldwell, 1970). As we will see, this is the same feature that was attributed to the first drugs that were successfully used to treat schizophrenia.

Most patients with schizophrenia receive medications for their illness. Is it possible that the neurocognitive deficits observed in schizophrenia are an unfortunate side effect of these medications? This question follows from the observation that medications can sometimes make patients appear sluggish. In addition, rigidity, tremor, and other types of involuntary movements are common side effects of antipsychotic medications that could potentially influence performance on neurocognitive tasks that depend on speeded responses. Let us consider how the modern medication treatments were first used for schizophrenia.

DEVELOPMENT OF ANTIPSYCHOTIC MEDICATIONS

In the 1940s, the French surgeon, Laborit, was attempting to solve a serious problem associated with the anesthesia for surgery. During or immediately following surgery, many patients would go into shock. In an effort to reduce autonomic activity and prevent surgical shock, Laborit tried a new drug, promethazine, which was a phenothiazine with antihistaminic properties. The results with promethazine were promising, so the search was on for more potent antihistaminic phenothiazines. In 1950, Charpentier synthesized chlorpromazine and Laborit used it with surgical patients shortly afterwards. Like the drug presumably used by Helen with her guests, chlorpromazine did not confuse or strongly sedate the patients. Instead it appeared to create a "disinterest" for the immediate environment as described by Laborit and colleagues. The impact on surgery was substantial: with an injection of chlorpromazine before surgery, much less general anesthesia was needed and surgical procedures became safer.

> In doses of 50–100 mg intravenously, it provokes not any loss in consciousness, not any change in the patient's mentality but a slight tendency to sleep and above all "disinterest" for all that goes on around him.
>
> These facts let us foresee certain indications for this drug in psychiatry ... (translated in Caldwell, 1970, p. 135)

Remarkably, Laborit and his colleagues suggested a psychiatric role for chlorpromazine in 1952 in their very first publication on the new drug. They thought that the drug worked by inhibiting excessive autonomic activity, which was seen as a basis for mental disease as well as surgical shock. At a rapid pace, the first trials of chlorpromazine with psychotic patients were underway and they confirmed the utility of this drug in treating psychosis. Chlorpromazine became the first of a series of antipsychotic medications that changed little for decades. Hence, a treatment for hallucinations and delusions originated unexpectedly from an attempt to control post-surgical shock.

At the time of its introduction, the beneficial effects of chlorpromazine were not well-understood. Laborit was looking for an antihistaminic agent, but the mechanism of action eventually centered on the affinity of the drug for the dopamine (D_2) receptor. Autonomic stabilization provided one general explanation of its effects. Moreover, the description of a pharmacologically-induced "disinterest" fit well with a model of schizophrenia that was also being developed in the 1950s. During this period, Broadbent (1958) proposed that attention in normal people operated like a mental "filter," which screened out irrelevant information. Some suggested that schizophrenic patients may have a defective "filter," which let in too much external stimuli. If so, a drug that leads to an environmental detachment might be quite useful as a way to reconstruct the mental filter.

To say that the introduction of chlorpromazine had a major impact on the treatment of schizophrenia would be a profound understatement. The discovery of new treatments for psychosis, coupled with a political emphasis on less restrictive treatment settings, led to a dramatic reduction in psychiatric inpatient beds. Drugs like chlorpromazine that block the D_2 receptor, called neuroleptics, became the mainstay of treatments for schizophrenia for the next 40 years. It was not until 1990 that the United States Food and Drug Administration approved a drug for the treatment of schizophrenia (clozapine) that had a mode of action substantially different than that of chlorpromazine. The observation that clinical potency of conventional agents correlated strongly with their affinity for the D_2 receptor supported the "dopamine theory" of schizophrenia. In brief, the dopamine theory postulated that schizophrenia resulted from a functional excess of dopamine activity. The dopamine theory of schizophrenia received additional support from the observation that dopamine agonists such as amphetamines can induce psychotic symptoms in otherwise nonpsychotic individuals. Although the dopamine theory was widely accepted in general form, the exact mechanism and the precise pathways that may be involved with schizophrenia have been the subject of considerable debate. Perhaps the greatest challenge to the theory has come from newer antipsychotic agents. As we will see later in this chapter, these new medications act on a broader range of neurotransmitter systems.

Although the antipsychotic medications have had considerable success, not all patients respond optimally to neuroleptics. Some proportion of patients (often estimated around 20–25%) are considered treatment-resistant. These patients with an intractable form of the disorder are a major public health concern because they require more frequent and longer hospitalizations. The introduction of new drugs with different neurochemical modes of action offers the possibility of symptomatic benefit for a subgroup of these treatment-resistant patients.

Aside from the clinical benefits, neuroleptics have clear drawbacks (Kane, 1996) (see Table 6.1). Most notably, they are associated with movement side effects. One area of concentration of D_2 receptors is the nigrostriatal pathway, which is involved with smooth execution of movement. Common problems with acute administration of neuroleptics are muscular rigidity and tremor, like those seen in Parkinson's disease. These side effects respond well to medications with strong anticholinergic potency (e.g., benztropine), which help to bring the dopaminergic and anticholinergic systems into a kind of balance. In fact, many patients routinely take two medications: an antipsychotic for control of symptoms and an anticholinergic for control of Parkinsonian side effects. Another side effect that can occur with acute administration is a type of restlessness called akathisia. Anticholinergic agents are also administered for this condition, but with limited success.

A more serious type of side effect is tardive dyskinesia. Tardive dyskinesia sometimes occurs after long-term neuroleptic administration (usually years) and is characterized by slow involuntary movements, especially of the lips and tongue. This side effect is more serious than the others because it is long-lasting and sometimes irreversible. Although there is no specific treatment for tardive dyskinesia, it can be suppressed, paradoxically, by increasing the dosage of the very agents that cause it.

Although movement side effects are clearly associated with neuroleptic treatment, they may also be associated with untreated schizophrenia. Kraepelin described what seemed to be tardive dyskinesia long before the advent of neuroleptics.

> The **spasmodic phenomena** in the musculature of the face and of speech, which often appear, are extremely peculiar disorders. Some of them resemble movements of expression, wrinkling of the forehead, distortion of the corners of the mouth, irregular movements of the tongue and lips, twisting of the eyes, opening them wide, and shutting them tight, in short, those movements which we bring together under the name of making faces or *grimacing*; they remind one of the corresponding disorders of choreic patients. (Kraepelin, 1971, p. 83)

Likewise, the Parkinsonian side effects are associated with drug administration, but Parkinsonian extrapyramidal symptoms have been observed in drug-naive patients who are experiencing their first psychotic break (Chatterjee et al., 1995). These patients with spontaneous extrapyramidal symptoms were more likely to develop Parkinsonian medication side effects with antipsychotic treatment. Hence, it is entirely possible that neuroleptics are exacerbating, not causing, certain types of movement disorders in schizophrenic patients.

TABLE 6.1   Movement Side Effects Associated with Neuroleptic Treatment

Parkinsonian Symptoms
- tremor
- muscular rigidity
- akinesia (reduced movement)

Acute Dystonia

Akathisia
- observed motor hyperactivity
- subjective restlessness

Tardive Dyskinesia
- writhing movements of lips and tongue
- slow movements of upper extremities

The presence of motor abnormalities in schizophrenia may identify a subgroup of patients whose motor systems are compromised early in development. Neurocognitive assessments have been used to validate such subgroups. For example, patients with tardive dyskinesia have greater neurocognitive deficits than those without (across a wide range of neurocognitive domains), and the severity of the tardive dyskinesia is correlated with the magnitude of neurocognitive deficit (Paulsen, Heaton, & Jeste, 1994). It is possible that group differences in neurocognition do not emerge until after the development of tardive dyskinesia, perhaps due to a shared neural substrate. An equally plausible alternative is that poor neurocognition is a risk indicator that predates the onset of tardive dyskinesia. In this case, the poorer neurocognition may reflect a brain that is already compromised and susceptible to further types of dysfunction when neuroleptics are administered.

Our discussion of the effects of pharmacological treatments on neurocognition in schizophrenia will include three sections. The first section concerns the neurocognitive effects of conventional neuroleptics with primary affinity for the D_2 receptor. Second, we will consider the neurocognitive effects of anticholinergic agents that are administered to control the Parkinsonian side effects of neuroleptics. Third, we will examine the neurocognitive effects of two newer antipsychotic agents, clozapine and risperidone.

CONVENTIONAL NEUROLEPTICS AND NEUROCOGNITION

A large number of studies have examined the neurocognitive effects of conventional neuroleptics (reviewed by Cassens, Inglis, Appelbaum, & Gutheil, 1990; Spohn & Strauss, 1989). These studies have used four primary types of designs (Spohn & Strauss, 1989):

1. A simple comparison of patients who are receiving medications to those who are not. With this design it is difficult to interpret group differences because it is not known whether patients were matched on task performance to begin with.
2. A test-retest design in which patients are assessed during a medication washout period and again while they are receiving medication. While more interpretable than the previous design, the limitation of this design is that it does not account for practice or placebo effects.
3. A counterbalanced crossover design in which patients serve as their own controls. One group of patients is tested in washout followed by a medication condition and another group is tested on medication followed by a washout period. Testing is conducted in a double-blind fashion so that neither experimenter nor subject knows which condition the patients are in. While this type of design offers considerable rigor, there is no agreement on what constitutes an adequate length of washout. If the washout period is too short, performance could be influenced by a lingering effect from the medication phase.
4. Independent-group, placebo-controlled design. In this design, patients are assigned to receive either medication or placebo under double-blind conditions. This type of design can be highly informative, assuming that the length of the medication trial is adequate.

The effects of neuroleptics on a large number of neurocognitive measures have been evaluated. We will select measures that were discussed in previous chapters.

Vigilance—Continuous Performance Test

Chronic administration of neuroleptics sometimes, but not always, has a beneficial effect on performance on a Continuous Performance Test (CPT). One study reported CPT improvement when patients were tested after 12 weeks of medication treatment following a washout period (Orzack, Kornetsky, & Freeman, 1967). A more rigorous independent-group, placebo-controlled study over an eight-week period showed improvement in CPT performance with medication (Spohn, Lacoursiere, Thompson, & Coyne, 1977), as did a cross-sectional study with medicated and unmedicated patients (Earle-Boyer, Serper, Davidson, & Harvey, 1991). In contrast to the improvement seen with chronic administration, acute administration of neuroleptics (less than three days) may have a negative effect on performance on a CPT (Latz & Kornetsky, 1965).

Reports of improved CPT performance associated with chronic administration of neuroleptics argue against the possibility that differences between patients and controls are explained by these medications. Instead, the findings raise an alternative possibility. Improved performance in these studies was associated with a concurrent improvement in clinical condition, so we do not know whether the changes in vigilance were associated with medications directly, or indirectly via symptomatic improvement.

Early Visual Processing — Span of Apprehension and Backward Masking

The findings from the Span of Apprehension are generally consistent with the findings from the CPT in that medication sometimes appears to offer performance benefits. The findings for the Span, however, depend on the dosage of the medication. With standard doses, treatment tends to improve performance on the Span (Marder, Asarnow, & Van Putten, 1984; Spohn et al., 1977), but high doses may reduce Span performance (Spohn, Coyne, Lacoursiere, Mazur, & Hayes, 1985). Similar to the findings with the CPT, treatment effects on the Span are associated with concurrent improvement in clinical state, making it difficult to disentangle these factors.

Regarding the effects of neuroleptics on backward masking performance, one report compared a group of patients receiving medication to a group that was unmedicated (Braff & Saccuzzo, 1982). As mentioned above, this type of design relies on the assumption that the groups are comparable on performance to begin with, although there is no easy way to test the validity of the assumption. Patients who received medication had better masking performance than those who did not, suggesting that neuroleptics had a beneficial effect on performance. Importantly, the neuroleptic-treated patients performed better on masking procedures despite being *more* symptomatic than the untreated patients. Unlike the previous studies on the CPT and Span, this study shows an effect of neuroleptics on performance that cannot be explained by clinical state.

Neuromotor Performance

Because neuroleptic medications are often associated with movement side effects, relationships have been evaluated between these medications and motor speed and dexterity (reviewed by Cassens et al., 1990). In general, the effects of chronic administration are minimal with few of the studies reporting significant differences. Two studies evaluated acute administration and both reported a dose-dependent reduction in motor performance when patients were tested within the first three days of administration. These initial (but not longer-term) effects on motor performance could be the result of Parkinsonian rigidity and/or tremor associated with acute administration.

A perusal of various other neurocognitive domains including abstraction and problem solving, learning and memory, visuospatial abilities, and verbal abilities reveals that the modal finding is no significant finding at all. The widespread failure to find significant effects of neuroleptic treatment on neurocognition may be puzzling initially because antipsychotic medications clearly have a substantive impact on psychotic symptoms. The dissociation of treatment effects speaks to the relative independence of certain types of neurocognitive performance and psychotic symptoms.

We started this section with the question of whether neuroleptic treatment can explain performance deficits in patients; clearly, it cannot. If anything, the administration of antipsychotic medications may, under some conditions, offer a slight benefit and reduce group differences on some measures (e.g., the CPT and Span). But, neuroleptics are not the only medication that patients receive. In many instances, they also receive medications with strong anticholinergic properties to help control the side effects of neuroleptic medication. What are the neurocognitive effects of these medications?

ANTICHOLINERGIC MEDICATIONS AND NEUROCOGNITION

Acetylcholine (ACh) and the cholinergic system is securely linked to memory. Animal studies have confirmed the importance of this neurochemical system for learning and memory and ACh agonists have been used for the treatment of dementia. With such a close association between the ACh system and memory, the administration of anticholinergic agents to schizophrenic patients potentially creates problems.

When nonpsychiatric controls receive short-term administration of the same anticholinergic drugs that are given to schizophrenic patients (e.g., benztropine), memory is detrimentally affected (Gelenberg et al., 1989). Likewise, in samples of schizophrenic patients who are receiving long-term administration of anticholinergic agents, serum anticholinergic levels have a negative correlation with memory performance (Perlick, Stastny, Katz, Mayer, & Mattis, 1986; Tune, Strauss, Lew, Brietlinger, & Coyle, 1982). Serum anticholinergic levels are not very specific because they reflect anticholinergic effects from a variety of agents, including neuroleptics. Studies that have specifically examined the effects of benztropine (Baker, Cheng, & Amara, 1983; Sweeney, Keilp, Haas, Hill, & Weiden, 1991) show an association with reduced verbal memory. Figure 6.1 shows a typical finding of benztropine's effects on memory.

While there is good agreement that anticholinergic agents can be detrimental to memory, there is no clear understanding of the range of neurocognitive abilities that might be affected. For example, not all forms of memory

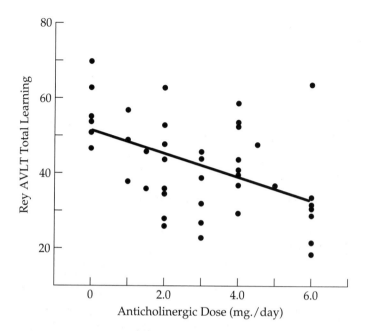

FIGURE 6.1   Anticholinergic Medications and Verbal Memory

Source: Reprinted from *Psychiatry Research, 37,* J. A. Sweeney, J. G. Keilp, G. L. Haas, J. Hill, and P. J. Weiden, "Relationships Between Medication Treatments and Neuropsychological Test Performance in Schizophrenia" p. 303, 1991. With kind permission from Elsevier Science Ireland, Ltd., Bay 15K, Shannon Industrial Estate, Co. Clare, Ireland.

appear to be affected to the same extent. The most consistent findings involve measures of "secondary" verbal memory such as recall tests of relatively long lists of words or stories. Despite effects on secondary memory, anticholinergic agents do not have a consistent impact on either immediate memory or recognition memory, suggesting that search strategies and active rehearsal are susceptible processes. The effects of anticholinergic agents on the CPT, Span, and backward masking are largely unexplored.

The findings provide two cautionary messages. First, when we see differences between patients and controls (especially for verbal memory), the role of anticholinergic agents should be considered. Second, treatment with anticholinergic agents should be subject to a careful cost/benefit analysis, similar to many other medications with more obvious side effects. While these treatments are often needed to control unwanted movements, they carry a neurocognitive liability that could negatively affect daily functioning.

NEW ANTIPSYCHOTIC MEDICATIONS AND NEUROCOGNITION

Currently, the pharmacological treatments for schizophrenia are undergoing profound change. As we enter a new pharmacological arena, conclusions about neurocognitive effects from studies of conventional antipsychotic medications that act primarily at the D_2 receptor will not necessarily apply to the next generation of medications.

Clozapine

Clozapine is effective for a subgroup of patients who had been refractory to conventional medications and has been used in Europe since the 1970s. Its approval in the United States was delayed until 1990 because of the risk of agranulocytosis, a rare, but potentially fatal side effect. This risk is minimized with weekly blood monitoring. Clozapine differs from conventional neuroleptics in that it has roughly equivalent affinity for both the D_1 and D_2 receptor, and it is a rather effective antagonist at the serotonin ($5\text{-}HT_2$) receptor. It also is an antagonist at the muscarinic cholinergic receptor, which might help explain why clozapine does not have the movement side effects of conventional neuroleptics and consequently, does not require co-administration of drugs like benztropine. Similar to the introduction of neuroleptics in the early 1950s, many patients who had been institutionalized for years showed symptomatic benefit with clozapine and were transferred to less restrictive settings.

The studies of the neurocognitive effects of clozapine have used two types of designs. Several studies used naturalistic, open label designs in which both patients and investigators knew which drug was dispensed. These studies examined within-group changes, and the possibility of practice effects needs to be considered when interpreting the results. In addition to these open label studies, two independent-group blinded studies have been conducted.

The open label studies that have evaluated the neurocognitive effects of clozapine have generally found only a few significant changes (Goldberg et al., 1993; Hagger et al., 1993; Hoff et al., 1996). Clozapine treatment was linked to improvements in verbal fluency and possibly motor speed, but it appeared to have detrimental effects on visual memory and possibly verbal working memory. Although clozapine's anticholinergic properties might explain these detrimental neurocognitive effects, it does not act like a typical anticholinergic agent. In animal studies, the pattern of performance with clozapine administration on a delayed response task was similar to that seen with conventional neuroleptics, but not that of typical anticholinergic agents (Rupniak & Iversen, 1993).

A single-blind and a double-blind study have generally supported the open label studies. In the single-blind study, clozapine failed to improve reaction time indices of attention compared with placebo or a conventional neuroleptic (fluphenazine) (Zahn, Pickar, & Haier, 1994). The double-blind study compared clozapine with another conventional neuroleptic (haloperidol) and found that clozapine had a beneficial effect on a measure of verbal fluency (Buchanan, Holstein, & Breier, 1994). Curiously, the treatment effects in this study were largely attributable to a decline in performance for the group assigned to the conventional neuroleptic.

Although clozapine's neurocognitive effects appear to be generally modest, it consistently has a positive effect on verbal fluency. Verbal fluency is a test of one's ability to generate search strategies to retrieve information from semantic memory. For example, subjects might be asked to name in 60 seconds as many words as they can think of that begin with the letter "C" or as many farm animals as they can think of. Such tests seem to rely on the functioning of the prefrontal region.

There appears to be an intriguing dissociation between clozapine's clinical and neurocognitive effects. Two studies (Goldberg et al., 1993; Zahn et al., 1994) reported essentially no noticeable cognitive changes despite substantial symptomatic improvement. These observations indicate that, similar to conventional antipsychotic medications, clozapine's neurocognitive effects may be quite divorced from its clinical impact, or at least the time course of the effects are quite different.

In general, these studies have used relatively comprehensive neurocognitive batteries that yielded a large number of dependent measures (Zahn et al., 1994 is an exception). The use of neurocognitive batteries is a direct outgrowth of the clinical neuropsychological approach to schizophrenia that was discussed in Chapter 2, and is not specially tailored to address questions of psychopharmacology. Using neuropsychological batteries insures a certain comprehensiveness; however, it also makes the data from these studies difficult to interpret. In the absence of clear hypotheses, the use of neuropsychological batteries runs the risk of generating positive results simply as a by-product of a large number of indices that are subjected to an equally large number of statistical tests.

In defense of this approach, there is an advantage in being overly inclusive when a research area is brand new. Investigators who make forays into a new area obviously do not have the benefit of previous studies to guide hypotheses. It is entirely reasonable for the initial studies to be hypothesis-generating. Subsequent studies in the next stage should be more focused and test specific hypotheses.

Despite these limitations, some tentative conclusions are warranted from these hypothesis-generating studies. It appears that clozapine may have a favorable effect on certain areas (e.g., verbal fluency and motor speed) and a detrimental effect on others (e.g., visual memory and verbal working memory). However, at this early stage of investigation, the effects of clozapine on most aspects of neurocognition do not seem to be substantial.

Risperidone

With only a few exceptions, the neurocognitive effects of conventional neuroleptics and clozapine appear to be fairly minimal. What about the neurocognitive effects of other antipsychotic agents? The next antipsychotic drug to receive approval after clozapine was risperidone (Marder & Meibach, 1994). Risperidone is a potent antagonist of the D_2 and 5-HT$_2$ receptor and is associated with fewer movement side effects than conventional neuroleptics.

Because risperidone has only been in general use in this country since 1994, little is known about its neurocognitive effects. So far, our laboratory has evaluated its effects on verbal working memory, spatial working memory, and psychomotor dexterity. Verbal working memory became a treatment focus for both theoretical and practical reasons. Working memory is of theoretical interest because it appears to rely on neural circuitry in the prefrontal region (Cohen et al., 1994; Fuster, Bauer, & Jervey, 1985; Goldman-Rakic, 1991; Grasby et al., 1993), an area that is considered relevant to the etiology of schizophrenia. Pragmatic interest in this area stems from findings that verbal working memory is consistently associated with skill acquisition in psychosocial rehabilitation programs (see Chapter 8). If impairments in verbal working memory limit the patients' ability to acquire psychosocial skills, the treatment of these deficits could potentially improve skill acquisition.

Studies that compare risperidone (or any other new agent) to a conventional neuroleptic face a thorny interpretive challenge: if treatment effects are uncovered, they could be either *direct* or *indirect*. Conventional neuroleptics require co-administration of anticholinergic agents more frequently than new agents. Hence, if we see a difference between treatment groups, the difference could be due to indirect effects of anticholinergic agents. Another possible route for indirect effects is through symptom changes. An indirect effect through symptom changes requires two assumptions: that one drug is more effective for symptoms, and that the symptom changes drive the performance changes.

A double-blind parallel-group study from our laboratory showed risperidone to have a beneficial effect on verbal working memory compared with a conventional neuroleptic (haloperidol) (Green et al., 1997). The measure of verbal working memory was a type of digit span task in which subjects listened to a string of digits (with and without distraction) and then wrote them down. Preliminary data from this study are shown in Figure 6.2. Importantly, the treatment effect was independent of anticholinergic agents,

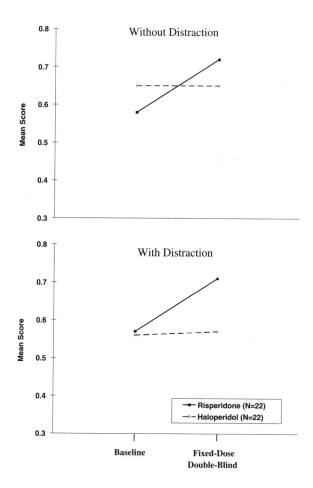

FIGURE 6.2   Effects of Risperidone on Verbal Working Memory

change in psychotic symptoms, and change in negative symptoms. These factors do not exhaust the list of possible indirect effects, however, the analyses include the obvious ones and suggest that risperidone's effects are at least partially due to direct effects. If risperidone has a direct effect on verbal working memory, what might be the relevant mechanism? It has affinity for both the D_2 and 5-HT_2 receptor. The D_2 system is unlikely to be the relevant mechanism because conventional neuroleptics that block the D_2 receptor do not have a consistent effect on verbal working memory. A more likely candidate is the 5-HT_2 system because under certain conditions, 5-HT_2 antagonists can improve learning and memory.

Several unpublished studies from our laboratory suggest that risperidone's neurocognitive effects are not limited to verbal working memory. All of these studies involved a comparison of risperidone with haloperidol. One study of spatial working memory by Susan McGurk showed a significant beneficial effect of risperidone that was explained by a detrimental effect of anticholinergic medications, which were given more frequently to the group receiving haloperidol. Hence, risperidone's effect on spatial working memory was indirect. The measure of spatial working memory differed from the measure of verbal working memory in that it involved delayed responses, which might be sensitive to anticholinergic effects. A second study by Robert Kern indicated that risperidone had a positive effect on psychomotor speed and dexterity. The effect remained significant even after statistically controlling for the relevant indirect effects (i.e., ratings of extrapyramidal movements, change in psychotic, and change in negative symptoms). This beneficial effect on psychomotor speed did not extend to motor learning, which was equivalent in the two treatment groups. Lastly, a preliminary study by Kimmy Kee examined a more complex social-cognitive function, perception of emotion. Risperidone had a significant beneficial effect on emotion perception. The mechanism for this result is not known, but it may be mediated by risperidone's effects on basic cognitive processes.

New Definitions of Efficacy

The neurocognitive effects of medications depend entirely on the type of medication. Conventional neuroleptics sometimes have a beneficial effect on vigilance and visual processing with long-term administration, and a detrimental effect on motor functioning with short-term administration. However, with most other aspects of neurocognition, the effects of these drugs are minimal. Anticholinergic agents such as benztropine that are given for side effects of neuroleptics have a detrimental effect on some aspects of memory. It is not known if they also have effects on other neurocognitive processes such as perception and vigilance. Although clozapine appears to have a positive effect on verbal fluency, it may have a detrimental effect on visual and verbal working memory. Its effects on other aspects of neurocognition, like those of conventional neuroleptics, seem to be slight. The neurocognitive effects of risperidone are only beginning to be evaluated. Compared with a conventional neuroleptic, risperidone has (possibly direct) beneficial effects on verbal working memory and psychomotor speed, and (possibly indirect) effects on spatial working memory.

Clozapine and risperidone are only the front runners of a new wave of antipsychotic medications that act on a wide range of neurochemical systems. This new generation of agents will spur a new generation of studies on their neurocognitive effects. Initial impressions are that the neurocognitive profiles of these drugs are different than those of conventional neuroleptics. The potential impact of these medications on neurocognition raises the possibility that novel antipsychotic agents act broadly in multiple treatment domains. Alternatively, an entirely separate class of drugs could eventually be used to reduce neurocognitive deficits. As discussed in Chapter 9, schizophrenic patients might someday take two types of drugs: one for symptoms and one for neurocognitive deficits.

The questions in this chapter have now come full circle. We started by asking whether conventional antipsychotic medications have detrimental effects on neurocognition and we are ending by wondering whether the new generation of drugs can help remediate the neurocognitive deficits of schizophrenia. This type of discussion forces us to rethink the definition of treatment efficacy. The notion of "efficacy" in psychopharmacotherapy has primarily been used to refer to reduction in symptoms (see Figure 6.3a). Symptom reduction will remain the primary goal of pharmacotherapy in schizophrenia; however, it may soon be possible to broaden the notion of efficacy to include amelioration of neurocognitive deficits. Why should we expand the definition of efficacy? We will see in Chapter 8 that neurocognitive processes are more closely associated with functional outcome (e.g., community functioning, social problem solving, and skill acquisition) than are psychotic symptoms. These neurocognitive deficits may act as "rate limiting factors" that restrict the functional adaptation of the patient. An expanded notion of efficacy (shown in Figure 6.3b) could extend beyond a narrow definition of symptom reduction and fit into a broader goal of *disability reduction*.

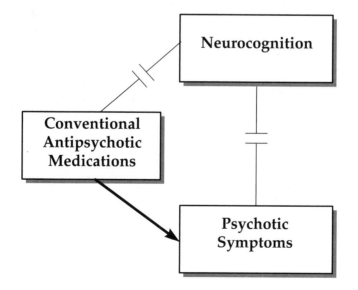

FIGURE 6.3a   Treatment Efficacy Defined as Symptom Reduction

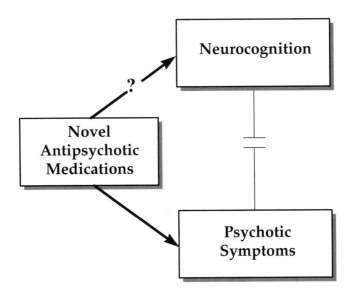

FIGURE 6.3b   Treatment Efficacy Defined as Disability Reduction

REFERENCES

Baker, L. A., Cheng, L. Y., & Amara, I. B. (1983). The withdrawal of benztropine mesylate in chronic schizophrenic patients. *British Journal of Psychiatry, 143,* 584–590.

Braff, D. L., & Saccuzzo, D. P. (1982). Effect of antipsychotic medication on speed of information processing in schizophrenic patients. *American Journal of Psychiatry, 139,* 1127–1130.

Broadbent, D. E. (1958). *Perception and communication.* London: Pergamon Press.

Buchanan, R. W., Holstein, C., & Breier, A. (1994). The comparative efficacy and long-term effect of clozapine treatment on neuropsychological test performance. *Society of Biological Psychiatry, 36,* 717–725.

Caldwell, A. E. (1970). *Origins of psychopharmacology: From CPZ to LSD.* Springfield, IL: Charles C. Thomas.

Cassens, G., Inglis, A. K., Appelbaum, P. S., & Gutheil, T. G. (1990). Neuroleptics: Effects on neuropsychological function in chronic schizophrenic patients. *Schizophrenia Bulletin, 16,* 477–499.

Chatterjee, A., Chakos, M., Koreen, A., Geisler, S., Sheitman, B., Woerner, M., Kane, J. M., Alvir, J., & Lieberman, J. A. (1995). Prevalence and clinical correlates of extrapyramidal signs and spontaneous dyskinesia in never-medicated schizophrenic patients. *American Journal of Psychiatry, 152,* 1724–1729.

Cohen, J. D., Forman, S. D., Braver, T. S., Casey, B. J., Servan-Schreiber, D., & Noll, D. C. (1994). Activation of the prefrontal cortex in a nonspatial working memory task with functional MRI. *Human Brain Mapping, 1,* 293–304.

Earle-Boyer, E. A., Serper, M. R., Davidson, M., & Harvey, P. D. (1991). Continuous performance tests in schizophrenic patients: Stimulus and medication effects on performance. *Psychiatry Research, 37,* 47–56.

Fuster, J. M., Bauer, R. H., & Jervey, J. P. (1985). Functional interactions between inferotemporal and prefrontal cortex in a cognitive task. *Brain Research, 330,* 299–307.

Gelenberg, A. J., Van Putten, T., Lavori, P. W., Wojcik, J. D., Falk, W. E., Marder, S., Galvin-Nadeau, M., Spring, B., Mohs, R. C., & Brotman, A. W. (1989). Anticholinergic effects on memory: Benztropine versus amantadine. *Journal of Clinical Psychopharmacology, 9,* 180–185.

Goldberg, T. E., Greenberg, R. D., Griffin, S. J., Gold, J. M., Kleinman, J. E., Pickar, D., Schulz, S. C., & Weinberger, D. R. (1993). The effect of Clozapine on cognition and psychiatric symptoms in patients with schizophrenia. *British Journal of Psychiatry, 162,* 43–48.

Goldman-Rakic, P. S. (1991). Prefrontal cortical dysfunction in schizophrenia: The relevance of working memory. In B. J. Carroll & J. E. Barrett (Eds.), *Psychopathology and the brain* (pp. 1–23). New York: Raven Press.

Grasby, P. M., Frith, C. D., Friston, K. J., Bench, C., Frackowiak, R. S. J., & Dolan, R. J. (1993). Functional mapping of brain areas implicated in auditory-verbal memory function. *Brain, 116,* 1–20.

Green, M. F., Marshall, B. D., Wirshing, W. C., Ames, D., Marder, S. R., McGurk, S., Kern, R. S., & Mintz, J. (1997). Does risperidone improve verbal working memory in treatment-resistant schizophrenia? *American Journal of Psychiatry, 154,* 799–804.

Hagger, C., Buckley, P., Kenny, J. T., Friedman, L., Ubogy, D., & Meltzer, H. Y. (1993). Improvement in cognitive functions and psychiatric symptoms in treatment-refractory schizophrenic patients receiving clozapine. *Biological Psychiatry, 34,* 702–712.

Hoff, A. L., Faustman, W. O., Wieneke, M., Espinoza, S., Costa, M., Wolkowitz, O., & Csernansky, J. G. (1996). The effects of clozapine on symptom reduction, neurocognitive function, and clinical management in treatment refractory state hospital schizophrenic inpatients. *Neuropsychopharmacology, 15,* 361–369.

Kane, J. M. (1996). Schizophrenia. *The New England Journal of Medicine, 334,* 34–41.

Kraepelin, E. (1971). *Dementia praecox and paraphrenia.* Huntington, NY: Robert E. Krieger.

Latz, A., & Kornetsky, C. (1965). The effects of chlorpromazine and secobarbital under two conditions of reinforcement on the performance of chronic schizophrenic subjects. *Psychopharmacologia, 7,* 77–88.

Marder, S. R., Asarnow, R. F., & Van Putten, T. (1984). Information processing and neuroleptic response in acute and stabilized schizophrenic patients. *Psychiatry Research, 13,* 41–49.

Marder, S. R., & Meibach, R. C. (1994). Risperidone in the treatment of schizophrenia. *American Journal of Psychiatry, 151,* 825–835.

Orzack, M. H., Kornetsky, C., & Freeman, H. (1967). The effects of daily administration of carphenazine on attention in the schizophrenic patient. *Psychopharmacologia, 11,* 31–38.

Paulsen, J. S., Heaton, R. K., & Jeste, D. V. (1994). Neuropsychological impairment in tardive dyskinesia. *Neuropsychology, 8,* 227–241.

Perlick, D., Stastny, P., Katz, I., Mayer, M., & Mattis, S. (1986). Memory deficits and anticholinergic levels in chronic schizophrenia. *American Journal of Psychiatry, 143*, 230–232.

Rupniak, N. M. J., & Iversen, S. D. (1993). Cognitive impairment in schizophrenia: How experimental models using nonhuman primates may assist improved drug therapy for negative symptoms. *Neuropsychologia, 31*, 1133–1146.

Spohn, H. E., Coyne, L., Lacoursiere, R., Mazur, D., & Hayes, K. (1985). Relation of neuroleptic dose and tardive dyskinesia to attention, information-processing, and psychophysiology in medicated schizophrenics. *Archives of General Psychiatry, 42*, 849–859.

Spohn, H. E., Lacoursiere, R. B., Thompson, K., & Coyne, L. (1977). Phenothiazine effects on psychological and psychophysiological dysfunction in chronic schizophrenics. *Archives of General Psychiatry, 34*, 633–644.

Spohn, H. E., & Strauss, M. E. (1989). Relation of neuroleptic and anticholinergic medication to cognitive functions in schizophrenia. *Journal of Abnormal Psychology, 98*, 367–380.

Sweeney, J. A., Keilp, J. G., Haas, G. L., Hill, J., & Weiden, P. J. (1991). Relationships between medication treatments and neuropsychological test performance in schizophrenia. *Psychiatry Research, 37*, 297–308.

Tune, L. E., Strauss, M. E., Lew, M. F., Brietlinger, E., & Coyle, J. T. (1982). Serum levels of anticholinergic drugs and impaired recent memory in chronic schizophrenic patients. *American Journal of Psychiatry, 139*, 1460–1462.

Zahn, T. P., Pickar, D., & Haier, R. J. (1994). Effects of clozapine, fluphenazine, and placebo on reaction time measures of attention and sensory dominance in schizophrenia. *Schizophrenia Research, 13*, 133–144.

7

Neurocognition and Neuroimaging

The modern era of neuroimaging dates from the 1970s, but the techniques for both structural and functional neuroimaging have been developing for most of this century. In fact, several modern review articles of the structural neuroanatomy of schizophrenia have confirmed general conclusions that were first arrived at during the Great Depression.

EARLY STRUCTURAL NEUROIMAGING

Pneumoencephalography (PEG) was the first method to provide information about brain structure in a living person. In PEG, air is introduced into the subarachnoid space through a lumbar puncture. The air displaces cerebrospinal fluid (CSF), and because air is about 800 times less dense than CSF, it increases visibility of the spaces normally filled with cerebral spinal fluid using ordinary radiography. The first use of air to obtain images of the ventricles was a complete accident (Oldendorf, 1980).

> E. K., 47 years old, machinist, was admitted to my service at the Harlem Hospital November 24, 1912, with the following history: Patient was struck by a trolley car and thrown to the pavement, receiving a laceration of the scalp. (Luckett, 1913, p. 237)

E. K. had sustained a fracture of the skull. Skull radiographs revealed a fracture of the frontal sinus and orbital plate. He stayed in the hospital for 12 days and then left against medical advice "at his earnest request." One week later he was readmitted to the hospital because of headaches, vomiting, and general listlessness. The skull radiographs on the second admission looked completely different than before (Figure 7.1).

> X-ray pictures … showed the ventricles enormously dilated with what was probably air or gas. Patient not having improved, but apparently getting worse, it was decided to do a cranial decompression. (Luckett, 1913, p. 238)

An operation was performed on E. K. to relieve the pressure in the ventricles. Initially an incision was made through the right temporal bone.

> A needle was then passed into the anterior horn of the lateral ventricle and the removal of the trocar was followed by two or three quick spits of air and fluid and then clear cerebrospinal fluid of the amount of 8 cc. (Luckett, 1913, p. 238)

An additional incision was made through the occipital bone and more air escaped through the cisterna magna. Following the surgery, E. K. did "remarkably well" for several days, but on the fourth day, he developed a high fever and died that night. Figure 7.1 shows the first visualization of brain structures with the introduction of air. The enlarged anterior portions of E. K.'s ventricles are clearly visible.

How did the air get into the ventricles? It was not present in the radiographs from the first hospitalization. The answer is in a gripping description provided by one of E. K.'s friends who visited him prior to his second hospital admission.

> Two days before the second admission to the hospital this friend called upon the patient and found him sitting down in a chair, holding his head in his hands and groaning. The patient said to his friend, "I just sneezed and had a terrific pain in my head, and then a flow of a large amount of clear fluid came from my nose—about a cupful." (Luckett, 1913, p. 140)

In all likelihood, air entered E. K.'s ventricular system through the fractured sinus and orbital plate when he sneezed. The air built up intracranial pressure, which was relieved through the discharge of CSF. His physician concluded that E. K. had "automatically decompressed himself."

The subsequent development of PEG relied on a careful exchange of air for CSF at the site of the lumbar puncture so as not to increase intracranial pressure. As the PEG procedure matured and developed, associated discomfort such as headaches, nausea, vascular hypotension, and syncope, was reduced, but not eliminated (Oldendorf, 1980). Despite its limitations, PEG provided the first images of the live brains of schizophrenic patients.

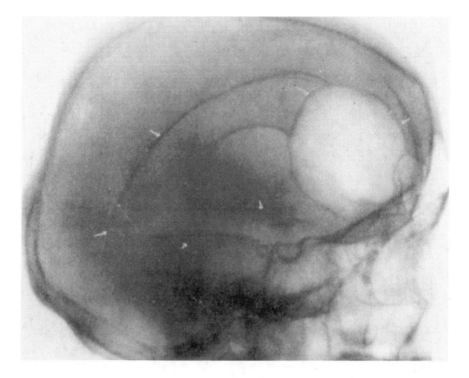

FIGURE 7.1

Source: By permission of *Surgery, Gynecology & Obstetrics,* 1913, 17, p. 238, now known as the *Journal of the American College of Surgeons.*

Figure 7.2 shows a PEG image from 1935 (Moore, Nathan, Elliott, & Laubach, 1935) for E. S., a 27-year-old woman with a diagnosis of paranoid schizophrenia. She had been ill for two and a half years without remission. She experienced "auditory hallucinations, delusions of persecution, mild degree of deterioration." Notice the extremely dilated sulci throughout the frontal and parietal lobes.

PEG also provided a means to quantify the volume of the ventricular system by measuring the amount of CSF removed during complete drainage of the ventricular system. (Complete removal of CSF was standard for PEG procedures in the 1920s and 1930s.) Of 57 schizophrenic patients who underwent complete drainage of the ventricular system, 49 had more than a normal quantity of CSF removed, indicating enlarged ventricles (Moore et al., 1935). By 1935, early PEG procedures revealed two major findings about brain structure in schizophrenia: (1) the sulci were enlarged, and (2) the ventricular system was enlarged. The differences in the brains of schizophrenic patients were generally interpreted to indicate deterioration or atrophy.

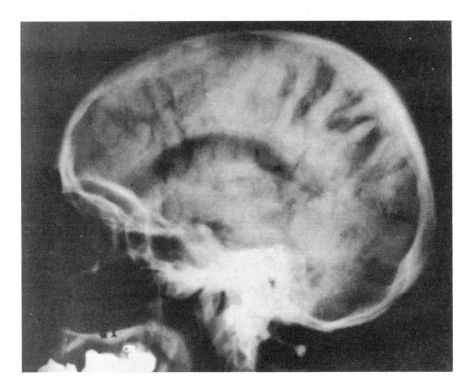

FIGURE 7.2

Source: From *American Journal of Psychiatry, 92,* pp. 43–67, plate 7. Copyright 1935, the American Psychiatric Association. Reprinted by permission.

MODERN STRUCTURAL NEUROIMAGING

Structural neuroimaging has employed two primary techniques: computerized tomographic (CT) scans and magnetic resonance imaging (MRI). CT scanning was the predominant imaging procedure in the schizophrenia literature from its first applications in the mid-1970s (Johnstone, Crow, Frith, Stevens, & Kreel, 1976) until it was largely replaced by MRI in the late 1980s. MRI has superior spatial resolution compared with CT and is more suited to repeat scans because it does not involve any radiation. The findings from these two techniques are generally comparable. Results from structural neuroimaging can be summarized according to the type of abnormality or according to the brain region of interest.

Types of Abnormalities in Schizophrenia

The literature on structural neuroimaging in schizophrenia is vast and well beyond the scope of this chapter (see Bilder, 1992; Raz & Raz, 1990 for reviews). From the wealth of neuroanatomical observations, a few highly reliable findings can be extracted. First, most studies show schizophrenic patients to have larger ventricles than control subjects. The size of the difference is roughly 0.70 standard deviations (Raz & Raz, 1990). The most commonly used variable is a ratio of ventricular size divided by brain size (ventricular brain ratio, VBR) to control for individual variability in overall brain size. The lateral ventricles have been emphasized in most studies, but enlargement of the third ventricle has also been reported and correlates with enlargement of the lateral ventricles. Figure 7.3 shows the brain of a schizophrenic patient and a control in which the area of the lateral ventricle appears somewhat larger on the patient's scan.

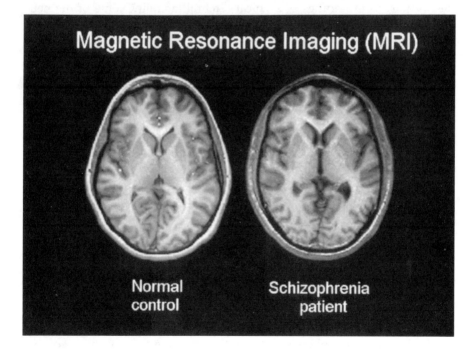

FIGURE 7.3

Source: With permission from M. S. Buchsbaum, MD, Neuroscience PET Laboratory, Mt. Sinai School of Medicine.

A second reliable finding is that patients have larger cortical sulci than controls (also detectable in Figure 7.3). Sulcal enlargement appears to be independent of ventricular enlargement, suggesting that these types of structural abnormalities represent different pathological processes. Ventricular and cortical abnormalities in schizophrenia might derive from different antecedents (Cannon, Mednick, & Parnas, 1989). The cortical abnormalities appear to be associated with family risk for schizophrenia, whereas ventricular abnormalities appear to be associated with a combination of family risk and obstetric complications.

A third finding that has sometimes, but not always, been replicated is that schizophrenic patients show abnormalities in hemispheric asymmetry. Normally, the brain extends further anterior on the right and further posterior on the left, a pattern of lateral asymmetry described as "torque." Schizophrenic patients have been found to have a reduction, or even a reversal, of this normal cerebral asymmetry (e.g., Luchins, Weinberger, & Wyatt, 1982). Apart from findings of atypical cerebral laterality, some of the neuroanatomical differences between patients and controls are more prominent in one hemisphere than the other. For example, ventricular enlargement and reduced volume of temporal lobe structures are sometimes observed only on the left. These structural findings are consistent with the notion that schizophrenia is primarily a disorder of the left hemisphere (see Chapter 2). However, large, well-controlled studies have failed to find any lateralized differences between schizophrenic patients and controls (Flaum et al., 1995), or have emphasized right hemisphere differences (Andreasen et al., 1994). At this point, the laterality of structural abnormalities in schizophrenia is an open question.

Regions of Interest

A few selected brain regions have attracted the lion's share of the attention in structural neuroimaging (Gur & Pearlson, 1993). Not surprisingly, the frontal cortex has been studied because of its presumed connection with symptoms and etiology of schizophrenia. The results have been inconsistent in that some studies, but not others, have reported decreased frontal lobe volume in schizophrenia. It is understandably difficult to draw conclusions from studies of a region that is so large and heterogenous as the frontal lobe. In addition, there are inherent difficulties in defining the boundaries of this lobe on two-dimensional images.

The findings are somewhat more consistent for the temporal lobe, both for the temporal cortex and for the medial aspects of the temporal lobe. Several studies have reported reduced volume of the superior temporal gyrus (both anterior and posterior regions) for schizophrenic patients. The reduction in size of the posterior temporal gyrus appears to be related to severity of thought disorder (Shenton et al., 1992) and to abnormalities in an electrophysiological component that reflects the processing of novel information (P300, McCarley et al., 1993). The medial temporal lobe includes structures, such as the hippocampus, that have also been reported to be reduced in size in schizophrenia (e.g., Breier et al., 1992). The reports of reduced hippocampal size coupled with the findings of abnormal cellular placement and orientation (see Chapter 1) strongly point to abnormalities in the development of this region.

Subcortical regions, such as the basal ganglia and thalamus, have also been the focus of investigation. For the basal ganglia, the results have been inconsistent. Whereas some studies failed to find differences between patients and controls, others reported *increases* in the size of basal ganglia structures such as the caudate. Follow-up studies of first-episode patients showed an increase in the size of the caudate nuclei over an 18-month period of treatment with conventional neuroleptics (i.e., D_2 antagonists), whereas control subjects showed a slight decrease in size over the same time period (Chakos et al., 1994). It was speculated that this somewhat puzzling finding might come about if the D_2 blockade of antipsychotic medications leads to an increase in dopamine receptors and hypertrophy (e.g., through collateral sprouting) of neural elements in the basal ganglia.

To ascertain the differences between groups of patients and controls, it is possible to compare an average schizophrenic brain with an average control brain. When this process was applied, specific regional differences between groups were observed in the thalamus and the adjacent white matter (Andreasen et al., 1994). The abnormalities in the thalamus supported "a parsimonious explanation for the multiplicity of signs and symptoms" of the disorder: "An abnormality in this structure could explain most of the psychopathology in schizophrenia, which can be readily understood as the result of abnormalities in filtering stimuli, focusing attention, or sensory gating" (p. 297). Note that a structural abnormality in the thalamus is viewed within a neurocognitive framework as a means of explaining the diversity of signs and symptoms in schizophrenia.

Neurodegeneration Versus Neurodevelopment

Initially, abnormalities detected with neuroimaging in schizophrenia were considered to be evidence of brain atrophy partly because ventricular and sulcal enlargement are seen in known degenerative disorders. However, subsequent findings raised questions about the origins of the abnormalities in schizophrenia. Structural abnormalities were found in untreated, first-episode patients, indicating that long illness and medications were not necessary for their occurrence. In addition, autopsy studies have generally failed to find evidence of gliosis. Because a reactive gliosis occurs with damage to a mature brain, the absence of gliosis suggests that structural changes most likely occurred in an immature brain, long before the onset of illness.

Aside from autopsy studies, the neurodevelopmental/neurodegenerative distinction can be addressed through longitudinal studies of repeated CT or MRI scans to determine whether ventricular enlargement progresses over time. The results have generally been mixed. Most studies failed to show any progression in ventricular enlargement, but a few studies reported a progressive increase in ventricular size (Bilder, 1992).

The bulk of the evidence supports the view that structural abnormalities in schizophrenia reflect a failure of normal neurodevelopment (e.g., hypoplasia) instead of neurodegenerative factors (e.g., atrophy). However, it may be overly simplistic to consider the question of neurodevelopment versus neurodegeneration as if there were only two alternatives. The few findings of progressive enlargement amid failures to find such patterns may indicate that a subgroup of patients (perhaps less than one-third) show deterioration, whereas other patients do not (Bilder, 1992). Moreover, both types of factors could be operating in the same individual. Perhaps the majority of the structural abnormalities are accounted for by neurodevelopmental processes, with some additional changes occurring after onset of illness.

Neurocognitive Correlates of Structural Abnormalities

Findings of structural abnormalities in schizophrenia provide compelling evidence that schizophrenia is, at least in part, a brain disease. The structural findings raise questions about the real-world significance of the reliably observed abnormalities. In other words, what difference does it make if patients have large ventricles?

Neurocognitive correlates of ventricular and sulcal enlargement have been examined with both neuropsychological batteries and intellectual measures. In general, measures of ventricular and sulcal enlargement show the same pattern of associations with neurocognitive measures. The majority of the studies have reported that ventricular and/or sulcal enlargement is associated with poorer neuropsychological performance. Drawing conclusions beyond this very general finding is difficult, partly because the brain measures (e.g., ventricular brain ratio) are regionally non-specific, and partly because the neuropsychological measures (e.g., global cutoff scores) are neurocognitively non-specific. The field will benefit from studies that examine neurocognitive correlates of localized brain volume in schizophrenia. For example, reduction in the volume of the medial temporal lobe and superior temporal gyrus appears to be associated with deficits in memory and abstraction (Nestor et al., 1993).

In contrast to these intuitive findings between structural indices and neuropsychological measures, the results for intellectual functioning have been decidedly mixed. Some studies have reported results in the expected direction (i.e., smaller ventricles with higher IQ), some have reported findings in the opposite direction, and many have not found relationships at all. Variability of the results can be explained by considering the types of intellectual abilities that are being assessed. Intelligence scales include some subtests that are sensitive to cognitive deterioration and decline following brain injury (e.g., Digit Span, Similarities). In contrast, other subtests change very little with brain injury and are rather good indicators of premorbid ability (e.g., Information and Vocabulary). Structural abnormalities in patients seem to be associated with subtests that are sensitive to brain injury such as speeded tasks, but not those that reflect premorbid abilities such as basic information and language (Bilder, 1992).

In one sense, the modern studies of structural neuroimaging in schizophrenia have confirmed what was known in 1935 from PEG: that schizophrenia is associated with ventricular and sulcal enlargement. However, the field has not merely been treading water. With newer imaging and analytic techniques, brain structure can be examined with much greater spatial precision. Modern between-group studies with sophisticated averaging and statistical techniques can isolate critical regions (e.g., the thalamus). Modern within-group studies can consider potential structural changes over time, as well as the correlation between the size of a particular sub-region (e.g., the posterior superior temporal gyrus) and a specific aspect of neurocognition. Importantly, the next phase of structural neuroimaging in schizophrenia will be in partnership with functional neuroimaging to explore elusive structure-function relationships.

FUNCTIONAL NEUROIMAGING

Functional neuroimaging has been applied to the study of schizophrenia in several different ways. At the level of basic neurobiology, functional neuroimaging techniques have used ligands to explore selectively the properties of receptor binding (Farde, Wiesel, Halldin, & Sedvall, 1988). In terms of phenomenology, studies have considered the functional neuroanatomy of certain symptoms, such as auditory hallucinations (e.g., Silbersweig et al., 1995). Our emphasis is on a third application: the use of functional neuroimaging during neurocognitive activation to identify characteristic differences in brain activity between patients and controls. The merger of neurocognition and neuroimaging in schizophrenia research is, in many ways, still in its infancy. The challenges of interpreting group differences on functional neuroimaging procedures have turned out to be substantial.

In structural neuroimaging, the subject's internal state is irrelevant. In contrast, the image in functional neuroimaging depends on what the patient is perceiving, thinking, and feeling. For this reason, the internal mental state of the subject is immensely critical for the image and should be as well-controlled as possible. Consider the problems of a resting state.

In clinical terms, the resting state can be likened to the appearance of patients sleeping in their beds: the commonality of psychiatric subjects with nonpsychiatric subjects is more prominent than the differences. (Brodie, 1996, p. 146)

This analogy illustrates some of the difficulty of using a resting condition without a specific neurocognitive activation task. If patients only differ from controls during certain neurocognitive activations, then group differences on functional neuroimaging will not be revealed in a resting state. The analogy captures part of the problem with imaging during rest. The other part of the problem is that, in the absence of a well-defined neurocognitive activity, there is no obvious way to interpret differences between patients and non-patients, or among subgroups of patients. To extend the analogy above, the resting state could be likened to a situation in which patients were observed to be tossing and turning in their beds but the controls are resting peacefully. The reasons for the disrupted sleeping (rumination? indigestion? bed bugs?) would not be discerned. Similarly, if groups differ in functional neuroimaging during a resting state, the reasons for the differences cannot easily be interpreted.

Several functional neuroimaging techniques have been used to study schizophrenia. Three representative methods were selected to illustrate applications to schizophrenia: regional cerebral blood flow (rCBF) with xenon, positron emission tomography (PET), and functional magnetic resonance imaging (fMRI). These three methods have fair to excellent spatial resolution, but their temporal resolution is limited compared with electrophysiological techniques. Most of the functional neuroimaging work in schizophrenia has used rCBF and PET. The fMRI procedure has only recently been applied and is included in this section as an indicator of new directions.

Regional Cerebral Blood Flow (rCBF)

In 1926, Walter K., a 26-year-old sailor, went to Peter Bent Brigham Hospital in Boston complaining of headaches and failing vision (Fulton, 1928). When physicians placed a stethoscope over the back of his head they heard a "loud, course systolic bruit over the left occipital region." The bruit was the result of a tumor of the left occipital lobe, and an operation was attempted. The tumor could not be removed due to hemorrhaging, but a decompression was made and the patient recovered. The bruit was still audible 16 months later when Walter K. returned for a follow-up examination. However, the bruit was not constantly present. Instead, it seemed to depend on what Walter K. was looking at.

> On listening to the bruit, it was obvious that it was much louder than when first examined on the day of entry. Subsequent observations were made during the following week, and it was not difficult to convince ourselves that when the patient suddenly began to use his eyes after a prolonged period of rest in a dark room, there was a prompt and noticeable increase in the intensity of his bruit. (Fulton, 1928, pp. 314–315)

The change in the intensity of the bruit occurred even if the patient's blood pressure remained constant. In addition, the changes were specific to visual stimuli.

> Activity of his other sense organs, moreover, had no effect upon his bruit. Thus, smelling tobacco or vanilla did not influence it, straining to hear the ticking of a distant watch produced no effect, and ordinary quiet conversation was without demonstrable influence. (Fulton, 1928, p. 315)

These observations were based on an extremely rare situation (a bruit over the primary visual area). Nonetheless, the case study of Walter K. strongly supports the notion that changes in mental activity are accompanied by changes in blood flow to specific regions. This connection between cerebral blood flow and mental processes served as the basis for the development of monitoring techniques for brain activity.

In the first study of cerebral blood flow in schizophrenia (Kety et al., 1948), subjects inhaled a mixture of oxygen, nitrogen, and nitrous oxide. Cerebral blood flow was estimated by the difference in nitrous oxide blood curves in the femoral artery and internal jugular vein. Schizophrenic patients did not differ from controls in this initial study, but the conclusion was tempered with a prophetic cautionary note.

> On the basis of these data a generalized change in the circulation or oxygen utilization by the brain of schizophrenics may safely be ruled out although there remains the possibility that local disturbances confined to small but important regions may still occur since the method used yields only mean values for the entire brain. (Kety et al., 1948, p. 767)

The modern studies of functional neuroanatomy in schizophrenia used an infusion or an inhalation procedure in which radioactive xenon gas was used as a tracer of cerebral blood flow. Despite rather poor spatial resolution, the xenon procedures produced some elegant and highly informative studies. The first study of regional cerebral blood flow in schizophrenia essentially replicated the conclusions of Kety et al. by finding a normal mean hemisphere blood flow in schizophrenic patients (Ingvar & Franzen, 1974). However, the blood flow of patients was characterized by relatively reduced blood flow in the frontal regions compared to the posterior regions, whereas the controls showed the opposite pattern (see Figure 7.4). This reduced frontal blood flow was referred to as a "hypointentional" condition based on the inference that the frontal lobes were essential for intentional behaviors. The hypofrontal pattern was sometimes, but not always, replicated probably because of the problems in using a resting state mentioned above.

The problem with variability in the resting state was overcome in a series of studies from the National Institute of Mental Health (NIMH) (Berman, Zec, & Weinberger, 1986; Weinberger, Berman, & Zec, 1986). These studies applied the xenon inhalation technique to patients and controls as they performed a neurocognitive task, the Wisconsin Card Sorting Test (WCST, see Chapter 3). The WCST was chosen because it was thought to reflect activity of the dorsolateral aspects of the frontal lobe, which was the brain region of primary interest to the investigators. Importantly for interpretation, subjects received a control task (number-matching) that approximated the WCST in terms of visual stimulation, eye scanning, button pushing, and physical location in the laboratory environment. During the WCST, normal controls increased their activation of the dorsolateral prefrontal lobe, but patients did not (Weinberger et al., 1986). No region distinguished patients from controls on the number-matching test. Performance on the WCST correlated with the amount of blood flow for the patients, indicating that the more patients activated the dorsolateral prefrontal region, the better they performed.

Reduced activation of the dorsolateral prefrontal cortex in schizophrenia could stem from a non-specific problem in attention or a lack of effort. To test these possibilities subjects received a version of the continuous performance test (CPT, see Chapter 3) in addition to the WCST during a xenon inhalation procedure (Berman et al., 1986). If deficits in the dorsolateral prefrontal cortex are non-specific indices of inattention or reduced effort, there should be decreased blood flow with the CPT similar to the WCST. However, there were no differences in blood flow for this region between the patients and controls during performance on this version of the CPT, even though the patients performed relatively poorly on the CPT. The results showed some selectivity for a deficit in the patients' ability to activate the dorsolateral prefrontal cortex under certain task conditions.

Normal Controls

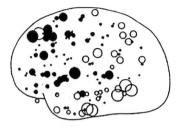

Chronic Schizophrenic Patients

Low Levels of Psychosis

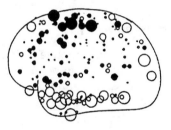

High Levels of Psychosis

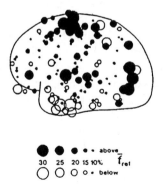

FIGURE 7.4

Source: From "Distribution of Cerebral Activity in Chronic Schizophrenia" by D. H. Ingvar and G. Franzen, 1974, *Lancet, 21*, p. 1485. © by The Lancet Ltd., 1974.

Clearly, the dorsolateral prefrontal cortex does not act in isolation but instead forms part of a neural circuit. Another study from the NIMH group examined the association between activation of the dorsolateral prefrontal cortex during the WCST and the anterior hippocampus, which forms part of a prefrontal-temporolimbic circuit. It included patients from the study of monozygotic twins discordant for schizophrenia that was described in Chapter 3 (Weinberger, Berman, Suddath, & Torrey, 1992). Activity of the dorsolateral prefrontal cortex was measured with xenon inhalation and volume of the anterior hippocampus was measured with MRI. For the affected (but not unaffected) twins, functional deficits in the prefrontal cortex were correlated with structural deficits in the anterior hippocampus. Specifically, smaller hippocampal volume was associated with less activation of the dorsolateral prefrontal cortex. These types of studies are especially revealing because they implicate dysfunctional neural circuits in schizophrenia. One of the key challenges facing neuroimaging in schizophrenia will be to move from identifying dysfunctional regions to implicating dysfunctional neural circuits.

Positron Emission Tomography (PET)

Although studies using the xenon inhalation technique were innovative and informative, neither its spatial nor its temporal resolution are optimal for imaging discrete cognitive processes. In addition, the technique can generate images from activity of the cortical surface, but is not well-suited for imaging subcortical structures. The introduction of PET scanning to schizophrenia allowed investigators to obtain images with better spatial resolution of both cortical and subcortical structures.

In PET, a radioactive tracer is injected into a person and carried through the bloodstream to the brain. The radioactive tracer emits a positron which travels a short distance and is annihilated by colliding with an electron. As it is annihilated, it generates two high-energy photons that travel in nearly opposite directions, separated by 180 degrees. It is these two photons that are sensed by coincidence detectors placed around the subject's head and used to form the image. Depending on the type of tracer, PET imaging can measure either metabolism or blood flow associated with changes in neural activity. When radioactively labeled glucose is used, the scans reveal brain metabolism. When radioactively labeled water ($H_2^{15}O$) is used, the scans reveal brain blood flow, which is closely linked to metabolism.

The initial studies with PET in schizophrenia used labeled glucose. The spatial resolution in these studies was superior to those using xenon, but the temporal resolution was poor because the half-life of labeled glucose is relatively long (about 110 minutes). Although findings from the PET glucose studies were generally consistent with the initial findings of Ingvar and Franzen in showing reduced metabolic activity in frontal brain areas, some found hyperfrontality instead (reviewed in Andreasen et al., 1992; Gur & Pearlson, 1993). The variability was probably due to differences across studies in the nature of the resting tasks, individual symptom profiles, and ways of defining the boundaries of the frontal lobe. The finding of hypofrontality was not attributable to a history of drug treatment because it was replicated with patients who had never received antipsychotic medication (Andreasen et al., 1992; Buchsbaum et al., 1992). Figure 7.5 shows an example of hypofrontality.

Unfortunately, hypofrontality is somewhat hard to interpret because it is remarkably non-specific; other conditions such as chronic alcoholism, autism, Alzheimer's disease, as well as exposure to organic solvents are associated with reduced frontal blood flow or metabolism (Deutsch, 1992). Because hypofrontality is reversible with the cessation of alcohol consumption and cessation of exposure to organic solvents, reduced frontal blood flow or metabolism does not necessarily reflect pathology of the frontal lobes. Beyond frontal abnormalities, some glucose PET studies have uncovered reduced activity in subcortical areas, such as the right thalamus

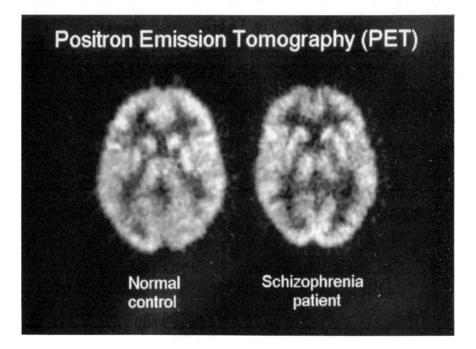

FIGURE 7.5

Source: With permission from M. S. Buchsbaum, MD, Neuroscience PET Laboratory, Mt. Sinai School of Medicine.

(Buchsbaum et al., 1996), consistent with the finding of structural abnormalities in the thalamus of schizophrenic patients (Andreasen et al., 1994).

It is informative to consider briefly how PET has been applied to questions of phenomenology in schizophrenia. Liddle, Frith, and their colleagues tested some rather specific hypotheses about the three syndromes of schizophrenia (negative/psychomotor poverty, disorganized, and psychotic/reality distortion). They obtained PET images of patients who were divided into these three subtypes (Liddle et al., 1992). Negative symptoms were associated with abnormality of the left dorsolateral prefrontal cortex, disorganized symptoms with the right ventral prefrontal cortex, and psychotic symptoms with the medial temporal lobe. A subsequent study from the same laboratory focused specifically on auditory hallucinations and found that activity in deep structures (e.g., thalamus, ventral striatum, hippocampus) was commonly activated during hallucinations (Silbersweig et al., 1995). Neocortical activations were also found, but they varied in location from patient to patient, perhaps reflecting differences in the content of the hallucination. Similar work on hallucinations is being conducted by my colleague Mark Cohen using fMRI, which will provide enhanced temporal and spatial resolution. These studies of functional neuroimaging and phenomenology provide excellent examples of ways to reduce variability by parsing broad questions into hypotheses about specific symptoms or subgroups.

More than for studies of phenomenology, the time frame of PET is an overriding consideration for studies of neurocognition. Glucose PET scans have a very long uptake period (about 30 minutes), placing constraints on which neurocognitive measures can serve as activation tasks. The CPT can be administered for this length of time, however, it would be desirable to have a shorter uptake period for many discrete neurocognitive tasks.

PET scans using oxygen reflect regional blood flow and can yield a scan for a 2–3-minute window because of the relatively short half-life of ^{15}O. Initially, oxygen PET was applied to the study of schizophrenia in the same manner as glucose PET: patients were compared to controls in a resting state. Such comparisons do not capitalize on the time frame advantages of the technique. Oxygen PET scans are well-suited for tasks that last a couple of minutes, including the WCST and measures of working memory, language processing, and selective attention. We will consider two examples.

Oxygen PET was used to examine selective attention in schizophrenia (O'Leary et al., 1996). Patients and controls were administered a dichotic listening test in which one stimulus was presented to the right ear while a different stimulus was presented simultaneously to the left ear. Although most people have a tendency to process verbal information that is presented to the right ear (because it projects primarily to the left hemisphere), subjects can typically direct their attention voluntarily to one ear or the other. When controls were asked to direct their attention to stimuli coming into their left ear, they increased activation of the right superior temporal gyrus and decreased activation of the left superior temporal gyrus. When given the same instructions, schizophrenic patients did neither. This study demonstrates how oxygen PET can provide an explanation at the level of regional activation for a commonly observed neurocognitive abnormality in selective attention.

The potential power of combining oxygen PET with a psychopharmacological manipulation was illustrated with verbal fluency as an activation task (Dolan et al., 1995). To assess verbal fluency, subjects were asked to generate words that begin with a certain letter. Responding was paced at one word every 5 seconds, which essentially equated the groups on level of performance. The control condition was a word repetition task that was administered after the verbal fluency task. Brain activity specific to verbal fluency was obtained by subtracting out the activity generated by the control task. In the resulting images, patients differed from controls by showing less activation of the anterior cingulate.

Next, the authors administered a dopamine agonist (apomorphine) or a placebo and readministered the neurocognitive and imaging procedures. During verbal fluency activation, the patients who received the dopamine agonist showed *enhanced* activity in the anterior cingulate compared with controls who received the agonist. Apparently, schizophrenic patients do not activate the anterior cingulate adequately under the specific task conditions. However, dopaminergic input had a regulatory effect on patients (not control subjects) that was seen with the activation task (not with the word repetition task). This study suggests that the dopamine system in schizophrenia is unusually sensitive. Importantly, it illustrates how neurocognitive, neuroimaging, and pharmacological procedures can be combined to explore the brain regions and neurotransmitter systems that underlie abnormalities in neurocognition.

Functional Magnetic Resonance Imaging (fMRI)

Initially, magnetic resonance imaging (MRI) was strictly a structural imaging tool. To obtain an image with MRI, an individual is placed in a strong magnetic field causing protons in the brain to align with this field. A brief radio frequency pulse is then applied, which pushes the protons out of alignment and introduces a phase coherence so that the protons are momentarily spinning together. Phase coherence is detected as a signal from a coil placed around the head, and the signal can be decoded and analyzed to yield images. When protons fall out of phase, the signal decays. Different tissues vary in their proton (i.e., hydrogen) concentrations and, consequently, they differ in MRI properties such as rates of signal decay. By capitalizing on differences in decay rates, MRI yields excellent contrast among various types of tissue.

The fMRI procedure is a modification of the MRI technique that is used to measure subtle changes in brain activity. It takes advantage of the fact that oxygenated and deoxygenated blood have slightly different magnetic properties and yield slightly different signals. As demonstrated in the case of Walter K., local brain activity is associated with an increase in regional blood flow, although the exact reasons for this association are not well-understood. The increase in flow exceeds the increase in oxygen consumption. As a result, more oxygenated blood passes through the active brain region, and the venous blood has a relative increase in oxygen levels in the activated versus the non-activated state (see Figure 7.6). This difference in oxygenated venous blood yields a small increase in MR signal (roughly 2–5% at a magnetic field of 1.5 Tesla). Hence, fMRI yields images of the difference between activated and non-activated states that are strictly dependent on blood oxygen levels.

The fMRI procedure has only become available recently and there have been few published studies in which it has been applied to schizophrenia.

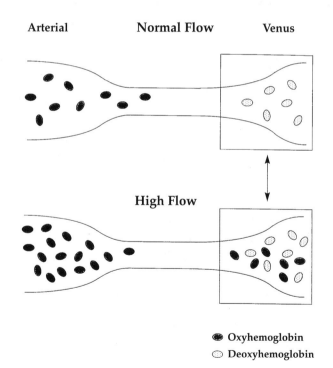

FIGURE 7.6

One such study used verbal fluency as the activation task (Yurgelun-Todd et al., 1996), similar to the oxygen PET study discussed previously. The responses in this task were not paced, making it difficult to compare this study directly to the PET study in which subjects were asked to produce one word every 5 seconds. Counting aloud served as a control task. Scans were obtained during each task and then subtracted to determine changes in blood flow associated with verbal fluency. This study considered only two regions: the dorsolateral prefrontal cortex and the superior temporal gyrus. Patients had less activation than controls in the dorsolateral prefrontal region, but more activation in the superior temporal gyrus. These results are somewhat consistent with the xenon inhalation findings mentioned earlier (Weinberger et al., 1992) in which functional deficits in the dorsolateral prefrontal cortex were related to structural deficits in the hippocampus. Both sets of findings implicate dysfunctional frontal-temporal circuits (albeit with different aspects of the temporal lobe) in schizophrenia.

Even at these early stages, optimism is high for applications of fMRI to schizophrenia research. In addition to confirming and extending findings from other neuroimaging techniques, this technique has the potential to open up entirely new lines of investigation. Because of its impressive temporal resolution (down to a tenth of a second, or better), the whole-brain imaging of brief neurocognitive processes will be possible for the first time. To examine neurocognitive processes that have shorter time frames, electrophysiological methods will be required. Figure 7.7 (Cohen & Bookheimer, 1994) shows a comparison of fMRI with other methods used to study brain function. The fMRI procedure has excellent temporal resolution compared with PET, and excellent spatial resolution compared with electrophysiological techniques. Because it is a safe procedure that does not involve radiation, scans can be repeated many times within a session or across sessions. Also, fMRI is well-suited for looking at data from a single subject so that individual differences in brain activation can be explored.

Interpretive Challenges

One potential difficulty in interpreting the results from fMRI and PET is that much of the research relies on the assumption that neurocognitive functions can be reasonably parsed into discrete components and then meaningfully subtracted from one another. This assumption may be safe for subtraction procedures with sensory and motor functions. However, such a compartmentalized approach for neurocognition may not apply well to higher mental functions, especially those that involve verbal mediation, strategies, and emotional components.

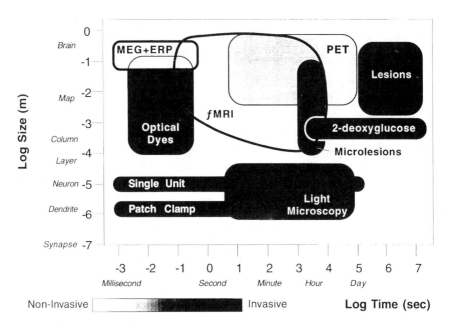

FIGURE 7.7

Source: From "Localization of Brain Function Using Magnetic Resonance Imaging" by M. S. Cohen and S. Y. Bookheimer, 1994, *Trends in Neurosciences, 17,* p. 269. Reprinted with permission of Elsevier Science.

... researchers often assume that if two tasks are similar, they can subtract blood flow induced by one from that induced by the other and what remains will implicate the brain basis of the cognitive steps that distinguish the two tasks. However, if the subjects believe that they have a challenging task ahead of them, they will prepare for it—and perhaps then try to organise the stimuli differently, or attend more closely. Such preparation can change which processes are involved in the task, inhibiting some while priming others. (Kosslyn, 1996, pp. 90–91)

In summary, it is difficult to overstate the impact of structural and functional neuroimaging on the way we view schizophrenia. Consider what happens when aspects of the disorder are attributed to a dysfunctional brain. Personal characteristics such as "craziness" and "laziness" become neurally based psychotic symptoms and avolition. Doubts that schizophrenia was a type of brain disease were commonly expressed in the 1950s and 1960s, but stark images of abnormalities in brain morphology tended to quell these doubts. On the contrary, compelling images of abnormalities in brain structure and function run the risk of creating the opposite bias, a type of "neuro-centrism," in which schizophrenia is viewed exclusively as a biological disorder without adequate appreciation for the importance of social and interpersonal factors.

Expectations for functional neuroimaging in schizophrenia are high, perhaps higher than for any other technology. However, the ability to interpret regional brain activity during a challenge task is strictly constrained by the extent to which the neurocognitive processes involved with the challenge task are understood. It has been argued that our ability to develop and interpret paradigms that inform us about the nature of schizophrenia have not kept pace with the impressive technical developments in functional neuroimaging. One of the pioneers in this area, Monte Buchsbaum, pointed out that "The neuroscience can be no better than the sophistication of the behavioural task probes and the neuropharmacological challenges that researchers employ" (Buchsbaum, 1995, p. 128).

On the other hand, newer functional neuroimaging techniques offer something unprecedented: the possibility of watching the response of the human brain to a neurocognitive challenge in nearly real time. Perhaps the payoff for schizophrenia research will be substantial when the field is better able to isolate and image the subcomponents of neurocognitive deficits; or when it moves beyond patient-control contrasts to explore broad issues of vulnerability, rehabilitation, coping strategies, medication effects, and protective factors. The coin of this realm is currently the promissory note.

REFERENCES

Andreasen, N. C., Arndt, S., Swayze II, V., Cizadlo, T., Flaum, M., O'Leary, D., Ehrhardt, J. C., & Yuh, W. T. C. (1994). Thalamic abnormalities in schizophrenia visualized through magnetic resonance image averaging. *Science, 266,* 294–298.

Andreasen, N. C., Rezai, K., Alliger, R., Swayze, V. W., Flaum, M., Kirchner, P., Cohen, G., & O'Leary, D. S. (1992). Hypofrontality in neuroleptic-naive patients and in patients with chronic schizophrenia. *Archives of General Psychiatry, 49,* 943–958.

Berman, K. F., Zec, R. F., & Weinberger, D. R. (1986). Physiologic dysfunction of dorsolateral prefrontal cortex in schizophrenia. *Archives of General Psychiatry, 43,* 126–135.

Bilder, R. M. (1992). Structure-function relations in schizophrenia: Brain morphology and neuropsychology. *Progress in Experimental Personality & Psychopathology Research, 15,* 183–251.

Breier, A., Buchanan, R. W., Ahmed, E., Munson, R. C., Kirkpatrick, B., & Gellad, F. (1992). Brain morphology and schizophrenia: A magnetic resonance imaging study of limbic, prefrontal cortex, and caudate structures. *Archive of General Psychiatry, 49,* 921–927.

Brodie, J. D. (1996). Imaging for the clinical psychiatrist: Facts, fantasies, and other musings. *American Journal of Psychiatry, 153,* 145–149.

Buchsbaum, M. S. (1995). Charting the circuits. *Nature, 378,* 128–129.

Buchsbaum, M. S., Haier, R. J., Potkin, S. G., Nuechterlein, K., Bracha, H. S., Katz, M., Lohr, J., Wu, J., Lottenberg, S., Jerabek, P. A., Trenary, M., Tafalla, R., Reynolds, C., & Bunney, W. E. (1992). Frontostriatal disorder of cerebral metabolism in never-medicated schizophrenics. *Archives of General Psychiatry, 49,* 935–942.

Buchsbaum, M. S., Someya, T., Ying Teng, C., Abel, L., Chin, S., Najafi, A., Haier, R. J., Wu, J., & Bunney, W. E. (1996). PET and MRI of the thalamus in never-medicated patients with schizophrenia. *American Journal of Psychiatry, 153,* 191–199.

Cannon, T. D., Mednick, S. A., & Parnas, J. (1989). Genetic and perinatal determinants of structural brain deficits in schizophrenia. *Archives of General Psychiatry, 46,* 883–889.

Chakos, M. H., Lieberman, J. A., Bilder, R. M., Borenstein, M., Lerner, G., Bogerts, B., Wu, H., Kinon, B., & Ashtari, M. (1994). Increase in caudate nuclei volumes of first-episode schizophrenic patients taking antipsychotic drugs. *American Journal of Psychiatry, 151,* 1430–1436.

Cohen, M. S., & Bookheimer, S. Y. (1994). Localization of brain function using magnetic resonance imaging. *Trends in Neurosciences, 17,* 268–277.

Deutsch, G. (1992). The nonspecificity of frontal dysfunction in disease and altered states: Cortical blood flow evidence. *Neuropsychiatry, Neuropsychology, and Behavioral Neurology, 5,* 301–307.

Dolan, R. J., Fletcher, P., Frith, C. D., Friston, K. J., Frackowiak, R. S. J., & Grasby, P. M. (1995). Dopaminergic modulation of impaired cognitive activation in the anterior cingulate cortex in schizophrenia. *Nature, 378,* 180–182.

Farde, L., Wiesel, F. A., Halldin, C., & Sedvall, G. (1988). Central D_2 dopamine receptor occupancy in schizophrenic patients treated with antipsychotic drugs. *Archives of General Psychiatry, 45,* 71–76.

Flaum, M., Swayze, V. W., O'Leary, D. S., Yuh, W. T. C., Ehrhardt, J. C., Arndt, S. V., & Andreasen, N. C. (1995). Effects of diagnosis, laterality, and gender on brain morphology in schizophrenia. *American Journal of Psychiatry, 152,* 704–714.

Fulton, J. F. (1928). Observations upon the vascularity of the human occipital lobe during visual activity. *Brain, 51,* 310–320.

Gur, R. E., & Pearlson, G. D. (1993). Neuroimaging in schizophrenia research. *Schizophrenia Bulletin, 19,* 337–353.

Ingvar, D. H., & Franzen, G. (1974). Distribution of cerebral activity in chronic schizophrenia. *Lancet,* 1484–1486.

Johnstone, E. C., Crow, T. J., Frith, C. D., Stevens, J., & Kreel, L. (1976). Cerebral ventricular size and cognitive impairment in chronic schizophrenia. *Lancet, 1,* 924–926.

Kety, S. S., Woodford, R. B., Harmel, M. H., Freyhan, F. A., Appel, K. E., & Schmidt, C. F. (1948). Cerebral blood flow and metabolism in schizophrenia: The effects of barbiturate semi-narcosis, insulin coma, and electroshock. *American Journal of Psychiatry, 104,* 765–770.

Kosslyn, S. M. (1996). Neural systems and psychiatric disorders. *Cognitive Neuropsychiatry, 1,* 89–93.

Liddle, P. F., Friston, K. J., Frith, C. D., Hirsch, S. R., Jones, T., & Frackowiak, R. S. J. (1992). Patterns of cerebral blood flow in schizophrenia. *British Journal of Psychiatry, 160,* 179–186.

Luchins, D. J., Weinberger, D. R., & Wyatt, R. J. (1982). Schizophrenia and cerebral asymmetry detected by computed tomography. *American Journal of Psychiatry, 139,* 753–757.

Luckett, W. H. (1913). Air in the ventricles of the brain, following a fracture of the skull. *Surgery, Gynecology and Obstetrics,* 237–240.

McCarley, R. W., Shenton, M. E., O'Donnell, B. F., Faux, S. F., Kikinis, R., Nestor, P. G., & Jolesz, F. A. (1993). Auditory P300 abnormalities and left posterior superior temporal gyrus volume reduction in schizophrenia. *Archives of General Psychiatry, 50,* 190–197.

Moore, M. T., Nathan, D., Elliott, A. R., & Laubach, C. (1935). Encephalographic studies in mental disease. *American Journal of Psychiatry, 92,* 43–67.

Nestor, P. G., Shenton, M. E., McCarley, R. W., Haimson, J., Smith, R. S., O'Donnell, B. F., Kimble, M. O., Kikinis, R., & Jolesz, F. A. (1993). Neuropsychological correlates of MRI temporal lobe abnormalities in schizophrenia. *American Journal of Psychiatry, 150,* 1849–1855.

Oldendorf, W. H. (1980). Computerized tomography in the perspective of past and future imaging methods. *The quest for an image of the brain.* New York: Raven Press.

O'Leary, D. S., Andreasen, N. C., Hurtig, R. R., Kesler, M. L., Rogers, M., Arndt, S., Cizadlo, T., Watkins, L., Boles Ponto, L. L., Kirchner, P. T., & Hichwa, R. D. (1996). Auditory attentional deficits in patients with schizophrenia. *Archives of General Psychiatry, 53,* 633–641.

Raz, S., & Raz, N. (1990). Structural brain abnormalities in the major psychoses: A quantitative review of the evidence from computerized imaging. *Psychological Bulletin, 108,* 93–108.

Shenton, M. E., Kinkinis, R., Jolesz, F. A., Pollack, S. D., LeMay, M., Wible, C. G., Hokama, H., Martin, J., Medcalf, D., Coleman, M., & McCarley, R. W. (1992). Left-lateralized temporal lobe abnormalities in schizophrenia and their relationship to thought disorder: A computerized, quantitative MRI study. *New England Journal of Medicine, 327,* 604–612.

Silbersweig, D. A., Stern, E., Frith, C., Cahill, C., Holmes, A., Grootoonk, S., Seaward, J., McKenna, P., Chua, S. E., Schnorr, L., Jones, T., & Frackowiak, R. S. J. (1995). A functional neuroanatomy of hallucinations in schizophrenia. *Nature, 378,* 176–179.

Weinberger, D. R., Berman, K. F., Suddath, R., & Torrey, F. E. (1992). Evidence of dysfunction of a prefrontal-limbic network in schizophrenia: A magnetic resonance imaging and regional cerebral blood flow study of discordant monozygotic twins. *American Journal of Psychiatry, 149,* 890–897.

Weinberger, D. R., Berman, K. F., & Zec, R. F. (1986). Physiologic dysfunction of dorsolateral prefrontal cortex in schizophrenia. *Archives of General Psychiatry, 43,* 114–124.

Yurgelun-Todd, D. A., Waternaux, C. M., Cohen, B. M., Gruber, S. A., English, C. D., & Renshaw, P. F. (1996). Functional magnetic resonance imaging of schizophrenic patients and comparison subjects during word production. *American Journal of Psychiatry, 153,* 200–206.

▶ 8

Neurocognitive Correlates of Functional and Clinical Outcome

Despite nearly a century of work to identify, measure, and characterize neurocognitive deficits in schizophrenia, there was remarkably little effort to determine the significance of these deficits for clinical outcome and daily activities. It may be informative to consider what happened in a separate, but related, area: vocational rehabilitation with psychiatric patients. Vocational rehabilitation has a longer tradition of identifying predictors of outcome and, consequently, it has a broader data base. However, a comprehensive review of the literature on vocational rehabilitation in 1984 came to a startling set of conclusions.

> ... a) knowledge of psychiatrically disabled persons' psychiatric symptomatology is *not* a valid indicator of their capacity to work; b) knowledge of psychiatrically disabled persons' functioning in a nonvocational environment is *not* a valid indicator of their capacity to work; and c) knowledge of psychiatrically disabled persons' psychiatric symptomatology is *not* a valid indictor of their functional skills (emphasis in original, Anthony & Jansen, 1984, p. 542)

The issue naturally generated debate. Although the reviews suggested that psychiatric symptoms were not related to vocational performance (Anthony, Cohen, & Danley, 1988; Anthony & Jansen, 1984), several investigators reported that psychiatric symptoms and diagnoses were related to vocational outcome (e.g., Massel et al., 1990; Tsuang & Coryell, 1993). A compromise position was advanced suggesting that work outcome is related primarily to negative, as opposed to psychotic, symptoms (Anthony, Rogers, Cohen, & Davies, 1995; Mintz, Bond, & Mintz, in press).

The most intriguing part of the debate was that it occurred at all. On the surface, it seems inconceivable that symptoms would not interfere with work outcome. After all, it is usually hard enough to be productive at work without battling psychotic symptoms such as hallucinations and delusions, or non-psychotic symptoms such as anxiety and depression. If symptoms are not obviously related to vocational outcome in schizophrenic patients, what is?

Perhaps neurocognitive limitations hold the patients back. Mental health practitioners have long noticed a dissociation between the reduction of symptoms and the resumption of full functioning. Schizophrenic patients frequently have difficulty navigating social and occupational waters, even after their symptoms have disappeared. Neurocognitive assessments offer experimental precision, but they often appear to be remote from the real-world activities of the patient. Colleagues frequently describe this investigative enterprise as esoteric. However, we will see that knowledge of patients' basic neurocognitive abilities can be useful for predicting and understanding outcomes in schizophrenia.

Outcomes in schizophrenia can be divided roughly into two categories: clinical and functional. Clinical outcome includes variables related to psychiatric symptoms such as time to symptom remission, rehospitalization rates, and eventual clinical state. Functional outcome includes a variety of domains involved with the acquisition and retention of skills that are needed for community functioning. Because clinical and functional outcome are not strongly interrelated, each area will be considered separately. In fact, there are probably several relatively independent outcome domains within each outcome category. However, the current literature does not permit clear subdivisions. The initial studies of neurocognitive predictors focused primarily on clinical outcomes and addressed a rather practical question for psychiatric treatment: What are the differences between patients who respond to treatment and those who do not?

NEUROCOGNITION AND CLINICAL OUTCOME

Shortly following the initial optimism that accompanied the introduction of antipsychotic medications, it became apparent that there was considerable variability in the response to medications. First, there is variability in the time to recovery from psychotic episodes. More importantly, about 20–25% of schizophrenic patients are considered refractory to pharmacological treatment. This range in treatment responsiveness raises two types of questions. First, can neurocognitive measures predict rate of recovery? If so, they would be an aid in treatment planning. Second, what is the difference between a treatment responder versus non-responder? Neurocognitive assessment may reveal intrinsic differences between groups of patients that could help link the activity of certain brain systems to treatment response.

To answer such questions, studies assessed baseline neurocognition and outcome measures such as length of time to recovery, level of persisting symptoms, or rehospitalization rates. Specificity of the neurocognitive measure is always a consideration. While it is useful to know that a global composite measure of neurocognition is related to rate of recovery from an acute episode (Smith, Largen, Vroulis, & Ravichandran, 1992), it is difficult to identify which neurocognitive processes are responsible for the relationship. For this reason, we will emphasize studies that have included specific neurocognitive measures.

Reaction time is an apparently simple, but highly informative, index that has been influential in generating complex theories about the nature of neurocognitive deficits in schizophrenia (e.g., DeAmicis & Cromwell, 1977). Two prospective studies (Cancro, Sutton, Kerr, & Serman, 1971; Zahn & Carpenter, 1978) showed a relationship between slower reaction time at an acute inpatient period and poorer clinical outcome. The interpretation was that patients who can respond faster and more reliably to environmental stimuli can recover faster and more completely from a psychotic episode. Note that this interpretation is more descriptive than explanatory because it does not provide a clear mechanism for the connection. One of these studies (Zahn & Carpenter, 1978) used a categorical analysis in which patients were divided into those who improved and those who did not. Baseline reaction time, but not any of the baseline measures of global psychopathology, discriminated groups at follow-up.

Whether or not a patient responds to treatment depends on an interaction between patient characteristics and the dosage of medication. The Span of Apprehension (see Chapter 3) has been helpful for understanding the relationships between clinical outcome and drug dosage. In one study, relapse rates were compared for patients receiving standard versus low doses of a conventional neuroleptic (fluphenazine decanoate) (Asarnow, Marder, Mintz, Van Putten, & Zimmerman, 1988). Patients were divided into those with good and poor Span performance. Among patients with poor Span performance, outcome was better with higher doses of medication (two-year, non-relapse rates of 86% vs. 22% for standard vs. low doses, respectively). In contrast, for patients with good Span performance, outcome was better with lower medication doses (one-year, non-relapse rates of 44% vs. 79% for standard vs. low doses, respectively). It appears that poor Span performance identifies patients who require higher doses of medication. The Span by dosage interaction can be seen in Figure 8.1, which shows the survival rates (i.e., the percentage of patients free of exacerbations).

Span performance was also evaluated in a group of treatment-resistant patients who were recruited because they were receiving very high doses of

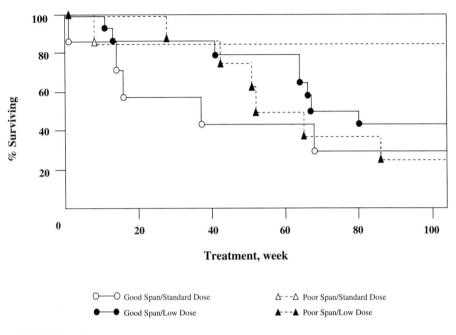

FIGURE 8.1

Source: From "Differential Effect of Low and Conventional Doses of Fluphenazine on Schizophrenic Outpatients with Good or Poor Information-Processing Abilities" by Asarnow et al., 1988, *Archives of General Psychiatry, 45,* p. 824. Copyright 1988, American Medical Association. Reprinted with permission.

antipsychotic medication. Their medications were converted to a standard antipsychotic (haloperidol) and systematically reduced. Patients who had poor Span performance at baseline assessment prior to medication reduction could not tolerate a reduction in their medications, but the other patients could (Green et al., 1993). Importantly, the patients in this study did not show differences at baseline in terms of psychiatric symptoms, concomitant medications, or medication side effects.

From these studies, it appears that poor Span performance identifies a group of patients who require higher doses of antipsychotic medications and are highly sensitive to changes in medication dosage. Moreover, the results from Asarnow et al. (1988) suggest that good Span performance may be a relative contraindication for a standard high dose of antipsychotic medications. The Span seems to be tapping a capacity that is relevant for treatment and that is not available from standard interviews.

The studies of prediction of clinical outcome can be viewed as having both practical and conceptual goals. At a practical level, a clinician who is faced with patients in acute episode would be aided by a valid way to determine which patients are likely to recover faster and which patients will require more time and greater intensity of services. The practical goal would be to increase the efficiency of treatment delivery. Based on a fairly small number of studies, neurocognitive measures seem to be helpful in this regard by providing information that is not available from standard clinical assessments.

At the conceptual level, the studies may provide clues about why certain patients respond to medications while others do not. For example, measures such as the Span can serve a dual function. On the one hand, it can help identify patients who are sensitive to medication changes, and on the other, it can implicate neurocognitive processes and brain regions that may be linked to medication responsiveness. With some of the functional neuroimaging techniques discussed in Chapter 7, it is becoming increasingly feasible to identify the relevant neural substrates of neurocognitive measures. Hence, measures like the Span may provide a neurocognitive "bridge" between specific relevant brain regions and treatment responsiveness.

NEUROCOGNITION AND FUNCTIONAL OUTCOME

Once one becomes aware of the scope of neurocognitive deficits in schizophrenia, it is natural to wonder how these deficits affect the way patients function in their daily life. Do the deficits make it difficult for patients to catch the right bus, prepare their dinner, or keep their job? Do they make it hard for patients to hold a conversation with a family member or to remember to take their medication? Despite a long tradition of research on the nature of neurocognitive deficits in schizophrenia, these fundamental questions have been largely ignored.

At a general level, it has been known that smarter patients usually function better than duller patients (reviewed by Heaton & Pendleton, 1981). However, the next question is one of specificity: Which specific neurocognitive deficits place limits on the achievement of particular outcomes? As an analogy, consider a chemical equation in which the rate of movement from one side of the equation to the other is limited by the availability of one compound. Similarly, deficits in some neurocognitive areas may restrict or limit patients' ability to retain, acquire, or re-learn skills. In essence, they act as neurocognitive "rate limiting factors" (Green, 1996).

Functional outcome in schizophrenia can be divided into three outcome domains that will be considered separately. The first section includes studies of *community functioning*. Naturally, community outcome can be subdivided into components of adaptive functioning (e.g., social and vocational functioning). However, most studies have used fairly global outcome indices, which limit the ability to examine the components of community outcome separately. The second section includes laboratory studies that have assessed *social problem solving*, a critical component of social functioning. The last section emphasizes rehabilitation and considers the role of neurocognition in the patients' ability to acquire *psychosocial skills* that are needed for community functioning.

Community Outcome

Several prospective studies have assessed specific aspects of neurocognition at baseline and then community functioning at follow-up (Buchanan, Holstein, & Breier, 1994; Goldman et al., 1993; Jaeger & Douglas, 1992; Johnstone, Macmillan, Frith, Benn, & Crow, 1990; Lysaker, Bell, & Beam-Goulet, 1995a; Wykes, Sturt, & Katz, 1990). Other studies have considered neurocognitive performance and community functioning concurrently, but prospective studies have an interpretive advantage in that assessments typically are conducted at baseline before patients show differences in outcome (e.g., while patients are hospitalized) and reveal how well neurocognitive measures predict future community functioning. The measures of community functioning differed from study to study, and included assessments of occupational functioning, quality of social networks, satisfaction with quality of life, and/or the degree of independent living (e.g., how much supervision the patient required).

Despite huge variability in the selection of neurocognitive measures, some replicated findings emerged. Secondary verbal memory and card sorting were reliable predictors of community functioning. Secondary verbal memory can be distinguished from immediate (or working) verbal memory and is assessed through recall and recognition of lists of words or stories, often after a time delay. Recollection of a newspaper article that you read this morning relies on secondary memory. In contrast, immediate verbal memory is a short-term store and is assessed with measures such as the digit span. A real-life example of immediate verbal memory occurs when you are told a phone number and you keep it actively in mind until you make the call; after you make the call the information is lost. The separation of immediate and secondary verbal memory is demonstrated by amnesic patients who tend to have dysfunctional secondary memory, but intact immediate memory. Card sorting in these studies refers to the Wisconsin Card Sorting Test (WCST, see Chapter 3), in which subjects are instructed to match cards, but are not told which rules they should use to do so. The WCST is considered a measure of executive functioning, concept formation, or cognitive flexibility. From this section, it appears that patients who have difficulty with secondary verbal memory and with executive functions will have more difficulty in achieving successful community adaptation.

Social Problem Solving

One component of successful community adaptation is the ability to solve social and interpersonal problems. Whereas measures of community functioning tend to be global, social problem solving is assessed with fairly specific laboratory-based measures. These measures usually involve videotaped vignettes in which subjects are shown an interpersonal situation (e.g., a husband and wife arguing over which TV show to watch; a customer discussing a billing mistake with a sales clerk). After viewing the vignette, subjects typically are asked to identify the problem, generate possible solutions to the problem, and then role play these solutions. Some assessments of social problem solving also include subjects' evaluations of the effectiveness of their solutions. Responses and role-playing exercises can be scored reliably by trained raters.

Several studies have explored the neurocognitive correlates of laboratory-based measures of social problem solving (Bellack, Sayers, Mueser, & Bennett, 1994; Bowen et al., 1994; Corrigan, Green, & Toomey, 1994a; Penn, Mueser, Spaulding, Hope, & Reed, 1995; Penn et al., 1993). Unlike the studies of community functioning, which were longitudinal and followed subjects as outpatients, the studies of neurocognition and social problem solving were cross-sectional and mainly included inpatients.

As in the previous section on community outcome, there was wide variability in the selection of neurocognitive measures, but some consistencies are apparent. Social problem solving was reliably related to secondary verbal memory and vigilance. Vigilance was measured in these studies by the continuous performance test (CPT, see Chapter 3), which measures subjects' ability to discriminate targets (signal) from non-targets (noise). Measures of immediate verbal memory and early visual processing (assessed with the Span of Apprehension) were related to social problem solving in a single study, but these findings were not replicated. Card sorting, which was a replicated finding for community functioning, was not associated with social problem solving. From this group of studies, it appears that patients who have deficits in secondary verbal memory and vigilance will have difficulty in solving social problems.

Skill Acquisition

One key determinant of community functioning is the ability to acquire or re-learn psychosocial skills. Psychosocial rehabilitation programs for schizophrenic patients provide instruction in areas such as medication management, conversation skills, leisure activities, and vocational skills. Content in these areas is presented through class instruction as well as behavioral role-playing exercises. Acquisition of the material can be reliably assessed with pre- and post-tests; and the adequacy of role-playing exercises can be scored by trained raters.

The studies that have evaluated the relationships between neurocognitive abilities and skill acquisition have been predominantly longitudinal and prospective (Bowen et al., 1994; Corrigan, Wallace, Schade, & Green, 1994b; Kern, Green, & Satz, 1992; Lysaker, Bell, Zito, & Bioty, 1995b; Mueser, Bellack, Douglas, & Wade, 1991; Weaver & Brooks, 1964). In most of these studies, neurocognition was assessed at baseline and psychosocial skill acquisition was rated over the course of a training program. Patients in these studies were primarily inpatients.

This group of studies had more consistency in the selection of neurocognitive measures than the other areas, rendering a more confident interpretation of results. Secondary verbal memory was consistently associated with skill acquisition, as it was for community functioning and social problem solving. In addition, immediate verbal memory was reliably associated with skill acquisition. Vigilance was consistently related with skill acquisition, as it had been with social problem solving. Associations between early visual processing and card sorting were reported, but these findings remain to be replicated.

Summary of Findings

From this complex array of findings a few major patterns can be extracted. Figures 8.2–8.4 summarize the findings across the various outcome areas. The findings can be reduced into three types: *Probable Associations* are findings that were replicated with independent samples. *Possible Associations* are non-replicated findings, either because of a failure to replicate, or because no other studies used a similar measure. *Negative Findings* indicate that at least two different studies failed to find a relationship, and no other studies found a significant relationship.

Figure 8.2 summarizes the results for memory measures. Secondary verbal memory was a strong predictor/correlate of outcome, regardless of the measure of functional outcome. In fact, all studies ($n = 7$) that included measures of secondary verbal memory found an association. Immediate verbal memory was associated with skill acquisition, but was only inconsistently related to social problem solving. The observed relationship between verbal memory and skill learning has some degree of face validity. To be successful with skills training programs, participants need to encode and recall material

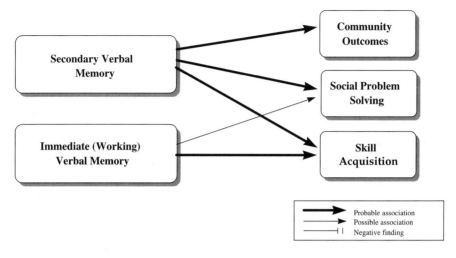

**FIGURE 8.2   Findings for Prediction of Functional Outcome—
I. Verbal Memory**

presented by instructors and through videotapes. Beyond the classroom, it is reasonable to expect that verbal encoding and mediation of daily activities are necessary for adequate functioning in the community.

The findings from other selected neurocognitive measures are included in Figure 8.3. Vigilance was reliably related to social skill acquisition and social problem solving. Vigilance in these studies refers to vigilance *level*, which is the ability to discriminate signal (target stimuli) from noise (nontarget stimuli) across an entire vigilance period. Vigilance *decrement* is the drop in vigilance level over the course of the test. Too few studies have evaluated this aspect of vigilance to allow us to draw any conclusions. The connections between vigilance and these areas of functional outcome have some face validity. Perhaps patients who are better able to distinguish signal from noise on the CPT are also better able to separate relevant from irrelevant information in the flow of continually changing social or instructional situations. If so, we would expect vigilance to be associated with community functioning, but that connection has not been tested yet.

Card sorting was consistently related to community outcome, inconsistently related to skill acquisition, and not related to social problem solving. One may initially have expected a neurocognitive measure of problem solving (i.e., card sorting) to be associated with interpersonal problem solving. However, the skills needed to sort cards within the very constrained setting of the WCST are probably quite different than the skills needed to solve multifaceted interpersonal problems.

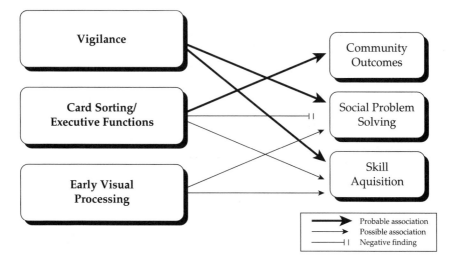

**FIGURE 8.3   Findings for Prediction of Functional Outcome—
II. Other Neurocognitive Measures**

If we extend the review to include studies that used *concurrent* assessments of neurocognition and community functioning, we can expect the relationships to be even stronger. As an illustration, consider a rather specialized example from a study of monozygotic twins discordant for schizophrenia (Goldberg et al., 1995). Among twin pairs who were concordant for schizophrenia, the intrapair differences in neurocognitive measures were used to predict intrapair differences in global outcome (measured with the Global Assessment Scale). A composite memory index alone accounted for 58% of the variance in outcome. Neurocognitive performance across several measures accounted for a remarkable 99% of the variance.

Several studies that examined functional consequences of neurocognitive deficits also included assessments of symptoms. The studies in the review were selected because they included neurocognitive measures, so they cannot be considered representative of the larger literature on symptoms and functional outcome. Nonetheless, the summary of findings in Figure 8.4 provides an indication of how symptoms compare to neurocognitive measures in the prediction of, and correlation with, functional outcome. Symptoms in these studies can be grouped into two types: psychotic and negative. Negative symptoms showed replicated links to social problem solving, but no relationships with skill acquisition. The relationships with community functioning were inconsistent.

Notably, psychotic symptoms were not significantly associated with functional outcome measures in any of the eight studies that evaluated them.

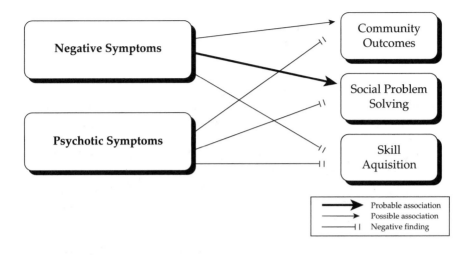

FIGURE 8.4 **Findings for Prediction of Functional Outcome—**
III. Symptoms

There are some considerations for this somewhat surprising absence of relationship. These studies used rather global measures of psychotic symptoms in which a cluster of psychotic symptoms were summed into a single value. It is entirely possible that a particular psychotic symptom is disruptive for functional outcome, but that this relationship was obscured by using composite measures of psychotic symptoms. For example, some especially intrusive symptoms (e.g., thought disorder or psychotic assaultiveness) may be incompatible with community adaptation, whereas others (e.g, hallucinations) may not be. In addition, when considering occupational functioning, not all jobs would be equally affected by symptoms. Jobs with minimal demands for interpersonal interactions would probably be less disrupted by ongoing psychotic symptoms. Despite these caveats, a central conclusion remains: If you wish to predict functional outcome and you can base the prediction on ratings of psychotic symptoms or verbal memory—pick verbal memory.

Another consideration is temporal: in some of the studies psychotic symptoms were assessed at one point in time, but outcome was assessed at a later time when patients could be in remission. However, even the cross-sectional studies in this review failed to find associations with psychotic symptoms. It is difficult to imagine that psychotic symptoms would not be related to outcome, but the following personal account demonstrates an ability to maintain a high level of functioning in the presence of severe symptoms.

I was convinced that this professor and I had a private means of communication and, because of this, interpreted most of what he said in class as personally relating to me. Sometimes the things I heard in class were bizarre and had no relation to the class purpose. One time the professor asked the room at large, "So your husband used to be a minister?" I had not divulged that information to him, but because I had recently told my babysitter that, I felt the incident was more than coincidence. I felt that there was a large network of people finding out about me, watching me on the street for some unknown reason. This feeling of lack of privacy soon grew into thinking my house was bugged, a fear that I would have off and on for the next 8 years. The bizarre and illogical statements I heard people make were later dismissed as auditory hallucinations. They seemed very real to me, however.

… These things caused me considerable anguish, but I continued to act as normal as I could for fear that any bizarre behavior would cause me to lose my job. I did not talk about these things, so the only noticeable signs of my illness were that I became silent and withdrawn, not my usual ebullient and smiling self. I did not think I was sick, but that these things were being done to me. I was still able to function, though I remember getting lunch ready very slowly as if working in molasses, each move an effort. However, my ability to study and write were not impaired because I got A's and B's for that semester. (Anonymous, 1990, p. 548)

Now let us circle back to the debate about the role of symptoms in vocational rehabilitation. Like the resolution of that debate, we also found that symptoms are related to outcome, but the associations hold mainly for negative as opposed to psychotic symptoms, and the strength of these associations is fairly modest. If the relationships between symptoms and outcome are modest at best, other critical variables must be missing. In all likelihood, some of those missing variables are neurocognitive in nature.

Figure 8.5 shows the relationships among neurocognitive deficits, psychotic symptoms, negative symptoms and functional outcome. In the top panel, the strengths of the associations are estimated at three levels (strong, weak, or questionable) based on the review of the literature. The relationships between neurocognitive performance and symptoms tend to be weak and typically stronger for negative than for psychotic symptoms (see Chapter 5). Likewise, the relationships between symptoms and functional outcome are weak, and stronger for negative than for psychotic symptoms. This pattern raises the very real possibility that the relationships between negative symptoms and outcome might be mediated through neurocognitive pathways.

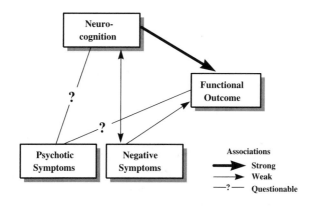

FIGURE 8.5a   Associations Among Neurocognition, Symptoms, and Functional Outcome

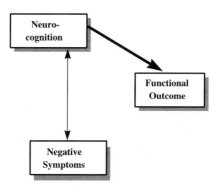

FIGURE 8.5b   Proposed Causal Pathways Between Negative Symptoms and Functional Outcome

Data from two separate laboratories suggest that this, in fact, is the case (Harvey et al., 1997; Velligan et al., 1997). Using a sophisticated path analysis, Velligan and colleagues found when the pathway from cognitive impairment to functional outcome was in the model, direct pathways from psychotic and negative symptoms to functional outcome were not needed. Their results suggest that cognitive impairment, rather than symptoms, influences functional outcome. How then do we explain the modest relationship between negative symptoms and functional outcome? Figure 8.5b depicts one causal path, which includes a strong association between neurocognition and functional outcome, coupled with modest shared variance between negative symptoms and neurocognition.

Practical Applications

Knowledge about neurocognitive "rate limiting factors" can be helpful in several ways. One potential application would be to assist in the planning of service delivery. Consider two inpatients who are similar in most respects except that one has poor, and the other has adequate, vigilance. The patient with adequate vigilance is likely to be more successful in a standard skills training program, whereas the other patient may need a program that is slower paced, offered in shorter segments, or includes more redundancy. Now consider two inpatients who differ in verbal memory ability and are about to enter the community. The patient with relatively poor verbal memory may need additional mental health support services to achieve and maintain optimal social and work outcome compared with the one who has good verbal memory. This use of neurocognitive assessment to provide estimates of intensity of service delivery creates a meaningful role for a new member of the treatment team: the clinical neuropsychologist. Clinical neuropsychologists have long provided assessments in psychiatric settings, but previously made little direct contribution to the treatment of schizophrenia.

A second, more speculative application of this information involves cognitive remediation efforts, which will be discussed in the next chapter. The term "cognitive remediation," as it is used in psychopathology, involves three types of designs: studies of rate limiting factors, feasibility studies, and generalization studies. The focus of this chapter has been on studies of neurocognitive rate limiting factors that examine the associations between neurocognitive variables and outcome. Feasibility studies are designed to determine whether performance deficits on a particular measure (e.g., Wisconsin Card Sorting Test, Span of Apprehension) can be modified under certain conditions. Generalization studies are the most ambitious and the least supported. In these studies, an intervention is directed at one level (e.g., vigilance) but the effects of the intervention are assessed in another domain (e.g., symptom reduction). Generalization studies face a substantial methodological problem: they require that experimenters make an *a priori* selection of which neurocognitive processes should receive the intervention and which outcome variables should be monitored. Without a clear understanding of the specific linkages between neurocognitive deficits and real-world functioning, such efforts to evaluate the generalization of remediation are destined to remain unfocused.

> Thus, before one embarks on the remediation of cognitive deficits, it would help to know a bit more how a specific deficit or pattern of deficits systematically relates to schizophrenic disability. (Hogarty & Flesher, 1992, p. 53)

In any case, little is known about precisely which information-processing deficits compromise social behavior in schizophrenia.... In light of this confusing picture, it is not clear which cognitive process or processes should be targeted for rehabilitation. (Bellack, 1992, pp. 44–45)

A CHANGE IN DIRECTION

It is natural to wonder about links between neurocognitive deficits and daily functioning. We intuitively feel that neurocognitive abilities help us to navigate through the obstacles and challenges of our world. We know that when we were cognitively compromised (perhaps courtesy of sleep deprivation, the flu, or prescription medications), routine activities become effortful and daunting. It is easy to understand how daily aspects of life could be more difficult and less satisfying if we had noticeable deficits in the neurocognitive abilities that we take for granted. Given the intuitive nature of this endeavor, the neglect of an experimental approach to this topic is all the more puzzling.

For the better part of a century, neurocognitive research in schizophrenia has "looked inward" to identify and characterize the deficits that are central to the disorder. Consequently, the lion's share of this book is devoted to the nature of neurocognitive deficits in schizophrenia. The last two chapters of the book represent a departure of 180 degrees: they are an attempt to "look outward." The distinction between looking outward and looking inward is somewhat illusory because practical findings inevitably lead to basic questions of mechanism. The central questions when looking outward are high-level versions of "So What?" What does the presence of neurocognitive deficits in schizophrenia tell us about response to treatments, about the need for services, and about the patients' daily life? The research that is looking outward has not yet reached maturity. It is rather easy to criticize these studies for having too few subjects, too many analyses, and hardly a hypothesis in sight. Nonetheless, they are the harbingers of a new direction of investigation. As such, they can be forgiven for being largely hypothesis-generating. Despite the limitations, these studies have provided a foundation for the next step, which should be a more focused, hypothesis-testing phase.

If neurocognitive deficits are restricting patients in terms of social, rehabilitative, and community outcome, then it might make sense to target these deficits for intervention. As mentioned in Chapter 6, conventional antipsychotic drugs provide a clear benefit for psychotic symptoms, but generally little or no effect on neurocognitive performance. In the last chapter, we will consider whether it is reasonable to consider behavioral or pharmacological interventions that might improve neurocognitive abilities.

REFERENCES

Anonymous. (1990). First person account: Behind the mask: A functional schizophrenic copes. *Schizophrenia Bulletin, 16,* 547–549.

Anthony, W. A., Cohen, M. R., & Danley, K. S. (1988). The psychiatric rehabilitation model as applied to vocational rehabilitation. In J. A. Ciardiello & M. D. Bell (Eds.), *Vocational rehabilitation of persons with prolonged psychiatric disorders* (pp. 59–80). Baltimore: Johns Hopkins University Press.

Anthony, W. A., & Jansen, M. A. (1984). Predicting the vocational capacity of the chronically mentally ill: Research and policy implications. *American Psychology, 39,* 537–544.

Anthony, W. A., Rogers, E. S., Cohen, M., & Davies, R. R. (1995). Relationships between psychiatric symptomatology, work skills, and future vocational performance. *Psychiatric Services, 46,* 353–358.

Asarnow, R. F., Marder, S. R., Mintz, J., Van Putten, T., & Zimmerman, K. E. (1988). Differential effect of low and conventional doses of fluphenazine on schizophrenia outpatients with good and poor information processing abilities. *Archives of General Psychiatry, 45,* 822–826.

Bellack, A. S. (1992). Cognitive rehabilitation for schizophrenia: Is it possible? Is it necessary? *Schizophrenia Bulletin, 18,* 43–50.

Bellack, A. S., Sayers, M., Mueser, K., & Bennett, M. (1994). Evaluation of social problem solving in schizophrenia. *Journal of Abnormal Psychology, 103,* 371–378.

Bowen, L., Wallace, C. J., Glynn, S. M., Nuechterlein, K. H., Lutzker, J. R., & Kuehnel, T. G. (1994). Schizophrenic individuals' cognitive functioning and performance in interpersonal interactions and skills training procedures. *Journal of Psychiatric Research, 28,* 289–301.

Buchanan, R. W., Holstein, C., & Breier, A. (1994). The comparative efficacy and long-term effect of Clozapine treatment on neuropsychological test performance. *Biological Psychiatry, 36,* 717–725.

Cancro, R., Sutton, S., Kerr, J., & Serman, A. A. (1971). Reaction time and prognosis in acute schizophrenia. *Journal of Nervous and Mental Disorders, 153,* 351–359.

Corrigan, P. W., Green, M. F., & Toomey, R. (1994a). Cognitive correlates to social cue perception in schizophrenia. *Psychiatry Research, 53,* 141–151.

Corrigan, P. W., Wallace, C. J., Schade, M. L., & Green, M. F. (1994b). Cognitive dysfunctions and psychosocial skill learning in schizophrenia. *Behavior Therapy, 25,* 5–15.

DeAmicis, L. A., & Cromwell, R. L. (1977). Reaction time crossover in process schizophrenic patients, their relatives, and control subjects. *Journal of Nervous and Mental Disease, 167,* 593–600.

Goldberg, T. E., Torrey, E. F., Gold, J. M., Bigelow, L. B., Ragland, R. D., Taylor, E., & Weinberger, D. R. (1995). Genetic risk of neuropsychological impairment in schizophrenia: A study of monozygotic twins discordant and concordant for the disorder. *Schizophrenia Research, 17,* 77–84.

Goldman, R. S., Axelrod, B. N., Tandon, R., Ribeiro, S. C. M., Craig, K., & Berent, S. (1993). Neuropsychological prediction of treatment efficacy and one-year outcome in schizophrenia. *Psychopathology, 126,* 122–126.

Green, M. F. (1996). What are the functional consequences of neurocognitive deficits in schizophrenia? *American Journal of Psychiatry, 153,* 321–330.

Green, M. F., Mintz, J., Bowen, L., Marshall, B. D., Kuehnel, T. G., Hayden, J. L., & Liberman, R. P. (1993). Prediction of response to haloperidol dose reduction by Span of Apprehension measures for treatment-refractory schizophrenic patients. *American Journal of Psychiatry, 150,* 1415–1416.

Harvey, P. D., Davidson, M., Mueser, K. T., Parrella, M., White, L., & Powchik, P. (1997). Social-adaptive functioning evaluation (SAFE): A rating scale for geriatric psychiatric patients. *Schizophrenia Bulletin, 23,* 131–139.

Heaton, R. K., & Pendleton, M. G. (1981). Use of neuropsychological tests to predict adult patients' everyday functioning. *Journal of Consulting and Clinical Psychology, 49,* 807–821.

Hogarty, G. E., & Flesher, S. (1992). Cognitive remediation in schizophrenia: Proceed … with caution! *Schizophrenia Bulletin, 18,* 51–57.

Jaeger, J., & Douglas, E. (1992). Neuropsychiatric rehabilitation for persistent mental illness. *Psychiatric Quarterly, 63,* 71–94.

Johnstone, E. C., Macmillan, J. F., Frith, C. D., Benn, D. K., & Crow, T. J. (1990). Further investigation of the predictors of outcome following first schizophrenic episodes. *British Journal of Psychiatry, 157,* 182–189.

Kern, R. S., Green, M. F., & Satz, P. (1992). Neuropsychological predictors of skills training for chronic psychiatric patients. *Psychiatry Research, 43,* 223–230.

Lysaker, P., Bell, M., & Beam-Goulet, J. (1995a). Wisconsin Card Sorting Test and work performance in schizophrenia. *Psychiatry Research, 56,* 45–51.

Lysaker, P. H., Bell, M. D., Zito, W. S., & Bioty, S. M. (1995b). Social skills at work: Deficits and predictors of improvement in schizophrenia. *Journal of Nervous and Mental Disease, 183,* 688–692.

Massel, H. K., Liberman, R. P., Mintz, J., Jacobs, H. E., Rush, T. V., Giannini, C. A., & Zarate, R. (1990). Evaluating the capacity to work of the mentally ill. *Psychiatry, 53,* 31–44.

Mintz, J., Bond, G. R., & Mintz, L. I. (in press). Assessment of work in mental health research. In N. E. Miller & K. MacGruder (Eds.), *Cost effectiveness of psychotherapy.* New York: Oxford University Press.

Mueser, K. T., Bellack, A. S., Douglas, M. S., & Wade, J. H. (1991). Prediction of social skill acquisition in schizophrenic and major affective disorder patients from memory and symptomatology. *Psychiatry Research, 37,* 281–296.

Penn, D. L., Mueser, K. T., Spaulding, W., Hope, D. A., & Reed, D. (1995). Information processing and social competence in chronic schizophrenia. *Schizophrenia Bulletin, 21,* 269–281.

Penn, D. L., Van Der Does, W., Spaulding, W., Garbin, C. P., Linszen, D., & Dingemans, P. (1993). Information processing and social cognitive problem solving in schizophrenia. *Journal of Nervous and Mental Disease, 181,* 13–20.

Smith, R. C., Largen, J., Vroulis, G., & Ravichandran, G. K. (1992). Neuropsychological test scores and clinical response to neuroleptic drugs in schizophrenic patients. *Comprehensive Psychiatry, 33,* 139–145.

Tsuang, D., & Coryell, W. (1993). An 8-year follow-up of patients with DSM-III-R psychotic depression, schizoaffective disorder, and schizophrenia. *American Journal of Psychiatry, 150,* 1182–1187.

Velligan, D. I., Mahurin, R. K., Diamond, P. L., Hazelton, B. C., Eckert, S. L., & Miller, A. L. (1997). The functional significance of symptomatology and cognitive function in schizophrenia. *Schizophrenia Research, 25,* 21–31.

Weaver, L. A., & Brooks, G. W. (1964). The use of psychometric tests in predicting the potential of chronic schizophrenics. *Journal of Neuropsychiatry, 5,* 170–180.

Wykes, T., Sturt, E., & Katz, R. (1990). The prediction of rehabilitative success after three years: The use of social, symptom and cognitive variables. *British Journal of Psychiatry, 157,* 865–870.

Zahn, T. P., & Carpenter, W. T. (1978). Effects of short-term outcome and clinical improvement on reaction time in acute schizophrenia. *Journal of Psychiatric Research, 14,* 59–68.

▶ 9

Intervention for
Neurocognitive Deficits

Schizophrenia may remain the same, but our perceptions of the disorder have changed dramatically over the last two decades. During the 1980s neurodevelopmental models substantially altered our views on the onset, course, and etiology of the disorder. Simultaneously, notions of the phenomenology of the disorder changed as the range of symptoms was broadened to include negative symptoms. The 1990s can be characterized as a period during which the neurocognitive aspects of schizophrenia have come into sharper focus. Jeffery Lieberman, an authority in the psychopharmacology of schizophrenia, observed that the focus on the neurocognition of schizophrenia is comparable to the heightened awareness of negative symptoms that occurred during the 1980s. Both neurocognitive deficits and negative symptoms are features of the illness that at the turn of the century were considered central to the disorder. Subsequently, they were considered secondary, or derivative of psychotic symptoms before being "rediscovered" as central features. In addition, for most of this century neurocognitive deficits and negative symptoms were not considered to be targets for intervention. Now they both are viewed as treatment-worthy.

Figure 9.1 summarizes some of the conclusions of earlier chapters.

1. Conventional neuroleptics are generally effective for psychotic symptoms, but their effects on most neurocognitive measures are weak or questionable.
2. The cross-sectional relationships between neurocognition and psychotic symptoms are generally weak or questionable.
3. Certain neurocognitive deficits are rather good predictors or correlates of functional outcome, whereas the relationships between psychotic symptoms and functional outcome are weak or questionable.

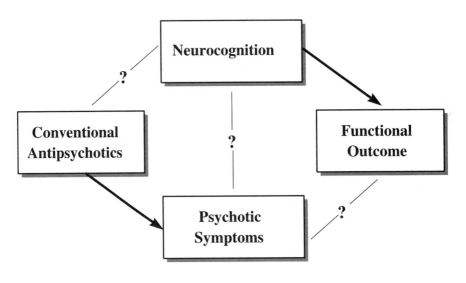

FIGURE 9.1   Pathways from Pharmacological Treatment to
Functional Outcome

To clarify, the argument is not that psychotic symptoms and neurocognitive processes are entirely separate, but that they are sufficiently separate. Psychotic symptoms and neurocognitive deficits cannot be entirely separate because we know that a temporal relationship exists between psychotic symptoms and Episode Indicators, and it is likely that some Vulnerability Indicators lie on a causal pathway leading to onset of the disorder. The argument is that the overlap is relatively small, and more importantly, that a model has greater explanatory power when psychotic symptoms and neurocognition are placed on separate pathways (e.g., consider the quite different associations with functional outcome).

Figure 9.1 depicts a problematic mismatch. Conventional neuroleptics have an impact on symptoms, but not neurocognition. However, functional outcome appears to be more closely related to neurocognitive abilities than to symptoms. This lack of correspondence generates some rather challenging questions. Should neurocognitive deficits become a treatment focus? Can neurocognitive deficits be modified either through cognitive/behavioral or pharmacological interventions? If so, is it reasonable to expect neurocognitive interventions to provide clinical or functional benefits to patients? We will begin with the prerequisite questions: Can neurocognitive deficits be modified at all, and if so, under what conditions (Green, 1993)? Our discussion will begin with cognitive/behavioral interventions and then consider pharmacological approaches and future directions.

NEUROCOGNITIVE DEFICITS AND
COGNITIVE/BEHAVIORAL INTERVENTIONS

We might or might not expect neurocognitive deficits in schizophrenia to be modifiable, depending on the nature of the deficits. As an analogy, consider a young man who wanted to be taller and stronger. To become stronger, he lifted weights. To become taller, he regularly performed stretching exercises and hung upside down in inversion boots. After several weeks his muscles became noticeably larger, but his height had not changed at all. Are neurocognitive abilities like muscles that grow with exercise, or are they more like height that changes very little once a certain level is achieved?

There is plenty of compelling evidence for brain plasticity. In a series of studies on "enriched environments," rats were raised in enriched or impoverished conditions. The enriched conditions included many animals in a spacious cage with novel items such as wheels, ladders, and mazes. In the impoverished conditions, animals were raised singly without objects or companions. It has been known for a long time that animals in enriched environments were better learners. In addition, there are neuroanatomical differences between the groups (Diamond, 1988). Animals from the enriched environments had a thicker cortex and more dendritic branching. These neuroanatomical changes are not limited to early development; they occur throughout the life span and can be seen even with adult rats. Figure 9.2 shows changes in cortical thickness for enriched and impoverished rats (compared with rats raised in a standard environment) who were placed in the experimental conditions at the age of 60 days. Environmental effects are surprisingly potent. The upper graph of Figure 9.2 shows clear neuroanatomical effects after only four days of environmental manipulation.

Basic research on brain plasticity provides some basis for cognitive rehabilitative efforts in a clinical setting. Attempts at remediation of neurocognitive deficits in schizophrenia have emerged from two different contexts. Both approaches tend to be labeled cognitive remediation, which only increases confusion in this area. In this chapter, we will discuss the approach that emerges from an *experimental* framework. These studies seek to determine the extent to which performance on discrete neurocognitive processes can be modified, with an emphasis on what remediation studies can tell us about the nature of the deficits. The other approach to cognitive remediation has emerged primarily from a clinically based, *psychosocial rehabilitation* framework in which the emphasis is to increase therapeutic effects for patients. These rather innovative clinically oriented programs are outside the goals of this chapter and have been described elsewhere (Brenner, Kraemer, Hermanutz, & Hodel, 1990; Gaag, 1992).

The first studies of cognitive remediation in schizophrenia were conducted in the 1950s and 1960s and were designed to improve reaction time

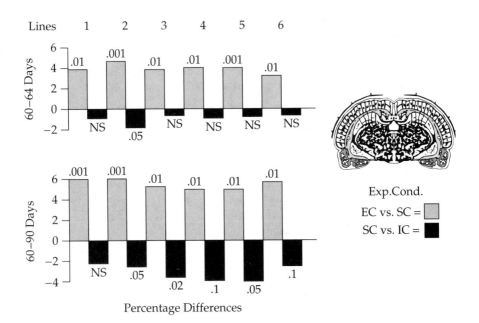

Lines   1   2   3   4   5   6

Percentage Differences

FIGURE 9.2   Measurements of Individual Lines in Areas 18 and 17

Source: Reprinted with the permission of The Free Press, a division of Simon & Schuster from *Enriching Heredity: The Impact of the Environment on the Anatomy of the Brain* by Marian Cleaves Diamond. Copyright © 1988 by The Free Press.

Note: Cortical thickness percentage differences between individual lines drawn on the cortex to determine if separate "columns" were responding to the environmental conditions. EC = enriched, SC = standard, IC = impoverished.

performance (Cohen, 1956; Rosenbaum, Mackavey, & Grisell, 1957). We can view these studies within the context of cognitive remediation only in retrospect. At the time they were conducted, the studies were guided by an attempt to manipulate the level of "motivation" in patients. Behavior modification procedures that involved aversive procedures improved reaction time, indicating that this deficit was malleable. Subsequent studies have moved beyond narrow aversive techniques to include more flexible cognitive/behavioral approaches. In this chapter, we will emphasize remediation studies on those capacities that were shown to be consistently related to functional outcome (see Chapter 8) such as verbal memory, vigilance, and card sorting.

Verbal Memory

In the 1970s a series of studies were conducted in the area of verbal memory (Bauman, 1971; Koh, Kayton, & Peterson, 1976). Because these studies were designed within a cognitive framework, they probably constitute the first true attempts at cognitive remediation in schizophrenia. Verbal memory deficits in schizophrenia had been well-documented by that time. It was suggested that patients used an inefficient encoding strategy when learning lists of words. When techniques were applied to increase the efficiency of encoding, the patients' verbal recall improved. In one study, the manipulation in the encoding process was done by asking the subjects to sort a list of words according to the degree of pleasantness-unpleasantness. To correctly sort the list, subjects had to process words to the level of their meaning. Patients were assessed under two types of recall (Koh, Grinker, Marusarz, & Forman, 1981). In the intentional recall condition, subjects were told to try to remember the words and no sorting procedure was used. In the incidental recall condition, the sorting procedure was used with a different set of words, and subjects were not told that they would need to remember the material. When the patients sorted the words, their incidental recall performance was roughly comparable to that of normal controls (see Figure 9.3). The results were in stark contrast to the intentional recall condition in which patients showed deficits. These initial studies were noteworthy because they showed that rather simple manipulations of encoding improved verbal memory performance in schizophrenic patients.

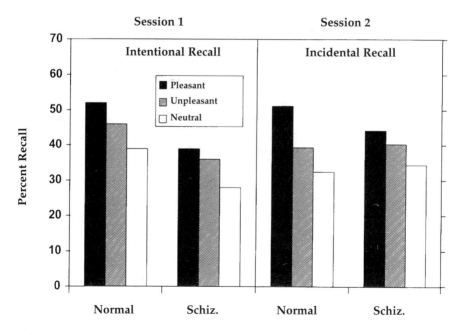

FIGURE 9.3

Vigilance

In addition to verbal memory, vigilance appears to be closely related to outcome. Vigilance is a convenient choice for intervention because available
rehabilitation programs for brain-injured patients frequently emphasize
"attention training," which is often a type of vigilance training. Such rehabilitation programs are usually built around computerized tasks that require
a speeded response from the subject. Task difficulty can be manipulated (e.g.,
by reducing stimulus duration or introducing distracting elements) and it is
increased as subjects improve. Two studies have used existing rehabilitation
packages with schizophrenic patients to determine whether: (1) schizophrenic patients show improvement on training tasks and, (2) the results
would generalize to improvements on another vigilance task (the continuous
performance test, CPT). Both studies showed the malleability of performance
on the training tasks; schizophrenic patients were able to benefit from training. However, generalizability to other tasks was equivocal. An unpublished
study by Alice Medalia and colleagues showed an associated improvement
on the CPT, and another study did not (Benedict et al., 1994). These two studies differed substantially in methodology (e.g., different versions of the CPT
were used and Medalia et al. matched groups on initial CPT performance,
whereas Benedict et al. did not), making it difficult to interpret the differences in CPT results.

Wisconsin Card Sorting Test

There has been a flurry of interest in the possibility of improving Wisconsin
Card Sorting Test (WCST) performance in schizophrenia. The amount of pre-
occupation with this particular measure defies full explanation. In part, the
interest stemmed from the assumption, based on functional neuroimaging
studies from the National Institute of Mental Health, that the test was a direct
index of the integrity of the dorsolateral prefrontal cortex. Regardless of the
soundness of this assumption, an experimental convergence on a single measure has been informative. An initial finding that performance on this measure could not be modified was viewed as evidence that the deficit was firm-
ly rooted in a dysfunctional prefrontal region (Goldberg, Weinberger, Berman,
Pliskin, & Podd, 1987). In contrast, subsequent studies demonstrated clear
improvement with instructions. The WCST has also provided a means to test
motivation effects on performance through manipulations of monetary reinforcement. The wide assortment of WCST findings raises a few key questions:
(1) What is the role of reinforcement? Are patients simply unmotivated or
uninterested? (2) What is the importance of the chronicity of the sample? Can
patients with severe forms of the illness learn? and (3) If a technique can bring
about improvement, how long will it last? Are the gains durable?

If patients are simply unmotivated or uninterested, then contingent reinforcement may have a beneficial effect. Two studies that reported improvement with instructions failed to find any effects of reinforcement alone (Bellack, Mueser, Morrison, Tierney, & Podell, 1990; Green, Satz, Ganzell, & Vaclav, 1992) but another study did (Summerfelt et al., 1991). The latter study used larger amounts of reinforcement (10 cents per correct response) compared to the studies that did not (2 or 5 cents per correct response). In an unpublished study from our laboratory by Susan Hellman, we randomly assigned patients to one of two reinforcement conditions (high vs. low). Performance gains were assessed immediately after training and at a one-week follow-up. The two groups showed no significant difference—and the results were in the opposite direction than predicted. Patients with lower levels of reinforcement showed slightly higher levels of performance gains immediately and at follow-up. These results suggest that manipulating the reinforcement value alone is unlikely to result in performance gains. However, we will see that contingent reinforcement can be valuable when used in combination with other interventions.

Inconsistency in training effects is not explained by differences in patient chronicity across studies. Samples of chronic, largely treatment-resistant patients have shown excellent performance gains (Kern, Wallace, Hellman, Womack, & Green, 1996), indicating that even chronic and cognitively compromised patients can benefit from training. Interventions for less severe patients may not need to be as intensive, but illness severity does not determine whether a patient is a good candidate for cognitive/behavioral interventions. The sophistication of the intervention method is probably a more important determinant of success than is illness severity.

For most of these studies, the durability of the training effects was either not addressed or not impressive. Generally, the training effects seem to last for a matter of days, with a substantial drop after a week. One instructional technique that has shown good durability in developmentally disabled samples is "errorless learning." Errorless learning instruction is based on two principles. First, training begins on simple task components that have a high likelihood of success. Second, increases in task demands are introduced very gradually so that high levels of performance (i.e., no or few errors) are maintained throughout the training process. Although training on the WCST cannot be entirely error free, it is possible to approximate errorless learning procedures with this task. When errorless learning principles were applied to the WCST in a single session with chronic psychiatric patients, the training effects proved to be highly durable (Kern et al., 1996). As shown in Figure 9.4, chronic inpatients were able to maintain their initial performance gains, without a significant drop, over a four-week period.

Errorless learning techniques are especially effective for samples of patients who have difficulty with *explicit* learning, but relatively intact *implicit*

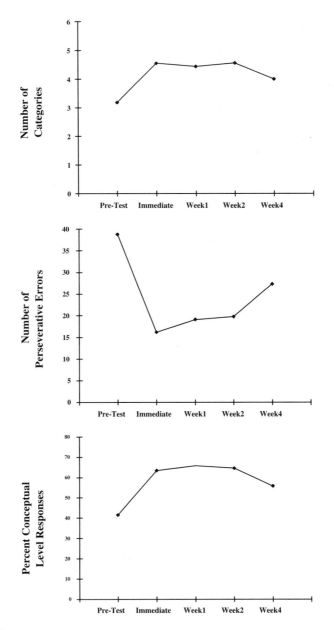

FIGURE 9.4

Source: Adapted from *Journal of Psychiatric Research,* R. S. Kern et al., " A Training Procedure for Remediating WCST Deficits in Chronic Psychotic Patients: An Adaptation of Errorless Learning Principles," Vol. 30, p. 289. Copyright 1996, with kind permission from Elsevier Science Ltd., The Boulevard, Langford Lane, Kidlington OX5 1GB, UK.

learning capabilities, such as amnesic patients (Baddeley, 1992). Explicit learning relies on conscious recollection of previous events and is reflected in tests such as list learning and recognition. In contrast, implicit forms of learning, such as acquisition of motor or perceptual skills, occur outside of conscious awareness. One great value of explicit learning is that it allows us to remember the mistakes we make and to correct them. Errorless learning techniques are thought to involve implicit forms of learning and are therefore suited for patients with intact implicit memory, even if they have deficits in explicit memory. Schizophrenic patients have clear deficits in explicit memory, but their implicit memory may be relatively intact (Kern, Green, & Wallace, 1997). Hence, errorless learning, with its reliance on implicit learning, may be very appropriate for schizophrenic patients.

CONCEPTUAL CHALLENGES

In addition to methodological considerations, all of the studies in this section present interpretive challenges. If we can modify a neurocognitive deficit, what does that tell us about the deficit, the disorder, or rehabilitation programs?

Vulnerability Issues

As discussed in earlier chapters, the nature of neurocognitive deficits in schizophrenia varies considerably. Some deficits are episode indicators that fluctuate with the presence and absence of psychotic symptoms. Other deficits are vulnerability indicators that are stable and enduring. It is easy to envision the remediation of episode indicators that are transient in nature. But can enduring vulnerability indicators also be modified?

The forced-choice Span of Apprehension (Span) has been implicated as an indicator of vulnerability (see Chapter 4). In one condition of the Span, subjects identify the letter "T" or "F" among a briefly presented array of 11 distractor letters. To explore whether the deficit on this measure is modifiable, chronic schizophrenic patients were assigned to one of four different interventions (Kern, Green, & Goldstein, 1995). Each patient was tested four times (three times in the same session): at baseline, during the intervention, at immediate post-test, and at one-week follow-up. The first, third, and fourth administrations were identical for all groups, but during the second administration each group received a different intervention. One group served as a control and received a repeat administration of the Span under standard conditions without any specific intervention. A second group received monetary reinforcement for each correct response. A third group received enhanced instructions that were designed to alert the subjects and remind them of the task demands. A fourth group received a combination of monetary reinforcement and the enhanced instructions. As shown in Figure 9.5, the group that received both reinforcement and instructions showed an improvement at the time of intervention and this improvement was maintained at immediate follow-up and one week later. The degree of improvement brought the patients up to the level of untrained normal controls. This study shows that monetary reinforcement in combination with enhanced instructions can yield improved performance. The intervention apparently does not need to be lengthy: An intervention that lasted less than 30 minutes had a beneficial effect that lasted at least one week.

What does it mean that performance on a vulnerability indicator can be modified? Do we now begin to doubt that it was really an enduring indicator of vulnerability? In fact, knowing that a particular deficit is an indicator of vulnerability tells us nothing about whether the deficit is modifiable. My colleague, Keith Nuechterlein, has argued by analogy that if

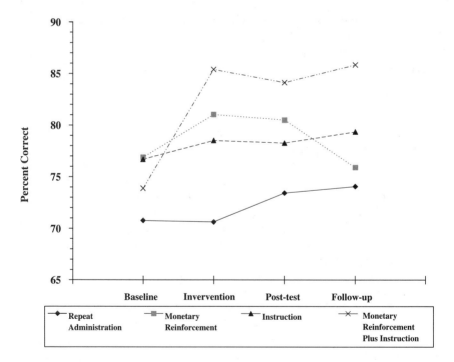

FIGURE 9.5

Source: From "Modification of performance on the Span of Apprehension, A putative marker of vulnerability to schizophrenia" by R. S. Kern, M. F. Green, and M. J. Goldstein, 1995, *Journal of Abnormal Psychology,* Vol. 104, p. 387. Copyright © 1995 by the American Psychological Association. Reprinted with permission.

dopamine dysregulation is a type of indicator of vulnerability to schizophrenia, it is modified every time patients receive a conventional neuroleptic. Although there is nothing inconsistent with a vulnerability deficit that can be modified, it should not be *easily* modified by events or instruction that would likely have occurred in the individual's personal history. Otherwise, we would expect the deficit to be naturally corrected through the course of events.

Validity Issues

Feasibility studies that attempt to modify discrete neurocognitive processes can have two quite separate types of goals. One goal is to learn about *interventions* and the other is to learn about *deficits.* Studies of interventions can inform us that, although monetary reinforcement alone may not be a potent intervention, it may be of value when combined with instructions. Likewise, the application of errorless learning to schizophrenia may provide a match between a particular type of intervention and a specific pattern of neurocognitive problems.

Alternatively, intervention techniques can be used as a means to explore the nature of a particular neurocognitive deficit. However, performance studies generally cannot view dysfunctional neurocognitive processes directly. Instead they assess the effects of an intervention on an *indicator* of the neurocognitive deficit, which raises the issue of construct validity. If one sees improvement on a training task (e.g., the CPT), it is difficult to know if the intervention is having an influence on the underlying construct (vigilance) or on some aspect of the task that is unrelated to the construct. One way to test construct validity with cognitive/behavioral techniques is to use multiple indicators of the same construct. However, these studies are hard to conduct and, because multiple methods are used, negative results are sometimes hard to interpret.

Another way to learn about the nature of neurocognitive deficits is to adjust the task parameters until the deficit is no longer modifiable (e.g., to map the boundaries of an intervention). An example from psychophysiology is illustrative. In the pre-pulse inhibition of the startle-blink (see Chapter 3), a mild tone shortly preceding the blink-eliciting stimulus reduces the amplitude of the eye blink. Interestingly, the inhibition of the startle-blink can be modified with simple instructions to attend to or ignore the pre-pulse stimulus. This modification is mediated by cortical mechanisms and is dependent on the interval between the pre-pulse and the blink-eliciting stimulus (Filion, Dawson, & Schell, 1993). Instructions can modify the blink amplitude at pre-pulse intervals of 120–240 ms, but not as early as 60 ms. The startle-blink paradigm involves several well-defined circuits: a basic startle (brain stem), inhibition of the startle eye blink (subcortical), and, at certain pre-pulse intervals, modification of the inhibition of the eye blink (cortical).

In some studies of schizophrenia, the most noticeable deficit is the failure to *modify* the inhibition of the startle-blink in response to instructions (Dawson, Hazlett, Filion, Nuechterlein, & Schell, 1993). Hypotheses about the time course can be tested by systematically altering the pre-pulse interval. For example, patients may modify their startle-blink inhibition to the same degree, but at later pre-pulse intervals than controls. Other neurocognitive measures such as backward masking are also suitable for systematic variation of time parameters, which can be used to map the time frame during which an intervention is effective.

Implications of Laboratory Studies

Although clinically based programs of cognitive remediation are not a focus here, we can consider how the lessons learned from the laboratory studies might be fruitfully applied to these interventions. In terms of intervention techniques, many of the clinically based programs rely heavily on repetition of tasks. Repetition, or "general stimulation," is a rather weak method of rehabilitation for brain-injured patients (Hanlon, 1991). The results from the Span and WCST indicate that repetition alone does not result in enhanced performance. However, in an unpublished study, Bruce Wexler and colleagues showed that repetition yielded improvement in perceptual and motor tasks when it was combined with contingent monetary reinforcement and when task parameters were altered to keep pace with changes in performance levels.

One feature of clinically based programs may be contraindicated for schizophrenic patients. The programs often use an interactive question and answer format in which the instructor asks open-ended questions to the group. The emphasis is on the generation and correction of responses from the patients. In contrast, an errorless learning approach to rehabilitation would arrange the questions hierarchically and phrase them in a way to increase the likelihood of correct responses.

Frequently, the clinically based programs are intended to bring about symptomatic improvement. On the surface this seems like a reasonable goal, but it presents an interpretive challenge. What would be the exact mechanism of the treatment effect? If the neurocognitive deficit was a Stable Vulnerability Indicator, its modification in a symptomatic patient would not be expected to yield any symptomatic benefit. If the deficit was an Episode Indicator that lagged behind the onset of symptoms, its modification would not likely yield clinical benefit. However, neurocognitive remediation might reduce psychotic symptoms under very specific conditions: if the neurocognitive deficit was an Episode Indicator, and if it was a causal part of the leading edge of symptom exacerbation.

Based on relationships between neurocognitive deficits and outcome (Chapter 8), we might expect that the clinically based programs should have their largest impact in functional outcome and areas that are separate from psychotic symptoms altogether. This may be reflected in benefits for non-psychotic symptoms such as social withdrawal, blunted affect, and hostility. Improvements in these areas have, in fact, been seen with such programs (Brenner et al., 1990).

PHARMACOLOGICAL INTERVENTIONS FOR NEUROCOGNITIVE DEFICITS

To review some of the points covered in Chapter 6, conventional neuroleptics do not cause neurocognitive deficits in schizophrenia and, for most areas of neurocognition, they do little to improve them. The situation with newer antipsychotic agents may be more promising. Clozapine appears to have a reliable positive effect on verbal fluency, which involves the ability to generate multiple examples of words and to retrieve information from semantic memory. Its effects on other aspects of neurocognition appear to be minimal.

Work on the neurocognitive effects of risperidone is just emerging. The agent appears to have a beneficial effect on verbal working memory that cannot be explained by its effects on psychotic and negative symptoms, or by the differential administration of anticholinergic medications. The new generation of antipsychotic medications will not require as much co-administration of anticholinergic agents compared with conventional neuroleptics. Because anticholinergic medications have detrimental effects on certain neurocognitive processes, the reduced use of these medications might yield neurocognitive advantages.

If the new generation of antipsychotic medications has an impact on two separate domains, neurocognitive processes and symptoms, it raises a basic definitional question about the nature of treatment efficacy. The notion of efficacy in the pharmacological treatment of schizophrenia has been defined narrowly in terms of symptom reduction. Primarily the term has referred to psychotic symptom reduction, but the effects of newer agents on negative symptoms have also been considered. Expanding the notion of treatment efficacy has been largely academic until recently because the medications in use did not have a substantial impact on neurocognition. However, if novel drugs act on multiple domains including neurocognition, then symptom reduction becomes too narrow. It is plausible, but as yet untested, that improvement in these critical abilities can translate into functional benefits for patients. Hence, newer medications could expand the narrow goal of *symptom* reduction into a broader goal of *disability* reduction (see Figure 6.3).

Construct validity is less of an issue for pharmacological studies than it is for cognitive/behavioral interventions. With a cognitive/behavioral intervention, improvement on a training task (the indicator) does not necessarily indicate improvement in the underlying neurocognitive ability (the construct). With pharmacological interventions, there is no training task so the interpretation of a treatment effect is simplified. If a drug improves performance on a test of verbal working memory, it is reasonable to conclude that the drug helps verbal working memory. Because pharmacological interventions largely bypass the issue of construct validity, they are easier to interpret in this regard.

If novel antipsychotic drugs offer promising neurocognitive effects, it is somewhat accidental because they were not developed with neurocognitive deficits in mind. However, other drugs were. One exciting area in drug development is the search for medications with beneficial neurocognitive properties, such as drugs that act on the glutamate system and appear to improve memory. Pharmacological treatments (cholinergic agonists) aimed at neurocognitive deficits are used with Alzheimer's disease, although the results have not been uniformly impressive (Davis & Powchik, 1995). Antipsychotic medications have not been selected based on their neurocognitive effects, but we may be approaching a time in which the neurocognitive properties of agents under development will be assessed routinely along with their effects on symptoms and side-effect profiles. In fact, pharmaceutical companies are starting to include neurocognitive assessments in clinical trials of new antipsychotic agents. Another possibility is that the novel antipsychotic agents will turn out to have a relatively small impact on neurocognitive deficits and that the field will turn to adjunctive medications (Davidson & Keefe, 1995). My colleague Stephen Marder has suggested that one day schizophrenic patients may receive two types of medications: one for symptoms and one for neurocognitive deficits.

FUNCTIONAL NEUROIMAGING AND NEUROCOGNITIVE INTERVENTIONS

A patient performs a neurocognitive task at a certain level. Following cognitive/behavioral or pharmacological interventions, the patient performs the task at a higher level. What exactly changed? For the first time, we can start to ask questions about the discrete changes in regional brain activity that accompany improved performance. It is now possible to explore the nature of dysfunctional neural circuits in schizophrenia by applying functional neuroimaging to performance changes. Such an approach has been used to examine the functional neuroanatomical changes in normal controls that are associated with procedural learning, which is a type of implicit learning (Grafton et al., 1992). Using subtraction techniques it is possible to distinguish the brain regions that are linked to learning a task, as opposed to execution of a task. Procedural learning tasks are well-suited for imaging experiments because the experimenters can be fairly sure that all subjects will show some degree of improvement. However, tasks such as the WCST that involve processes of relevance for schizophrenia can be used as well.

In a continuation of their work on functional neuroimaging during the WCST, a team from NIMH obtained PET images on normal controls before and after training on the WCST (Berman et al., 1995). The intention was to determine whether a network of brain areas (including the dorsolateral prefrontal cortex) is active only while learning the task, or if activity in the network is always involved with execution of the task. Any region or network that was active even after the task was learned and practiced would probably be mediating some constant aspect of the test, for example, a working memory component. In fact, the dorsolateral prefrontal cortex was activated both before and after practice, suggesting that this region was associated with a constant property of the test. Learning (as opposed to executing) the WCST may be associated with activity of other brain regions. This study is an excellent example of how repeated functional scans can be used to dissect learning components within the context of performance changes. When applied to schizophrenia, this type of study would enable investigators to evaluate whether the pattern of brain activation involved with learning a task differs between patients and controls. It would also determine the processes through which neurocognitive deficits are normalized in schizophrenia. These types of studies may even be more interpretable with schizophrenic patients because the magnitude of the changes would be greater than with normal controls. A limitation of the study by Berman et al. is that the normal controls performed fairly well before instructions and practice, and therefore had little room for improvement.

The neuroimaging of improved task performance is not limited to cognitive/behavioral interventions; applications to pharmacological interventions are also warranted. For example, if a new medication has a direct beneficial effect on a construct (e.g., risperidone's effect on verbal working memory), patients could be scanned on PET or fMRI during the cognitive activation task once while receiving a conventional neuroleptic and again after random assignment to a conventional medication or a novel agent. In this way, we could determine what type of changes (e.g., magnitude of activation, regional distribution of activation) appear to accompany performance change. It may soon be possible to obtain something quite unheard of previously: a functional neuroanatomy of neurocognitive improvement in schizophrenia.

BEYOND THE SYMPTOMS OF SCHIZOPHRENIA

It is inevitable. Anyone who spends a large proportion of their time study-ing, treating, or living with schizophrenia will be asked by an interested lay person to explain what the disorder is. Typically, the answer will take the form of a listing of psychotic symptoms. Sometimes the answer will be more comprehensive and will include a brief description of negative symptoms. But rarely will neurocognitive deficits be mentioned as part of the answer. In comparison to psychotic symptoms, neurocognitive deficits are not as noticeable, not as odd, and they are not part of any formal diagnostic system.

It is reasonable at this time to ask whether the neurocognitive deficits themselves should become a focus of treatment. Functional neuroimaging, cognitive/behavioral interventions, and psychopharmacology can be com-bined to learn what it takes (at the performance, neuroanatomical, and neu-rochemical levels) to make the deficits go away. Neurocognitive intervention studies provide information of both scientific and practical value. There is scientific value in knowing which components of neurocognitive deficits can be modified and which cannot, and under what conditions. In practical terms, neurocognitive deficits appear to be more closely related to function-al outcome than psychotic symptoms. It is entirely possible that remediation of certain neurocognitive deficits will lead to more satisfactory and more complete social and occupational functioning for patients—but this remains a hypothesis to be tested.

Figure 9.6 is a revision and extension of Figure 9.1 in which components have been added and strengths of relationships have been included. Novel antipsychotic agents were added above conventional agents, negative symp-toms were added next to psychotic symptoms, and adjunctive pharmaco-logical and cognitive/behavioral interventions were added as possible influ-ences on neurocognitive deficits. Even with these additions, the diagram is woefully oversimplified. For example, there is no doubt a universe of medi-ating variables between neurocognitive deficits and functional outcome (e.g., social schema formation, degree of family support, awareness of and attitude toward illness). Relationships with clinical, as opposed to functional out-come, are not included and probably involve a separate host of factors. Another limitation of the figure is that strengths of the relationships are only rough estimates. Nonetheless, the figure shows the mismatch of current treatments to functional outcome and the possibilities that exist with the newer medications. Importantly, the figure depicts neurocognitive processes as a major intersection for pathways in the model.

Our view of schizophrenia has shifted dramatically and irreversibly over the past couple of decades. Neurodevelopmental factors have taken on increasing importance for a disorder that was seen as one of deterioration.

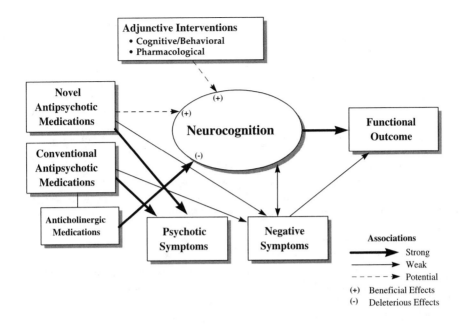

FIGURE 9.6

Notions of phenomenology have expanded to include negative symptoms. These rather substantial changes were driven by insightful investigators, compelling data, and a deep-rooted feeling that existing paradigms and concepts were not adequately explaining important aspects of the disorder. Viewing schizophrenia from a neurocognitive perspective necessitates yet another shift—one that may be particularly fundamental. Like the shifts of recent decades, it too is driven by data that cannot be ignored and a deep-rooted feeling that somehow, somewhere, critical aspects of the disorder are being missed. It goes further by asking us to accept the counter-intuitive premise that the most dramatic features of the illness are not the most important features of the illness. Our challenge is to reach a vantage point from which we can see beyond the symptoms of schizophrenia.

REFERENCES

Baddeley, A. D. (1992). Implicit memory and errorless learning: A link between cognitive therapy and neuropsychological rehabilitation? In L. R. Squire & N. Butters (Eds.), *Neuropsychology of memory* (pp. 309–314). New York: Guilford Press.

Bauman, E. (1971). Schizophrenic short-term memory: The role of organization at input. *Journal of Consulting and Clinical Psychology, 36,* 14–19.

Bellack, A. S., Mueser, K. T., Morrison, R. L., Tierney, A., & Podell, K. (1990). Remediation of cognitive deficits in schizophrenia. *American Journal of Psychiatry, 147,* 1650–1655.

Benedict, R. H. B., Harris, A. E., Markow, T., McCormick, J. A., Nuechterlein, K. H., & Asarnow, R. F. (1994). Effects of attention training on information processing in schizophrenia. *Schizophrenia Bulletin, 20,* 537–546.

Berman, K. F., Ostrem, J. L., Randolph, C., Gold, J., Goldberg, T. E., Coppola, R., Carson, R. E., Herscovitch, P., & Weinberger, D. R. (1995). Physiological activation of a cortical network during performance of the Wisconsin Card Sorting Test: A positron emission tomography study. *Neuropsychologia, 33,* 1027–1046.

Brenner, H. D., Kraemer, S., Hermanutz, M., & Hodel, B. (1990). Cognitive treatment in schizophrenia. In E. R. Straube & Halweg (Eds.), *Schizophrenia: Concepts, vulnerability, and interventions.* (pp. 161–192). New York: Springer-Verlag.

Cohen, B. (1956). Motivation and performance in schizophrenia. *Journal of Abnormal and Social Psychology, 52,* 186–190.

Davidson, M., & Keefe, R. S. E. (1995). Cognitive impairment as a target for pharmacological treatment in schizophrenia. *Schizophrenia Research, 17,* 123–129.

Davis, K. L., & Powchik, P. (1995). Tacrine. *Lancet, 345,* 625–630.

Dawson, M. E., Hazlett, E. A., Filion, D. L., Nuechterlein, K. H., & Schell, A. M. (1993). Attention and schizophrenia: Impaired modulation of the startle reflex. *Journal of Abnormal Psychology, 102,* 633–641.

Diamond, M. C. (1988). *Enriching heredity: The impact of the environment on the anatomy of the brain.* New York: The Free Press.

Filion, D. L., Dawson, M. E., & Schell, A. M. (1993). Modification of the acoustic startle-reflex eyeblink: A tool for investigating early and late attentional processes. *Biological Psychology, 35,* 185–200.

Gaag, M. v. d. (1992). *The results of cognitive training in schizophrenic patients.* Rijksuniversiteit, Groningen.

Goldberg, T. E., Weinberger, D. R., Berman, K. F., Pliskin, N. H., & Podd, M. H. (1987). Further evidence for dementia of the prefrontal type in schizophrenia? A controlled study of teaching the Wisconsin Card Sorting Test. *Archives of General Psychiatry, 44,* 1008–1014.

Grafton, S. T., Mazziotta, J. C., Presty, S., Friston, K. J., Frackowiak, R. S. J., & Phelps, M. E. (1992). Functional anatomy of human procedural learning determined with regional cerebral blood flow and PET. *The Journal of Neuroscience, 12,* 2542–2548.

Green, M. F. (1993). Cognitive remediation in schizophrenia: Is it time yet? *American Journal of Psychiatry, 150,* 178–187.

Green, M. F., Satz, P., Ganzell, S., & Vaclav, J. F. (1992). Wisconsin Card Sorting Test performance in schizophrenia: Remediation of a stubborn deficit. *American Journal of Psychiatry, 149,* 62–67.

Hanlon, R. E. (1991). Neuromotor activation in the facilitation of language production: Rehabilitation applications. In R. E. Hanlon & J. W. Brown (Eds.), *Cognitive microgenesis: A neuropsychological perspective.* New York: Springer-Verlag.

Kern, R. S., Green, M. F., & Goldstein, M. J. (1995). Modification of performance on the Span of Apprehension, a putative marker of vulnerability to schizophrenia. *Journal of Abnormal Psychology, 104,* 385–389.

Kern, R. S., Green, M. F., & Wallace, C. J. (1997). Declarative and procedural learning in schizophrenia: A test of the integrity of divergent memory systems. *Cognitive Neuropsychiatry, 2,* 39–50.

Kern, R. S., Wallace, C. J., Hellman, S. G., Womack, L. M., & Green, M. F. (1996). A training procedure for remediating WCST deficits in chronic psychotic patients: An adaptation of errorless learning principles. *Journal of Psychiatric Research, 30,* 283–294.

Koh, S. D., Grinker, R. R., Marusarz, T. Z., & Forman, P. L. (1981). Affective memory and schizophrenic anhedonia. *Schizophrenia Bulletin, 7,* 292–307.

Koh, S. D., Kayton, L., & Peterson, R. A. (1976). Affective encoding and consequent remembering in schizophrenic young adults. *Journal of Abnormal Psychology, 85,* 156–166.

Rosenbaum, G., Mackavey, W. R., & Grisell, J. L. (1957). Effects of biological and social motivation on schizophrenic reaction time. *Journal of Abnormal and Social Psychology, 54,* 364–368.

Summerfelt, A. T., Alphs, L. D., Wagman, A. M., Funderburk, F. R., Hierholzer, R. M., & Strauss, M. E. (1991). Reduction of perseverative errors with schizophrenia using monetary feedback. *Journal of Abnormal Psychology, 100,* 613–616.

Index